DIRTY MARKS

DIRTY MARKS

The Education of Self, Media and Popular Culture

John F. Schostak

Pluto Press
LONDON • BOULDER, COLORADO

First published 1993 by Pluto Press
345 Archway Road, London N6 5AA
and 5500 Central Avenue,
Boulder, Colorado 80301, USA

British Library Cataloguing in Publication Data
A catalogue record for this book is available from the British Library

Library of Congress Cataloging-in-Publication Data
Applied for.

ISBN 0 7453 0430 3 hb
ISBN 0 7453 0431 1 pb

Designed and produced for Pluto Press by
Chase Production Services, Chipping Norton.
Typeset from author's disks in Palatino by
Stanford Desktop Publishing Services, Milton Keynes.
Printed and bound in Great Britain
by T.J. Press, Padstow.

CONTENTS

ACKNOWLEDGEMENTS

Study leave provided by the University of East Anglia contributed to making this book possible. The idea for it arose from a conversation with my colleagues Terry Phillips and Maggie MacLure. The title *Dirty Marks* I owe to Terry. The remainder is a text loosened from responsibility, available for play.

1

INTRODUCTION

Can anyone be sure that the opinions, faiths and knowledge that they hold most dear are freely their own? undoubtedly true? What was it people were willing to die for when the Gulf War started in 1991? Oil or Ideals? The late twentieth century is proving to be a very volatile, dangerous time. Is a New World Order developing, or is it just the same old conflicts of greed and power? The central question for all individuals is how to make up their own minds in order to act on their own behalfs. This is an age of the mass moulding of opinion and belief, emotions and attitudes, conduct and action. It is an age when nationalism and blind faith are both the most desired qualities of the population by leaders but are the most dangerous to the survival of the world.

For the individual the process most critical to freedom and survival is education. However, the education system is itself subject to political interference and in many instances around the world *is* the agency of suppression. The system of education is not limited to schools. The sources of information are the media, the family, neighbours, friends, the subcultures of gangs and groups. It is in this matrix of overlapping and competing institutions and groups that the individual develops and takes decisions affecting the course of his or her life, including the decision to kill or to die for a cause. This book is about the struggle of the individual to know, to speak out, and to act, and about the experiences of repression, struggle and liberation. The basic principle is that of education and the focus of examination is the discourse that forbids, inhibits, represses, covers up and silences.

What can be said, seen, heard or done in any particular place, private or public, is subject to conventions, rules and laws. It is freedom within the law, the convention, the peer group value system. What cannot be said, seen, heard or done can be variously experienced as repression, censorship, protection, security against corruption and degradation. Different cultures, different faiths, different belief systems mark the boundaries inside which freedom is to be experienced in different places. What is good in one, is bad in the other. In a society where neighbours are likely to believe differently, where the media provides images of alternative belief systems and conduct, the diversity can be experienced either as overwhelming, ugly, evidence of conflict, or it can be seen as an opportunity to choose, to debate, to take critical positions on that which has become so familiar it can hardly be seen except from the outside.

This attitude, I believe, is critical to the development of education as an independent discipline. Its subject matter is to be found in the processes of freedom and repression through which societies, communities, groups and individuals develop. Education takes place not in the crude delivery system of approved packages of knowledge and conduct which dominates modern schooling. It takes place in the processes through which freedom is experienced, its nature, its ethical foundations. Conversely, it must therefore focus always upon the question of the forbidden, how it is constructed, the ethics through which it is conceived, the implications for freedom. This twin discourse on the relations between freedom and repression and the forbidden I call the forbidden discourse.

Since discourse is a key term of the book, its use needs to be clarified. It is helpful to make a distinction between language and discourse. Language is not just the total set of all words but consists also of the rules, codes and conventions through which those words may be combined to form meaningful units, such as phrases and sentences. Language is learnt socially. It is through language that objects are distinguished from each other, world views and a sense of self are constructed. When language is used in this way, 'language systems and social conditions meet' (Hartley 1982: 6). Discourse is socially and historically produced. Discourses are produced around every kind of social activity. There are the discourses of academic activity, the discourses of the family, domesticity or of the gang. To speak then of a forbidden discourse is to indicate a specialised use of language historically, culturally produced. Foucault (1981: 52–3) made specific reference to the forbidden discourse as referring to political and sexual discourses. More fundamentally, he argued that

> … discourse is not simply that which manifests (or hides) desire – it is also the object of desire; and since, as history constantly teaches us, discourse is not simply that which translates struggles or systems of domination, but is the thing for which and by which there is struggle, discourse is the power which is to be seized.

The forbidden discourse, as I use it, refers then to a structure which inserts itself into or twists the routine discourses of business and domestic life to repress, inhibit, cover over or subliminally suggest something other than what is apparently being presented. Education is central to the recovery and the analysis of the contents and processes of the forbidden. As such it is a meta-discourse, a discourse about all possible discourses. The forbidden discourse is an inherent potential in all possible discourses; an 'underside' to be recovered through analysis of the historical and social structures which erect taboos, the dark places, silences. Through the perspective of education a study of contemporary Western discourses can be made which provides a source of resistance against reductive and censorial thought and action. Through the study of the images and myths of contemporary culture it explores what can and cannot be said, what can and cannot be shown, what can and cannot be done.

As a meta-discourse the field of education includes study of the kind of self that emerges in the discourses of contemporary mass culture, the constraints on the self's actions by media representations, and the potential for real development. At every turn the questions of freedom are raised. How free are we when we make decisions which fundamentally affect our own lives and the lives of others? Through the forbidden discourses at play in society the personal is fragmented, the sense of self de-centred, dis-ordered, marketed and rendered inert under the play of market propaganda. We are currently at a crossroads between freedom and its loss. But the crossroads is a moving crossroads. People always have been and always will be at the crossroads of possibility. This book is about the crossroads as it appears in the late twentieth century as we play with the possibilities for the future on the basis of our experience, our reflections and the ways our memories are and have been re-written in order to re-think our futures. The method is comparative, that is, through comparing a range of institutions and social structures and processes the commonalities and resemblances can be drawn out for analysis.

Myth, narrative, story are central to the discourse practices through which selves are produced and a world made known. They compose the everyday curriculum materials, the stocks of common knowledge essential for competence in the world, informing decisions and actions. They are set pieces of discourse which explain why things are, why they have to be and provide a sense of the known, the stable, the right, the moral, the good. Thus, the elaboration of educational practice consists of de-constructing the ready-made materials, to identify the means of their construction, and the structures and processes through which these ready-made materials are circulated from generation to generation and person to person. In so doing, the hidden is uncovered, the repressed revealed and the processes and structures of the forbidden made known. What is at stake in the process is to ascertain what a person can become and what prevents these potentials flowing freely.

The prime discourse, the catalyst and paradigm for all other discourses begins in the family, or family-surrogate. Chapter 2 discusses the role of the myth of The Family in the production of the social self. It discusses how the idea of The Family is employed in political discourse to close down debate and subtly regulate the institutions of education and information. These institutions may be those that are well recognised as having 'educational' functions such as schools, the media, the family. They also include those that are less well recognised such as gangs or peer friendship groups which form the basis of education into counter-cultural discourses. At this point, education is being used in its popular catch-all sense of shaping and moulding the individual through the transmission of information, ideas and values, and of introducing the individual to the discourses typical of the groups which operate in the different institutions of life. Out of these discourses, the course of life of any one individual develops.

In Chapter 3, the course of life as the individual moves from the institution of The Family to the institutions of public life is charted in terms of the construction of the Other as Stranger and public space as being territorialised in terms of the different dramatis personae, and the kinds of 'stories' that can be told about such spaces as the individual moves from territory to territory. The stories act like the curriculum materials through which the individual is 'educated' or more typically, 'schooled' into the required discourses, behaviours and attitudes. The territories divide according to what can be made known and done within those territories. Some become forbidden areas in which the forbidden aspects of the self may be expressed under cover. Others are for the public self. The boundaries are policed whether with internal or external controls, systems of surveillance and processes of repression. The major territories of public life are policed by the Heroes who epitomise 'goodness', 'propriety' and 'courage'.

The Heroes and their Villains are explored in Chapter 4. Comics provide a useful insight into the construction of the Heroic in terms of the Family Romance and the process through which the Family as a basic myth structures or re-territorialises the outside world in its image. Thus, at the beginnings of the Gulf crisis of 1989 Saddam Hussein is set within a comic-like drama between Good and Evil, the Hero and the Monster in which a World is to be Saved. World Loss and World Saving are fundamental constructions in the Hero mythology in which mass populations are to be schooled. This leads then to the problem of the representation of the repressed, the unsayable, the silenced.

Forbidden forms of representation arise in response to the need to represent split-off, alienated, silenced aspects of the self; the need to counter the processes of repression, to represent alternative voices; the need to explore alternative ways of being and of living. Within the forbidden are quite different kinds of experiences, intentions, emotions. The whole issue of censure and censorship is raised. For those who want to represent the counter-cultures and the oppressed in society, dilemmas arise particularly in the areas of rights to free speech. The dilemmas are particularly acute in relation to blasphemy, racism and pornography, where granting one person's rights to free expression wounds and degrades another. These processes and issues are discussed in Chapter 5.

The demarcation between the Private and the Public faces through which the permissible and the forbidden are constructed is central to Chapter 6. The use of scandal by the tabloid press creates a superficial sense of the newspaper being 'investigative' or 'telling it like it is'. This contrasts with those forms of investigation which challenge official discourses, revealing the contradictions, the shady deals, the interconnections or 'conspiracies' between the institutions of power in business, politics, the media and the military which form the secret state. The difference is between schooling into comfortable belief and educating into discomforting awareness.

Revelations of the political nature of representation reveal the deeper, hidden, denied connections between the disavowed politics of fascism, racism and social exploitation and the public politics pervading market economies which are typically structured according to patterns of domination and subordination in association with division of labour and inequalities of wealth, privilege and power. In Chapter 7, the forbidden politics is discussed in relation to the kinds of challenge (itself a forbidden discourse and a forbidden politics) that may be 'educated', that is, constructed as a counter discourse.

Chapter 8 considers the relationship between self-assertion and violence. The framework for understanding the relation is that of the official and counter-discourses which the media typically represent as a battle between 'Culture' and 'Anarchy', a distinction drawn by Arnold in the nineteenth century. More fundamental distinctions, however, have to be drawn in order to re-conceptualise the place of violence in society and in the assertion of rights. What is the relationship, if any, between the Male Hero of Violence and the forms of violence which suddenly 'explode' as in the random killings of the Hungerford massacre of 1987, or the political terrorism of radical or revolutionary groups? Is there ever a moral, educationally sound basis to violence?

The tensions leading to the potential fragmentation of society have in some way to be defused. The anxieties of the comfortable groups demand action. Yet action is not always possible. The sense of guilt which may arise when confronted with poverty, degrading exploitation, violence has in some way to be assuaged. In constructing a counter discourse which focuses awareness, the old unities of the Hero and the Villain are de-fused, taken apart and the foundations upon which they are built laid bare. The politics of representation is a battle between discourses. The explosive pressure of political tensions can be pre-empted or released without in any way changing or resolving them. The concentrations of pressure can be diffused around the system, rendering them strategically ineffective. Counter to these are the discourses which canalise energies to prise apart the knots, the agglomerations, the sedimentations of defences against knowing, understanding and action. These processes are explored in Chapter 9 in relation to the Thatcher years, providing a basic description of the conditions framing education and empowerment.

The final chapter develops a framework through which empowerment in terms of education can take place. It provides examples and arguments through which reconstructions can take place. The educational process is clearly not limited to, nor dependent on, the acts of teachers in schools. the educational process has relevance to all those involved in the critique of society, popular culture, the media and the political process. It is the perspective that unifies critique and practice in the pursuit of cultural freedoms.

Underlying the forbidden is the discourse of knowledge, ignorance and innocence which either closes down, or reformulates in order to open up the possibilities of alternative discourses. This dialectic pervades each chapter.

The process and function of education is a complex task. It delves towards what is forgotten, unseen, overlooked, disapproved, repressed, forbidden. The knowledge required for day-to-day interactions is limited because so much is simply taken for granted – no questions asked – and:

> ... most human acts in a developed society do not proceed according to a merely individual circuit but, on the contrary, a more or less large part of their trajectory goes through social circuits which are often extraordinarily far removed from the immediate reality of the individual's concrete action. In order to account for a relation as apparently straightforward as the wage-rate paid to a labourer for his work, it is necessary to get beyond it up to and including capitalist competition on an international scale. In fact it is the *immense extent of the detour* between the starting-point of an individual's action and its return to itself, which explains *the basic spontaneous unconsciousness of the individual of the real bases of his personality.* (Sève 1978: 224)

To engage in education is to embark upon an unpredictable course. Unlike schools its curriculum cannot be charted beforehand. Instead, the curriculum is the historical course of reflection, expression and action undertaken in the process of uncovering and recovering. It uncovers the forgotten or darkened social circuits through which meaning and material existence in everyday life are constructed. It establishes the networks of association which underlie the surface appearance of discontinuity. It records and expresses what is discovered and formulates plans of action.

The great desire is to know, not just to guess, or to have plausible evidence, but *really* to know. Science and religion represent alternative ways of banishing the darkness of ignorance. Science claims to provide *the facts* based upon rational experimentation, and analysis to develop theories or models of the world. Religion depends upon revelation from divine sources. Where science must question and question again until no doubt remains, religions must banish questioning in order to have the faith that knows because it no longer can question. Yet, for many, the two forms of knowing, of seeking knowledge, or banishing ignorance, are not so different. They represent, merely, alternative belief systems amongst many, alternative codes of conduct, alternative ways of forming a world in which to live, find an identity with others with whom the world is shared and feel some security. With science, there is possible the belief in progress, in the ultimate perfectibility of the human being. In utopia a true innocence, or near perfectibility might be achieved through knowledge. For the religious, there is the Innocence of the past, the Garden of Eden, which through faith may be recoverable on earth, or at least found in Heaven after death. These two forms of discourse, the scientific and the religious, illustrate the relationships between knowledge, ignorance, and innocence. The discourse that integrates them as merely alternatives along an indefinite range of other possible alternatives is the discourse that allows the emergence of the forbidden.

To believe one possesses the truth, or at least the true method, necessarily excludes other possibilities. Depending upon one's culture, those who hold alternative views of the world can be seen as enemies, heretics, devils, mad or merely bad. A society may invest considerable effort in suppressing, repressing and forbidding access to knowledge of the existence and nature of alternatives. *There is no alternative* is the rule of the society or group which believes it has found the one and only true answer. Why are there inequalities of wealth and power? *It is only natural,* cry the true believers. Doubt must be suppressed. This can be done through a variety of means. Killing and torture are the more brutal methods of instilling the fear that freezes critical thought in the masses. Humour, ridicule, criminalisation and labelling as insane are more sophisticated methods. The object is to produce a social discourse which renders alternatives unnatural, mad, bad; and renders *the one true way* natural, sane, good.

Societies have always controlled access to knowledge through the operation of taboos, the belief in deities, or the enforcement of laws and the training of conduct. Special buildings or areas – educational institutions, churches, various other public service institutions and businesses – have been designated for the transmission of and production of socially desired kinds of knowledge and conduct and discourse. Between them there exist the boundaries necessary to a complex society. The kinds of discourse appropriate for a business meeting or the kinds of challenges to belief routinely undertaken in a university seminar would not be appropriate in a church service. If a society considers both are appropriate and socially acceptable in their place, there needs to be a sense of social disapproval if the one is carried into the other. The members of a society must not know too much about the society itself, must be prevented from pondering the contradictions. When entering a Church founded upon the belief that 'thou shalt not kill' a soldier must suspend his or her awareness of contradiction. For the soldier there should be no words to articulate the contradiction which eases into mind the doubt. Paulo Freire, in writing of his work as a teacher in Latin America, referred to a 'culture of silence' where 'Externally, the alienated society as a whole, as the mere object of the director society, is not heard by the latter. On the contrary the metropolis prescribes its word, thereby effectively silencing it. Meanwhile, within the alienated society itself, the masses are subjected to the same kind of silence by the power elites' (1970: 16). Here the masses are silent and kept silent by the strategy of the oppressor defining 'the word' for the masses and by preventing them from speaking. However, when the masses, as Freire writes, do begin to find their own words, and to speak them, the director society violently suppresses them. The work of education is to draw out the authentic word of those suppressed by the culture of silence and thereby *educate,* or draw out, 'an increasingly critical attitude toward the world and so to transform it' (1973: 34). Education draws upon and draws out the forbidden as a precursor to freedom.

The point of reflecting on the forbidden is that through its structures of resistances, it marks out the new freedoms. In psychoanalytic terms the process has been conceived of medically, as a cure. In religious terms it has been seen as a process of battle and of being saved from the devil, the lord of the forbidden. In political terms it is a process of the preservation of the state, the status quo, against attack from within and without against enemies who would take over and destroy. But the forbidden is all and none of these. It is about looking fully at the self in all its forms and in all its expressions and actions. There is no cure here from the self; there is no saving from the self; nor is there any way to exclude and destroy the enemy within. Instead, there is the possibility of open and honest exploration and development. This is the educational course of the forbidden.

2

HAPPY FAMILIES:
Knowledge, Ignorance and Innocence – the drama begins

To speak of the family is to speak of a world which is both intimate and strange. Through the family, the world is reproduced not just in the biological sense, but also in the sense of 'Like father like son; like mother like daughter.' Laing (1976 edition: 52) wrote of a family who 'had buried their dead *in each other*'. Each day we labour to make live all the forms of this society bequeathed by parents long since forgotten by name but personified as Our Father in Heaven, Our Fatherland, or as some living representative who makes us His or Her children: Queen, King, Great Leader. With no hint of irony we speak of large institutions from schools to multinational companies as families. And if here we do not find a home, then there are the gangs, the alternative family of brothers and sisters and godfathers.

The family is the primal mediating structure between the larger social structures and the individual – it most intimately deals with the body. Thus, everywhere, the family acts as a continuous thread by which to read each into the whole. To understand this process, what is most familiar to all – the family – will be rendered unfamiliar, alien. In familiar terms the family is a scene of private, intimate actions. In unfamiliar terms, these private and most intimate acts are already the property of a public director society. One's private and most intimate acts do not 'proceed according to a merely individual circuit' as Sève (1978) has noted. It is the extent to which the ordinary individual act 'goes through social circuits which are often extraordinarily far removed from the immediate reality' that is suppressed from ordinary consciousness and discourse. To raise this discourse is an essential act of education: the discourse that emerges from the suppressed can be called a forbidden discourse while it remains the object of coercive acts aimed at neutralising and inhibiting it, by what Freire calls the director society. We begin, therefore, with the social circuits which provide the context for the emergence of the family and an individual's acts within the family.

IDEOLOGY, POLITICS AND THE FAMILY

In modern societies politics has as its central aim the management or control of masses. A human mass is not quite like the grains of sand that form the mass of the sand dune, to be blown whether by arbitrary or well directed winds. Grains of sand do not ask 'Why am I here?' or proclaim 'God is love', or shout 'Eureka!' Nor do they stand up in protest, nor kill for an ideal, out of greed, or out of obedience or fear. People congregate into face-to face patterns of which the most fundamental and general are kinship based. The modern Western family is a particular case. The family is a face-to-face organisation which in its abstract structure is the paradigm for mass social organisation providing such abstract formulae as: head–led; authority–obedience; seniority–obedience; powerful–powerless; male dominance–female subservience – and so on. The values, attitudes and beliefs underlying the family as an instrument for organising masses into manipulable units is thus a vital starting-point for the discovery of forbidden alternatives. For this reason the family has received considerable attention from a variety of radical perspectives as well as those perspectives which act as apologists for the political *status quo*. Ideologically and politically, what are the central functions of the family? In her *The Politics of Reproduction*, Mary O'Brien (1981) writes:

> The family appears in political theory, as it does in history, in a number of ways: it has been perceived as the 'basic unit' of political society, as the economic unit of society, as the repository of tradition, custom and morality, as a mode of safely siphoning off the disorderly dangers of sexual passion. It has also been perceived as the most practical mode of rearing children and replacing those lost in battle, or of replacing the labour power of the industrial proletariat. The wide variety of views of the family, together with the marvellous variation in family forms which have appeared in history, all have two properties in common. One is the conviction that the family is necessary. The second is that the family is the proper sphere of women. (p. 11)

In her book, O'Brien's central argument concerning the family focuses upon the nature of reproduction. This term, in her argument, functions like a hinge which opens one way towards the world of work and the labour of men and the reproductive forms of society; then turns towards the world of domesticity, the family and the labour of women in the reproduction of the species. This double circuitry in which acts of 'reproduction' are united is a warp which twists individuals into structures not of their making but which they reproduce in their every act. These structures weave together individual, family and social structures external to the family. The family therefore at every step serves a double function. Its inner organisation services the needs of the state while serving the needs of individual members. As such it is a unit of political economy. The family as a face-to-face unit organises individuals into basic relationships with powerful cognitive and emotional ties. The sense of self, of personality and identity emerges from these face-to-face interactions. As an inter-generational unit the family relays the experiences, customs, traditions learnt by an older generation to a younger generation within a context of control and authority. As such it is a repository of custom, tradition and authority. The family as a sexually based union controls the relationships of sexual reproduction. It manages the sexual expression of adults and the emergent sexuality of children. The patterns of sexual ties between members of the family have been analysed by Freud in terms of the Oedipus complex. The sexual theme of the forbidden discourse arises here. But this is only a starting-point in a society which is beginning to critique and even rebel against its patriarchal forms. At stake in the rebellion of the brothers and the sisters against the father and at stake in the articulation of alternative forms of sexual expression, is the social order itself, the social order predicated on patriarchal forms. At this point then, the discourse has already developed four channels for its conversations about the family as:

a. a unit of political economy servicing the needs of the state: reproduction of workers, soldiers etc
b. a repository of custom, tradition and authority
c. a device for the control of sexuality: the Oedipal family
d. a vehicle for the management of rebellion, war and protest

The first three will be developed in turn, the last will be discussed in later chapters.

The Family as a Unit of Political Economy

The general social task of the family is to weave the tangled threads of culture into the child, smacking and caressing the cries and gurgles and uncoordinated limbs into a voice, a well behaved person. The task of politics is to coordinate the actions of persons. Fundamental to this are the forms of reproduction, not only of goods and services and of the species but of social institutions, roles, classes, personal identities, privilege and power: in short, all the cultural forms associated with patriarchal authority. Thus, at the heart of reproduction are the processes of enculturation itself: language and the forms of discourse through symbolic structures and processes of all kinds. The family prescribes a symbolic order of a certain kind. There are plays of variations along the theme of male and female. One major set of variations for male and female are: husband, father, son of, real man, breadwinner/employee of; and, wife, mother, daughter of, real woman, housekeeper. All these are terms of face-to-face relationships which tie individuals not only to each other but also to the forms of society. Playing through the variations, alternative themes and their variations arise by association. Prior to father or mother is lover. Lover associates with themes of romance, faithfulness, rejection, betrayal, adultery, promiscuity, jealousy and so on. Real man and real woman have in their shadows their opposites in which themes of failure, impotence, and weakness create other possible discourses for male and female to play out in their everyday lives. It is in these plays of opposition that the possibility for the forbidden discourse arises. It is through the ever-present possibility of alternatives that the family in its prevailing ideological form is under threat.

So, for example, in her analysis of 'reproduction' and of 'labour' O'Brien reveals the major oppositions at the heart of the family and at the heart of economic relations. One set of oppositions exists between those who labour and those who do not; the other set, apparently unrecognised by Marx, are the genderic oppositions 'between those who labour reproductively (women) and those who do not (men)' (p. 36). Reproduction, in this latter sense, articulates a forbidden discourse concerning women and the place of women in men's lives which produces a series of oppositions which O'Brien sees at the core of male–female relations in a patriarchal society. These are:

1 The man and the child, who may not be his;
2 The woman who labours to bring forth her child and the man who does not labour;

3 The man who is separated from biological continuity, and the women whose integration with natural process and genetic time is affirmed in reproductive labour;
4 Following from 1, individual man and all other possible potencies, men in general. (p. 36)

Since only the mother can know for certain who fathered her children, there is a particular male anxiety concerning the lineage of children behind the construction of the laws of ownership, marriage and inheritance. Only by constructing laws and beliefs concerning the sanctity of marriage, faithfulness, and the legitimacy and illegitimacy of children can the father attempt to ensure that the children he calls his, are his and so maintain purity in the lines of descent. Clearly, the woman's 'knowing' in this instance is different from the man's 'knowing'. The man's 'knowing' has to be rationally and socially constructed through the production of laws (whether secular or religious) and social norms. In this relationship between the two kinds of 'knowing' arises in the man a deep seated ignorance of the status of the child and hence the purity of the line of inheritance which reliance upon laws and customs cannot fully eradicate.

Man's and woman's knowing reveals a discourse which is maintained at three levels: the conceptual, the material and the level of social conduct (cf. Sayer 1984). Each level reads back into the other. So at the conceptual level in patriarchal societies the very ideas of Father, Mother, Child, of Husband and Wife, of Brother and Sister, of Male and Female, of Boy and Girl have a material counterpart in the patterns of political, economic and social life. The material structures of Home, House of God, School, Place of Work signify or point to the concepts of domesticity, religiousness, instruction and work which sustain them. Between say, the idea of God and the material structure of a church are the equally material forms of social conduct through which religiosity is sustained in human practice. The forms of discourse, the patterns of behaviour, the forming and fashioning and dressing of the body – these signify the idea of God and godliness. No individual act occurs without subjection in some way to the scrutiny of what it means to be a religious person, or similarly, a real Husband, Wife, Man, Woman and so on. To take on the role of father is to take on what it means to be a father within a prevailing moral order. To change the concept of father is to strike at the very roots of a given social order. The relationships of Father, Mother, Husband, Wife, Child are held together under the concept of the Family, the Church, the Citizen. Each member of the family has their proper conduct. Change the conduct and the whole concept of the family is at stake.

In summary, the scene of action of the family is supported by the material arrangements of society. There is the family home which is materially separated from the place of work in current Western society, although not in previous times and perhaps not in the future. This enables a division between the world of public action and the domain of domesticity where the man can find relief from work or the affairs of state. It is the sphere of women and child-rearing where the young are drawn towards their adult roles. In its arrangements it neatly mirrors or echoes the face-to-face forms of other social institutions and patterns of relationships.

The family, considered as a basic political and economic unit, offers a powerful control structure for the political regulation of everyday affairs in both domestic and public life. It is essentially a simple structure organising millions of individuals into face-to-face patterns through which control is routinely exercised in a way which is familiar to all and largely accepted as 'only natural'.

> The power of the family resides in its social mediating function. It reinforces the effective power of the ruling class in any exploitative society by providing a highly controllable paradigmatic form for every social institution. So we find the family form replicated through the social structures of the factory, the union branch, the school (primary and secondary), the university, the business corporation, the church, political parties and governmental apparatus, the armed forces, general and mental hospitals, and so on. (Cooper 1971: p. 6)

Recently, the family as a central instrument in the collection of 'ideological state apparatuses' (Althusser 1977), along with school, church, and the mass media has been placed at the forefront of political action. For the Thatcher government of the 1980s in the UK, for instance, when in 1983 it revealed its plans to solve Britain's social problems by resuscitating the family as a traditional good, it had in mind the happy family which was conceived as the centre of good house-keeping, dutiful children and hence a model of economic propriety and good citizenship. A committee of senior cabinet ministers produced a report, which included such traditional proposals as: the encouragement of mothers to stay at home, the training of children to manage their pocket money and to 'examine the extent to which professionals, such as social workers, teachers, doctors, architects tend to undermine individual responsibility' (*Guardian*, 17 February 1983). More striking were statements by senior ministers in the Thatcher government at a time of major street riots throughout Britain in 1981. Rhodes Boyson, for example, the then Junior Education Minister spoke of the undermining of the traditional authority patterns in homes and schools. The *Times Educational Supplement* (17 July 1981) reported him:

> Speaking at the Royal Grammar School, Surrey, last week, he said: 'In many RE lessons Christianity tends to be presented as an undemanding tour round a museum of quaint religious doctrines, instead of providing clear insight into the beliefs and principles of our fathers.'
>
> Children must meet firm yet fair discipline in schools or they would not grow up to appreciate the rule of law. 'If we destroy the authority of the headmaster and his staff, society will reap dragon's teeth in the form of juvenile revolt' he said.
>
> Without respect for traditional values, many young people grow up without beliefs, pride or confidence in themselves, Dr Boyson added. They found their identity, not through participation in a common national purpose, but in their own particular dress, colour, class or minority group. And assorted 'pied pipers and exploiters of both Left and Right' moved into the vacuum.

This expressed not simply a response to an immediate set of circumstances but a mood of the times. It was a response to the so-called permissiveness of the 1960s. Thatcher herself spoke of the 1960s 'claptrap' which undermined the traditional family through permissiveness:

> 'We are reaping what was sown in the Sixties. The fashionable theories and permissive claptrap set the scene for a society in which the old virtues of discipline and self-restraint were denegrated. Parents, teachers and other adults need to set clear consistent limits to the behaviour of children and young people. Children need, respond to and too often lack clear rules.
>
> 'Only in this way will they be able to grow up in a framework of certainty and learn the self-control necessary to cope with the problems of life.' (*Sunday Times*, 28 March 1982)

This framework of certainty is constituted out of what children should know and what they should be prevented from knowing, what they should do, and what they should be prevented from doing. A framework of laws and financial measures have been developed, principally in the 1988 Education Reform Act, to ensure that these ideas and principles for conduct should be materially reinforced. The debate that led to this act made clear what was at stake. It covered such subjects as sexuality and sex education, the necessity for teachers to teach about the profit motive, the eradication of debate in schools concerning the social implications of scientific advances, the eradication of peace studies from the curriculum and the necessity to promote a set of good books. Major newspapers on the right wing of British politics rallied to the cause:

> Brainwashing of British schoolchildren by extremist Left-wing teachers has become common-place, according to a shock report obtained by the Daily Express.
>
> Based on interviews with parents and pupils, it reveals how the extremists have infiltrated classrooms in primary, comprehensive and even famous public schools.
>
> 'Nowadays every subject in the curriculum may be used as a vehicle to put across an ideology', says the report compiled by research student Mr Tim Evans.
>
> The report comes on the eve of a crucial vote in the Commons on whether to ban political bias from the classroom.
>
> (*Daily Express*, 9 June 1986)

The attempt to stifle political debate in schools concerning such issues as racism, sexism, the promotion of peace, the understanding of the basis for social organisation was nowhere more stark than in the pronouncements of a right-wing group of educationists whose work had a major influence on the government in framing its policies. Their views were expressed in a pamphlet titled *The Wayward Curriculum: A Cause for Parents' Concern?* which attacked what they considered to be the dubious subjects of anti-racism, women's studies and peace studies. They considered also that sociology and politics were being studied at too early an age. In this, Professor Anthony Flew wrote 'anti-racism appears to have become second only to "peace studies" as a fig leaf hiding a massive and altogether unprecedented campaign of political falsification and indoctrination within state schools'.

In this way, the pattern of patriarchically defined male–female and adult–child relations begins to connect together the relations between knowledge and ignorance, innocence and the forbidden. Politically, the family as a repository of traditional virtues is the key instrument for articulating the values of a society. It is at the centre of this debate on education and the nature of society carried out by the British Conservative party. Popular capitalism was to be brought about, on the one hand, by giving parents greater control over school activities and on the other, as householders, as tax-payers, as fundamental units in the market economy, greater power to participate. Peter Walker, then Secretary of State for Energy, was reported as urging lessons in capitalism for all children:

> 'The educational system should be changed so that every child in his last year at school devoted one week of that year to be told the mechanisms of proprietorship.
>
> 'They could have explained to them the manner of becoming home owners, the availability of mortgages, the availability of improvement grants, the manner in which older properties can be improved and enhanced in order to see that they swiftly get on the road to house proprietorship.
>
> 'They could be told of the mechanism of the Stock Exchange, the methods by which you can buy and sell shares, the hazards and the opportunities. They could be taken through all the schemes that are available for the start of your own business. They could be addressed by those who had been successful proprietors in small and large companies.' (*Independent*, 4 March 1987)

Anthony Bevins, the political editor, went on to comment that the spreading of home ownership would 'create an increasing impediment to a return of socialism'. The family is a political tool by which to organise society. As a repository of 'tradition' it can be manipulated to serve ends far removed from the ordinary concerns of its members. By defining the family as a repository of 'traditional' (that is, conservative) virtues, a culture of silence is imposed upon it. The family has no word of its own except as the 'family'.

By the end of the 1980s a considerable array of laws affecting freedom of debate were in place. To these can be added the self censorship of newspaper and TV journalists. Such was the concern to the international journal *Index on Censorship* of these tendencies that it devoted its entire 1988 issue to censorship in Britain. Perhaps one of the most absurd and potentially dangerous acts of censorship was the veto by the Thatcher government during the summer of 1989 of a study of British sexual habits which for the first time would have provided national information necessary to the control of AIDS. It was felt that it would provoke 'unseemly speculation' (*Sunday Times*, 17 September 1989). As the *Sunday Correspondent*, 21 January 1990, commented, such studies could 'taint' the government. However, such interference was not limited to the survey but 'has led to the censorship of advertising campaigns, the pulping of educational material and the marginalisation of high-risk groups in a way that is putting young people at increased risk'. The outcome, intended or not, is an attempt to construct a sense of childish innocence or purity which has to be protected from the dirtiness of sex, even at the cost of putting people's lives at risk. This control of knowledge and ignorance is a central function of the traditional imagery associated with the family.

The Family as a Repository of Tradition

It is the family that is at the heart of all moral panics when there is the perceived loss of traditions, declining standards, decaying values. The Thatcher and Major governments in Britain and the Reagan and Bush administrations in America consistently pointed to the youth movements and political ethos of the 1960s as the source of decline. The 1960s achieved mythic status, at once a sign blurred by nostalgia for youth lost, and a mark of rebellion splattered on the containing walls of Victorian values. In 1988 the Law and Order Minister at the Home Office, John Patten, was reported by the *Sunday Times* as saying 'a world that was full of park keepers, of train guards, of bus conductors and other authority figures who acted as restraining influences had largely vanished'. Shortly after taking up his duties as Secretary of State for Education, he blamed increases in vandalism on the lack of religious values inculcated by parents and schools. The existence of external and internal authority figures creates a sense of there being no hiding place. To the loss of such instruments of surveillance, he and his colleagues attributed increases in lawlessness generally.

The pattern of authority as a guardian of knowledge and innocence and a shield against ignorance and corruption enshrined in the image of the Victorian family and its replication in the institutions of society is set against its twin, the myth of social permissiveness and lawlessness. It takes its strength from the fall from grace myth which guides so much of popular culture. Victorian values of the strong, religious family, the mother in the home and the father working hard provide the ingredients of the tradition, the golden age from which the modern age has fallen. The 1960s have taken on the status of a period of temptation, the tempters being the 'trendy lefties', the Pinko Liberals who subverted the youth, luring them to taste of the forbidden values which brought a knowledge of evil. The happy family was a guardian of the knowledge–innocence–ignorance structure which kept evil at bay. Schools as a surrogate family had to be cleansed of trendies and pinkos. In Britain a powerful movement of Educational Reform culminated in the 1988 Education Act. Its main object of attack has been the forms and content of teaching associated with the myth of the 1960s. This same movement found expression also in attacks made upon freedom of speech in the media and also freedom of information in politics and in particular, the secret services. To exist, the happy family not only must be aware of its enemies, it must *have* enemies. Like the Mafia, the happy family offers a protection service. It sets up the threats and offers to protect you from them. The happy family always knows what is in the best interests of its members. This yearning towards some imagined golden age of virtue and innocence is, of course, not new. No matter what date in history we choose, the people of the time will point to some period just twenty or forty or fifty years before it as the golden age (cf. Pearson 1983):

> The tendencies of modern life incline more and more to ignore, or disparage social distinctions, which formerly did much to encourage respect for others and habits of obedience and discipline ... And if it be true, as is so frequently asserted, that the manners of children are deteriorating, that the child of today is coarser, more vulgar, less refined, than his parents were, then, it must be admitted, whatever be the proficiency attained in arithmetic, and however much the intelligence may be sharpened, that the education presented to the children of the poor falls lamentably short of its ideal, in a most important particular.
>
> In selecting a TEACHER, *moral* influence is less easily tested than intellectual attainment. Of the two, it is the *more important*.
>
> (Mr C. G. Heathcote, Stipendiary Magistrate for Brighton, 1898. Source: Pearson 1983)

Nearly 100 years later, during the 1980s, the same refrain was heard by the Thatcher government in Britain and the Reagan presidency in America. And the form of the family which supports traditional values is always under threat from the same sources: bad parents (typically from the lower classes and groups defined as ethnic or minority), bad teachers (typically leftwing, permissive, trendy), bad influences (the gang, the boyfriend/girlfriend, television/radio, etc), and the predatory (drug pushers, pimps and so on). The myth of the 1960s now acts as a symbol for all that is threatening. And it is sex, its expression and its control, that is the motive. Under threat was the role of the family in regulating sexuality, sublimating sexual energies in ways approved for the reproduction not only of the species but also of society in all its forms.

The Oedipal Family

The argument is that the happy family has within it a buried and closely guarded secret. The secret concerns the relations between the family members as each jostles with the other for favours, security, position, power or the satisfaction of sexual desires. It is not that the Other-who-is-dangerous is outside of the family, but that it is within. The boundaries which separate the permitted from the forbidden are already a part of the warp of the family itself. This myth provides us with a particular drama of the family which Freud saw as the basis for the development of the socialised individual, which Lacan sees as framing the conditions under which the child is drawn into language and into society and which influenced Althusser in his conceptions of ideology. It is thus a particularly fertile myth for the modern imagination.

The drama, as is well known, involves the relations of forbidden desire between father, mother and child. The general direction of the argument leads us to consider the formation of a particular kind of discourse which we have been calling the forbidden which thrives upon and is articulated in the ambivalent, shifting, ironic structures of family relations. A history of the family cannot easily be written. The family, like women and children, does not have a history written about it in the way that there are histories of wars, politicians, kings and queens. It is appropriate, therefore, that the study of the forbidden begins also in a study of the forgotten and the social processes of forgetting. The Oedipus myth in psychoanalysis represents a particular form of patriarchal consciousness which has dominated

Western forms of culture and is thus a powerful agency in the repression of women and children and the regulation of sexual energies (cf. Mitchell 1974). It is thus from a feminist perspective that we may first begin to gain an appreciation of the forbidden within patriarchal forms of social organisation.

Underlying the Oedipus drama are not only the rights of succession between father and son but also the prohibitions regarding sexual relations between parents and children. In this sense, the Oedipalised family is a primary articulation of the realms of the sanctioned and the realms of the forbidden. Drawing upon the work of Lévi-Strauss (1970) and Ortigues, Lemaire (1970) describes the relation between family, the forbidden and society as follows:

> What is forbidden is coincidence between kinship relationships (blood relationships) and relations of alliance (marriage relationships) on pain of abolishing the Family. The Family appears as a symbolic structure which is irreducible to any natural structure: animal promiscuity. It is also irreducible to awareness of the psychological relations actualized by reproduction on the one hand and by love on the other hand.
>
> This means that the family structure manifests a transcendence of all natural order by the establishment of Culture. It alone allows each and every one to know who he or she is. In total promiscuity no one could in fact be called father, son or sister and no one would be able to situate himself or recognise others by the particular place they occupied. In this sense, the name, in so far as it is an element conveying relations of proximity, is a token of the recognition of individuals by one another. (pp. 61–2)

The role of the forbidden is dual: it establishes the structures of the individual and the relations of the individual with others in the symbolic order of the community. To this extent, the forbidden is a force which gives rise to culture itself.

However, the forbidden discourse is not straightforwardly expressible. It arises in a complex of relationships. It is in the nature of the forbidden for its structures and its intentions not to be clearly expressed, but to be recoverable through a kind of semiotic reconstruction which involves as its first move a de-construction of ordinary day-to-day discourse about experience.

TOWARDS THE FORBIDDEN SELF: OEDIPAL MIRRORS

It is through the family that the self first sees itself in relation to others and the objects and circumstances of the world. How the self finds itself through the family is the subject of much complex theorising. A powerful metaphor in theorising the development of the self has been that of the mirror.

A sociological perspective, symbolic interactionism, has provided insights into the development of the self which places its genesis within social interaction. For George Herbert Mead, the self has two 'sides': the 'I' and the 'me'. The 'I' is the original, impulsive centre of experience and source of behaviours. The 'me' is the social dimension which reflects upon the actions of the 'I' in the light of what is socially approved. The 'me' is constructed out of what significant others – mother, father, close relations, teachers – say about the self. Thomas Cooley used the term 'the looking glass self'. Mead likened this process of the development of the self in relation to significant others with Freud's superego. It has a censoring function. However, it is not simply an image of the self, or a set of roles and identities which compose the repertoire of the self that is internalised by the looking glass. Of greater importance, it seems to me, is that whole networks of relationships and patterns of action are also internalised.

One way of conceptualising this pattern is in terms of Berne's *Transactional Analysis*, where people internalise and play out life-time scripts and psychological games. In his view, individuals internalise a tripartite division of the self: the child, the adult, the parent. Each of these accord with real experiences of being a child, experiencing the actions of adult rationality (either as they grow into them or as they are personified by others) and all have had parents (or parental figures). There is then an inner stage upon which the various actors play out a repertoire of games, some of which structure a whole lifetime and are called life-scripts. These games and scripts are formularised in terms of typical relationships, how people are hooked into playing them, the moves that may be made and the pay-offs received. Many fall into the fairytale patterns such as 'Little Red Riding Hood', or 'Sleeping Beauty'. Those who play out negative games are seen as frogs (who never transform into the Prince) while those who play positive games are princes or princesses.

The mirror that is constructed reflects a whole world. However, it is not a unified construction. It is not a pure mirror. The mirror is flawed, it sometimes – perhaps always – distorts, it conceals, as well as reveals, it is misted. Anyway, the mirror is a deceptive surface, presenting a stage without substance, its depths are not its own. Within its framework, the significant others, to use Mead's term, play games of censorship, both inviting and repelling the child. Some of the 'I's' behaviours are warmly received, others are slapped. A split occurs between the 'good me' and the 'bad me', as well as the 'good parent' and the 'bad/hurtful parent'. Gradually, there is the construction of a covert self, the expression of which cannot be uttered; however, it comes to be the centre of initiative and action for the appeal to the forbidden.

This developing exploration of the mirroring metaphor provides a level of analysis which reaches into the individual through the process of the imaginary – basic to ego subjectivity – which Lacan places at the centre of the development of the social self. It is particularly fruitful in the analysis of media 'mirrors', an approach employed as the basis for an analysis of the way film and television is used to represent social reality and ordinary experience. It is useful to follow through the argument.

It is argued that the biological individual is shaped by structures outside. The assumption is that at six to eighteen months the child's visual capacities are sufficiently mature, well beyond other motor capacities. By identifying with the image of the mother or mother-substitute, the child is able to perceive at the level of fantasy his or her own body as a unity like the mother's. This serves to unify perception, constituting the subject as images and reflections just as a mirror frames the objects of a room. The mirror provides reflected images of the self, framed in terms of bounded relations with other reflected objects. This constitutes the 'imaginary'. In the face-to-face relationship one sees or constructs oneself with reference to the image re-presented by the other. What is most intimate is thus represented in a way that is 'distant', 'outside' and strangely ungraspable. The image that stares back from the mirror is culturally determined whilst intimately felt. Through the conception of the imaginary in relation to the wider circuitry of cultural structures, the ordinary discourse of the subject is indissolubly connected to cultural organisation. Or so it appears.

First, one conceives of a structure independent of a given individual: social, material, symbolic relations. Then one conceives of an inner capability – visual organisation – through which the outer structure is taken into the inner, imposing the outer structure upon the inner through a process of imaginary identifications. This is the basis of a broad family of psychological and sociological theories. It is convenient to the extent that it allows some other to peer into the 'inner' of another. It facilitates the development of a theory of representation where the public and the private have become confused and the mark of the self no longer cleanly marks identity. That is, the self is no longer simply identical to self. The barriers between self and other are down. But all is not clear.

According to Silverman (1983: 130–1) Lacan 'asserts that the signifying activities of both the unconscious and the preconscious are centred on the Oedipal experience, and that the Western symbolic order derives its coherence from the phallus or paternal signifier'. The mirror is an Oedipal mirror. The experience underlying the construction is that of lack. Lacan assumes that there was an original whole which is then divided in half, leading at every stage to the desire to recover the missing complement. This division was sexual in nature and the only solution, for Lacan, is heterosexual union and procreation. This original loss is not socially or linguistically constructed. Following this is a second loss. It results in the 'pre-Oedipalisation' of the body. The sexual territories of the body begin to be marked out. There are injunctions concerning what can or cannot be touched, how it can be touched, who does the touching; there are prohibitions concerning what is clean or unclean, what can be shown or cannot be shown:

> The child's body undergoes a process of differentiation, whereby erotogenic zones are inscribed and libido is canalized (i.e., encouraged to follow certain established routes). Specific somatic areas are designated as the appropriate sites of pleasure, and the areas which are so designated are all ones which open onto the external world – most importantly the mouth, the anus, the penis and the vagina. The mother is the usual agent of this inscription, defining the erotic zones through the care she lavishes upon them.
>
> The territorialization of the infant's body provides the means whereby the outpouring of libido can be directed and contained. By indicating the channels through which that libido can move, the mother or nurse performs a social service, assists in the conversion of incoherent energy into coherent drives which can later be culturally regulated. Indeed, by organizing the infant's body in relation to its reproductive potential, the mother or nurse already indicates the form which that cultural regulation will take: the orchestration of the drives around sexual difference. (p. 155)

This territorialisation of the self is not like a map which unambiguously sets out the possible routes one may take from one place to another, presenting the shortest routes to arrive at a desired destination. If anything, it is incomplete, perhaps set out like those ancient maps of the world where the unknown is designated with the words 'here be dragons'. To enter certain areas of the map requires becoming 'dirty', or 'saucy', or 'bold'. However, this is not a map, but a body. It is me that is dirty here, or bad when I do that, or shamed if I reveal this. These aspects of me, if I do them, feel them, can be called the forbidden self. It is a self created by the Oedipalised family, implied in the smiles and frowns of the 'mirror' through which my 'official' self is organised as a coherent self by mother and father in relation to others and to objects in the world. It is a self I cannot talk about, it haunts me like a shadow behind the reflected official self. The mirror is always at least a double-mirror. It does not reflect me in any unambiguous way. It presents to myself an overlayed set of reflections, partially hierarchised in terms of 'real self', 'inner self', the 'self that mummy loves', 'the self that daddy desires', 'the self that yearns to be like my brother/best friend' and so on. In my family my selves are known and are paraded according to circumstances. There are those selves I can talk about or reveal to all, those I can talk about or reveal to some, those I can only talk about or reveal to special people, and those I can never talk about or reveal.

Lacan's views are complex. Macey (1988) has argued that Lacan's followers (e.g. Jacques-Alain Miller) have presented his writings as if they made a coherent whole, with the journal *Screen* in 1973 appropriating Lacan as a major figure, unproblematic, representing 'a body of categories, a theory which requires no contextualisation or explanation' (p. 20). They are used in this book not for their power to explain, but for their suggestiveness of a way of thinking, of analysing, of blurring. Lacan provides a particular account of the story of three, in his analysis of Poe's 'The Purloined Letter'.

The queen receives a letter which she does not wish the king to see. Unfortunately the king enters the room. She places the letter on a nearby table. An ambitious minister enters who notices the queen's discomfort and infers that it is the unopened letter that is the mark of this discomfort. He steals the letter under the queen's eyes by a clever manoeuvre, knowing that she dare not stop him. The minister conceals the letter. No matter how carefully the police search they cannot discover it. The letter is recovered by a clever detective (as Poe calls him, a famed analyst) who also sees what the ordinary police cannot see. Like the king, the police do not see, or cannot read, the obvious.

The motivation for the events of the story is the letter, the text of which is never revealed, paralleling the contents of the unconscious and the way it motivates conscious actions. This relationship between the one who sees, and sees the import of a particular sign, the one who needs to conceal and those who are continually deceived is fundamental to political manipulation. The hidden motivation is the text that must not be read, and if read will lead to tragic consequences.

The Oedipus story, like 'The Purloined Letter', involves a threesome – king, queen and son – and the unconscious contents that provide, in this case, the terrible denouement. These are stories that can be generalised like other forms of triangular relationships, not those that rest upon a stable base, but those that divide by pulling in opposite directions each of the three points A, B, and C. So, in the relationship between A and B, C becomes the hidden third, the secret lover, the dark other. When A and C relate, then A and B is suspended, put out of play, the light is shifted and B slides into the dark of the triangular relationship. These shifts of light and dark correspond to the play of sexuality from public expression to private fantasy. When a newspaper proclaims prim family values on one side of the page and exhibits a nude pin-up on the other, private fantasy is made both publicly acceptable as 'just a bit of fun' yet still consumable in private fantasy. To reveal the darkened connections is to be caught out, accused of having a dirty mind to see such connections. An unstable oscillation between the prim and the titillating occurs which is continually denied. It is the essence of the unstable triangle to generate such oscillations. This oscillation results from a deeper tension.

Buried in the Oedipal relationship is a brutal drama: child abuse, incest, abandonment, patricide, vengeance. Like the purloined letter it is a text stolen. The text cannot be voiced, but if said, cannot be believed unless transformed into fantasy, lies. It is both the family normalised and the family scandalised. For Freud as for Lacan to negotiate the Oedipus process successfully is to enter normal society, in which sexual energies are appropriately directed towards the opposite sex. However, to realise the Oedipal drama, to open out its processes is a scandal. It is a possibility that has to be both recognised and denied. Child abuse is not a subject that adults are willing to talk about. To postulate the Oedipal process as fundamental in society raises the unthinkable. The implication that child abuse or incest is widespread seems fantastic in a society where people think of themselves as civilised, caring and moral. For Freud the solution was to say that the Oedipal drama takes place in imagination only, thus accounting for the generality of the process without having to postulate widespread violence and sexual abuse. Alternatively, the Oedipal triangle, with its abuse, betrayal and sexual tensions, can be projected more widely to include the relations between state or media personalities as parental figures providing competing love objects or betrayers, and the mass or audience as child figure or lover. There are different levels at which the reality of such processes can be realised. However, the reality of child sex abuse and violence within the home cannot be lightly dismissed.

During recent years people have been increasingly made aware of it as a major problem. Ives (1985) in a New Society article reported that 'Each year more than 5,000 children in England and Wales are battered badly enough for them to come to the attention of the authorities. And each year more than 50 children are killed by their parents – far more than by the strangers we teach our children to be wary of.' Two kinds of batterer were described: the stress batterer and the disordered batterer. The first is described as 'typically a woman struggling to bring up one or more children with too little help from a partner, if indeed she has one.' The second is typically 'a man whose problem lies in his past, he will probably have been seriously abused himself as a child, and this leaves a distorting imprint on his mind. He is left in adult life with a very poor impression of himself (though he may disguise this from outside observers with a "life and soul of the party" front. To him, harsh physical punishment is probably an accepted, even integral part of family life.' There is a sense in which the two kinds can be said to be connected. They are both part of the imagery of certain kinds of male and female stereotypes: the hard man whose only solutions reside in violence, the fraught woman stressed by the demands of domesticity who loses control. Perhaps both respond to the impossible demands of the stereotypes of what it means to be a 'real man – the head of the family' or a 'real mother', the one having infinite strength and authority, the other having infinite care and calm.

The effects of such cases do not remain within the domains of the perpetrators and their victims. They stand as an implicit criticism of the family, and in particular the father. This brutalising Other is revealed and inserts itself within the idea of the family leading to a public reaction against the accusers. In the spring of 1987, psychologists in Cleveland in the northeast of England claimed that a large number of child sexual abuse cases had been discovered. There were two dimensions to the shock: the first was that so many could be discovered; the second, was the apparent ease with which children could be taken away from families. The form of diagnosis – anal dilation – was controversial. The doctors involved came under intense media attention, and the social services were reviewed. There was considerable outrage on every side of the issue. The issue remained. The *Sunday Times* in 'The legacy of Cleveland' (Brian Deer, 9 July 1989) reported that two years on, the issue was no clearer. The occasion of the article was a BBC2 play 'Testimony of a Child', where 'although it was the father who was suspected of abusing his two children – who were then briefly taken into care – viewers were finally confronted with the apparent paradox of the children joyfully returning home. The post-Cleveland twist was that the local social services wrote the parents a letter of apology.' What is at issue is carried in the final paragraph of the article: 'Unfortunately, children are rarely given the power that makes them feel able to refuse sexual intimidation. Nor do they often have the sort of relationship with parents in which they discuss issues like these without the fear of being blamed, disbelieved or even taken away. The biggest thing missing from Testimony of a Child was what children have to say.' There are those things which cannot be talked about. The underlying structure is that of silence, the unseen, the unsaid, the unheard. Through this there is a split in experience, a discontinuity, a fragmentation where things no longer make sense, where reasons fail to connect with actions.

This was nowhere truer than in the Nottingham ritual abuse controversy during 1990 where children's testimony was the centre of the controversy. As described by Judith Dawson (*New Statesman and Society*, 5 October 1990), a social worker, the problem arose in the summer of 1987 when it was considered by a care worker that eight children in a family suspected of incest should be removed. Seven children in the extended family were already in care. It was a family that had first been suspected twenty years earlier 'and, in 1975, the father (now the grandfather) had been imprisoned for incest with his daughters.' This led to twenty-five children being taken into care as the case progressed. Nine adults were convicted and imprisoned, eight from the same family. 'Lord Justice Farquarson singled out the social workers for praise in court and the Prime Minister also praised them in parliament.' The children, once in care, described fears and activities which were clearly unusual. Their homes had been paedophilic meeting places where they had been systematically tortured and abused:

> Their accounts built up a clear picture of children being abused for the gratification of adults interested not in sex itself, but in its use as a tool for the promotion of ritualistic acts. They say that they were made to stand in circles, being orally and anally penetrated by adults in strange costumes; that they were forced to eat excreta and to drink blood from animals; that animals and human babies were killed before their very eyes. We do not know if these events all took place, but we do know that the children believe they did, and are able to describe it in the most minute detail.

The media derided the emerging evidence. The social workers were accused of being too influenced by consultation with occult groups, 'but the children's disclosures came first'. The police, according to the article, did not want the evidence to be revealed. They were accused of being too gullible on the one hand and too powerful on the other. The controversy continues. In the view of Dawson the media response has been 'designed to protect "innocent family life" against the new urban myth of the "satanic" abuse of children inspired by evangelical fundamentalists'. Campbell in the same publication focuses on the dismissal of the children's evidence where children are 'designated tendentially dishonest and undeserving' and an inquiry team 'mocked their allegations that they had been abused by posh people in posh houses. How could a disgraceful, scruffy family keep company with the rich and respectable?' Campbell sets the issue within the wider oppression that children and women experience.

The function of the family is to organise processes of denial, to generate outrage and panic in its own protection as an institution preserving innocence. Allegations and evidence of abuse and ritualistic practices de-stabilise the myth of innocence, re-inserting the dark Other into the family relationship. Yet abuse occurs and if children believe it, and their testimony is not arbitrary then the ritual use of sex should also be taken seriously. Proof and the need to deny creates an oscillation between the horror directed towards perpetrators and the denigration that is continually raised against those who attempt to reveal such practices. It produces a situation in which real investigation, real strategies by which to handle allegations of abuse in any of its forms are inhibited. The effect of this oscillation is to disconnect events from the underlying structures and processes in which they occur.

In an article by Janet Watts ('Why do men do it?' *Observer*, 6 August 1989) on convicted child sex offenders, the elements of incomprehension and distaste are apparent throughout. A man says 'I just want to know why I do it'. The title of the article suggests it will give an answer. No answer is provided. Instead, the terror of the men's identities being recognised through the article is described, a probation officer is reported as needing to take a bath after work to wash away the feelings, another says 'sometimes you can go out and see perpetrators everywhere.' And another says, 'I'm not sure that's not the truth.' Worse, the perpetrators look normal, 'one of us'. Research is drawn on showing that the single common denominator of offenders is their capacity to deny:

> They minimise their offences in a multiplicity of ways. As: 'It was a one-off', a 'coincidence', an 'accident'; 'It just happened'. They put the responsibility on to the children: 'She wanted it, too'; 'She really seduced me'; 'These three-year-olds can be really provocative'.

The American literature is reported in summary to refute these 'reasons':

> Offenders rarely commit 'one-off' offences: a group of 159 intrafamilial offenders disclosed (under guaranteed confidentiality) 12,927 acts against girls; 44 offenders had committed 2,741 acts against boys. The majority of offenders molest both boys and girls, and both inside and outside the family. Conviction rates are a gross underestimate of sex offending: a population of 561 non-incarcerated offenders, including all types of paraphilia, had committed 291,737 acts.

The Director of the Child Assault Prevention Programme, Michele Elliott (letter to the *Sunday Times*, 14 October 1984) reported studies showing that 46 per cent of children had hidden sexual experiences before 12 years of age, involving older men some of whom were relatives; '1.2 million children are annually exploited in child prostitution and child pornography.' The *Guardian* (19 October 1983) reported the National Society for the Prevention of Cruelty to Children concluding that one child a week dies at the hands of parents and 'a further 50,000 suffered the "lesser deaths" of gross neglect, physical and mental torture, sexual abuse or emotional starvation.' However, counting the cases year after year does not make it more knowable. Paradoxically, as the Cleveland and Nottingham controversies show, it marginalises the issue, takes it out of the normal range and sets up the spectre of these dangerous-others who prey upon children, who turn families rotten. It turns attention from examining the structure of the family itself and the role it plays in the constitution of society, providing the conditions in which the dismissal of children's and women's evidence and their real abuse can be hidden. Such a structure cannot be counted in order to find its sense or its impact. It is found in the ways in which roles and identities are organised in society across the sexes, the social classes, the ethnic, cultural and religious discriminations and the age groups of each. It is not the numbers of incidents, but the structures implied in the incidents, each incident revealing a little more about their essential, or common properties. Through each incident the roles are displayed, the conduct, the belief systems, the logic of relationships between roles, between institutions, between systems of institutions. The numbers gloss over the intricacies of structure and of detail through which all are implicated in the realities of the drama.

If it is just numbers, then the solution is simple: it is a matter of training, the increase in the number of 'experts', or of increasing funding for the 'problem'. Thus, for example, it was reported (*Times Educational Supplement,* 8 July 1988) that the Department of Education and Science (DES), following the Butler-Sloss inquiry into the Cleveland affair, recommended that 'every school designate a "senior teacher" as being responsible for "co-ordinating action" on child abuse in all its forms'. However, the DES 'insists that no additional costs should be incurred for training teachers,' although money was to be made available for training social workers. Apart from raising awareness little is accomplished. The cases continue. The targets move. In reports in the *Sunday Correspondent* (25 March 1990) institutional neglect on a national scale over the last twenty years was revealed. 'Families are split up and children removed because of fears about the quality of their parenting.' The children that result from the system of state 'care' were described as rootless, having 'higher levels of delinquency, crime and unemployment'. In another article on the same page, 'Teenagers in care in one of London's largest children's homes are becoming involved in robberies, stabbings, underage sex, vandalism and prostitution'. Official care is reported as failing. A report by the National Children's Bureau (*Independent;* 13 December 1990) reported that 'the number of children living in poverty has doubled in the past 10 years'. In America Abramovitz (1991) wrote of social policy being in disarray. Generally, there has been a depression of average family income over the past decade, with 12.8 per cent (31.5 million) Americans living below the poverty line. African Americans earned 10–26 per cent less than whites. For the first time, sons and daughters in their lifetime expect to have a lower standard of living than their parents. However, the Census Bureau reported that 'for the most affluent fifth of all households, wealth rose 14 per cent from 1984 to 1988, after adjusting for inflation' (*New York Times*, 11 January 1991) Poverty, its effects upon children and its associated issues make a scandalous text, the true import of which must be kept from the eyes of the comfortable.

None of this is a new problem. It has a long history. De Mause (1975) described the history of childhood as a nightmare out of which we are only just awakening. His contributors showed the historical pervasiveness of abuse, and of harsh discipline based upon moral imperatives founded on deeply internalised texts or discourses of original sin and absolute obedience. Child-rearing patterns began to change towards the modern form during the nineteenth century. Although Walvin (1982) characterised the emergent family ideal of the nineteenth century as that of domesticity for the middle- and upper-class families, the working-class family was regarded otherwise. Moreover:

> By the mid-century there were, notably in London, armies of children living beyond the family pale and surviving in wretched groups. When trying to save such children, and to render them more amenable to training and a useful adult life, reformers created artificial family arrangements. Such waifs were put into 'homes' where they were given foster parents and where they were encouraged to feel part of a wider family group. Even in the proliferating public schools there emerged the concept of *'locus parentis'* to provide those schools with the morally and socially approved sanctions of family over the pupils. (p. 14)

Although children in literary circles had begun to be conceptualised in terms of innocence rather than original sin, discipline was still a central feature of general child-rearing practices. Regarding school:

> Bishop Blomfield used to say that if a child were whipped before it arrived at the age of three, it would need no floggings afterwards.
>
> Parents and children themselves when the matter is put logically before them, admit the need of corporal punishment, and if teachers would only consult parents before administering it to the children, sentimentalists who get so much out of this subject would have little copy to work on. As a child, I myself received hidings which I richly deserved, and only wonder now that I was so lightly let off. (Swinburne 1911: 14)

Corporal punishment continued in British schools for most of the twentieth century until August 1987. The issue of discipline, however, has not gone away. Many would still like to see a return to corporal punishment. In the family, smacking still has its place.

What is the relation between discipline, corporal punishment officially administered, smacking by parents, hitting in the school playground between peers, the hidden but apparently widespread child abuse and – it has to be added – wife-beating?[1] It's all in the family. It all forms a part of a cultural obsession with violent forms of control. Is there a continuity between the 'smack' and 'brutal abuse'? Is there a resemblance of structure sufficient for the smack to be interpreted as a 'part' through which the whole context of violent and authoritarian forms of control and 'respect' is reconstituted in the mind of the abuser? If this is so, then the alien acts of the abuser are rendered uncomfortably familiar. This is not to say that the process of reconstituting the whole context from the part is straightforward or simple. There is a need for detailed case studies to provide the range of variation through which commonalities and resemblances can be discerned.

One such illustrative study can be made of the Schreber case. This is a case made famous because it was used by Freud to support his theory of the relationship between paranoia and homosexuality. Freud based his analysis exclusively on a heavily censored account written by Schreber of his experiences. However, of more importance for the discussion at this point is not Schreber's account, nor Freud's analyses, but the role of the father and the suppressed text of the father's beliefs and actions in Freud's account. Schatzman (1973) drew attention to the fact that Schreber's father was a famous and

1 Although there are incidents of abuse against husbands these are a minority compared with abuse against wives, girlfriends, women generally.

influential educationist in Germany whose pamphlets on child-rearing were translated into many languages. Freud could not have but known this. Thus, the childrearing beliefs and practices of the father should be central to interpreting the son's experiences. The father practised total behavioural control over the child, employing instruments that would fix the child's body into the 'correct' position whether sitting, standing or lying. Psychological strategies demanded that children 'love, honour, and obey their parents', teaching parents 'a method explicitly designed to force children not to feel bitterness or anger towards their parents, even when the feelings might be justified' (p. 47). The father's text (in the broadest sense of the term) was hidden from the child. All actions were designed to ensure the child would have no access to the text. It is doubly ironic that Freud also made no reference to the many texts that the father published. The power of the suppressed text is a model of textual suppressions and manipulations politically practised through the name of The Family, or family values, or Lacan's nom du père which conceals the like-sounding non du père.

Through smacks, threats, injunctions against seeing, doing, hearing and saying, sexuality and social behaviour become regulated within the Happy Family. The child is Oedipalised according to psychoanalysts, socialised according to sociologists, civilised according to politicians. The child, in any case, learns to live with, even become the mirror of her or his self presented by the significant others within the family and the community. The images of what it means to be a man and a woman are presented and internalised. If those images involve strict discipline, then that becomes internalised as normal. The macho man, the strong father, leader of the family or the gang structurally merge to present images of authority and leadership. If the discipline is harsh – even brutal – then this only proves the real 'manliness', the real 'leadership' qualities as any John Wayne film testifies. The smack within this context is considered normal; the image of the smack thus comes to represent the whole set of values of the good, strict father able to control and discipline and thus build the character of his children. What is abnormal is the same action carried out to excess, or for reasons that are sexual and lead to enjoyment. The difference is crucial. But so is the similarity. Within this ambiguity of relation stands the public face proclaiming values and virtues as reasons for the control; behind it, in its shadow is the confused mixture of feelings – power, terror, righteousness – which are denied and repressed as the forbidden self. The unruliness, the cheekiness, the insolence of the other must be repressed in the name of authority. This self that emerges that must at once be denied and punished may be seen everywhere: the gangs of children up to no good, the mischievous child at the back of the class, the child who refuses to do as he or she is told.

It is common for teachers, politicians and people in general to talk of children's family backgrounds as the reason for their behaviour – a lack of parental control, a family breakdown, a single parent family. Typically, the images conjured up are also framed in terms of social class and racial discriminations. There are whole classes of people who for centuries have been regarded as the 'dangerous classes', the 'criminal classes'. It is upon these that the forbidden is projected, as they become the darkened 'third' in the relationships of the family, which are even re-packaged and sold back as entertainment to thrill, excite and 'scare' the docile classes.

The project of the happy family is still at work throughout society. Its implications are not fully realised. The remaining chapters of this book are devoted to de-constructing and re-working the experience and the expression of being an individual, being alive and being free to create and express one's self in society.

3

STEPPING OUT ALONG THE COURSE OF LIFE

The move from family to outside world is already prepared, the curriculum is well formed, its syllabus composed of the stories told from the cradle to the playground, to the streets. The first step that consciously raises the possibility of leaving the family creates the boundary between the territory of the family and that of the outside. In the outside, there is the sanctuary of the out-of-reach, the hiding place where the surveillance of parents and parental figures cannot disturb or impose upon the expression and behaviour of the child. It is a place of new possibilities which allow the identity for the family to be managed alongside the identity-for-friends/peers/strangers. Relationships to strangers and to friends are added to family relationships: re-constructing the triangle of relationships already well known from the processes of Oedipalisation. The territories of strangers, friends and families are re-sexualised at every transition point in the life of the individual. They can be the 'new fathers' or 'mothers' from whom to learn new things, on whom to project feelings and needs. Of the three, strangers generate most instability in the triangle as potential threat. The course of an individual's life in relation to family, friends and strangers is not arbitrary in the sense that what happens is so bizarre that these sequences of events do not fit within some known pattern.

At its most stereotypical, audiences and readers will always recognise the life pattern of 'the middle-class business family','the town drunk', 'the goody-goody', 'the drug addict', 'the moral campaigner', 'the schoolgirl mum', 'the wife-beater', 'the gambler' and so on. These are so recognisable that many sociologists will write of the 'career' of the drug addict, the rapist, the victim just as one would talk of the career of the accountant. These career patterns, through which individuals find not only an identity but a way of life, are part of the cultural repertoire of families, communities, societies.

Such careers, enacted in their appropriated territories, divide between those that are good and those that are bad. It is the structure of the forbidden discourse – institutionalised in schools, churches, policing and so on – that creates this binary division, at once holding the two apart and together. Through the discourse a repertoire of injunctions, sly looks and covert gestures evokes the paths to be trod, the fruits and pay-offs to be found.

The repertoires are evoked in the myth of leaving, the myth of 'making one's way in the world', the myth of 'making something of oneself'. The myth is not a frozen story as in the case of a Grimm's fairy story, but is rather a form which finds expression through a myriad of possible tellings and re-tellings. It is something which becomes part of the explanatory force of an individual's, a group's, or community's identity, history and way of life. The myth is carried through anecdotes, popular sayings, partially remembered stories or characters from books or television or cinema, the imagery surrounding 'stars', war heroes and legendary events.

Lurie (1990: 189–204), in her book on children's stories, comments that 'children's games and rhymes and jokes do not exist in isolation: they have echoes in history, anthropology, archaeology, literature, popular culture and art.' Thus:

> When a child climbs a pile of stones and shouts 'I'm the king of the castle, get down you dirty rascal!' he is repeating a Roman children's taunt; when an older boy or girl shows a baby the 'two little birds, sitting on a hill, one named Jack and the other named Jill', she or he is rehearsing a nursery entertainment known on four continents.

The stories, rhymes and jokes of children rehearse roles, attitudes and conduct over the range of experience that the myth of the happy family would protect them from: the sexual, the violent, the wicked and the heartless. Yet the rhymes and songs proclaim them with great pleasure:

> Look, look, mama,
> What is that stuff
> That looks like strawberry jam?
>
> Hush, hush, my child,
> It is papa,
> Run over by a tram.
> (Francella Butler)

My mommy lies over the ocean
My daddy lies over the sea
My daddy lies over my mommy
And that's how they got little me.
(Lurie)

Such rhymes express not only forbidden knowledge and feelings but also provide a sense of power over situations and over others, seducing them, trapping them, making fools of them:

- What's the difference between a mailbox and a hole in the ground?
- I don't know.
- Well, I certainly wouldn't send you to mail a letter.
(Lurie)

When one individual meets another in a public or private place and they seek to know something of each other the work is carried out through a range of symbolic practices already coded in the stories, the rhymes, the jokes. In the encounter each is a mirror to the other, a mirror which does not simply represent, but also evokes images that seduce, repulse, and manipulates the sense of the real held by the other. The task is to construct the specular, the spectacle and the spectacular. Together they construct the spectatorium: the place where all that can be seen is shown. In a space where values are given to the hidden, the covered, the buried, trading takes place: 'I'll show you mine, if you'll show me yours.' Margins are created for secret viewing. Alongside this is the auditorium where all that can be said is said and in its margins, secrets are traded, the unsayable whispered. Thus, the world is territorialised into places where things can be seen, done, heard here, but not there.

The course of life, then, is arranged with its public spaces constructed out of what can be seen and heard in that space, and the margins to these. In any encounter in any space, the style of gesture used, the fashion of clothes worn, the haircut, the colour of skin and hair, the body and facial type, the manner of speech, the vocabulary used, the topics of conversation – all these and a myriad of other clues to the nature of the other will be used to say 'I know what sort of person/place this is', and 'I know the kinds of things this person does or what can be done in a place like this.' By such clues the person will be judged as either appropriate or inappropriate to the space, either an insider or an outsider to the group that dominates that space, uses it for their own purposes.

Both self and other are inscribed by the cultural signs and symbols of their respective groups. Through the inscriptions partitions between one group and one way of life and another are drawn. Knowing how to read and knowing how to present or manage the signs and symbols associated with people and places is crucial. During a study of police training in Australia, as we drove through a well-known area in the city, a police officer told me how some people could walk safely through its streets at any time and others get mugged: 'It's how they look. You just know the kind of person.' Clearly in his mind was the image of 'mean streets', and 'mean people'.

A young female police officer talked of why she wanted to join the force. She said it was the sense of power which compensated for a sense of lack of power in her youth. The important thing for her was:

> to be out in the streets, to be seen. If you're seen there's no crime at all. There might be something round a block where a building's blocking you. If you're seen out in uniform it's a deterrence straight away. It's like the little old lady on the train, she likes to see you in uniform. If you're standing there in plain clothes, she doesn't know who in the hell you are. You can be Jack Smith across the road. But if you're in uniform that lady feels safe, therefore she has no worries of getting mugged on the way home. Walking down the street, I find that's great being seen in uniform. Being seen, is a major thing. When you're driving, driving a, down the street in the police truck is great, just to be seen in the area. But if we're not seen in the area equally the crime rate ....
>
> I'm actually a beat person my self, walking the streets. I find that's great, just being seen in uniform, speaking to people, finding their views on what we should do and where we should go to find these crimes because we'd have no chance of solving crimes if it wasn't for the police and people out there.

There are interesting inversions in this passage. The powerless child – who incidentally had had no family, having been orphaned – now has power and becomes the authority caring figure, invoking also a traditional male role looking after the 'lady'. Through this reading of the signs and symbols of the street, the participants of an encounter are positioned. That is, they are established in their authority and control relations as either 'one of us', or 'one of them'. And an area is constituted out of the kinds of encounters that occur between the already dramatised role-players. Being fooled by a misleading sign can be dangerous.

There are those who are expert in the management of misleading impressions (Goffman 1970). Participants in such encounters can have different levels of awareness concerning the openness or hiddenness of intentions (Glaser and Strauss 1967) These levels of awareness range from total openness, where all information is believed to be above board, to the belief that the other is lying or concealing relevant information. In each encounter, one person may believe that all is open, the other may not. All encounters are structured through a process of positioning and partitioning – you are here, you are Us; you are not there, not Them – and the control of access to information. The positioning and partitioning of face-to-face relations does not occur randomly; they pick up or mimic the patterns of relations already pervading the institutions and social strata of society.

The course of life in this perspective is a process of negotiating position and place with a continual danger of misrecognition. In the simplest view of it, it is like the flat image of the chess board. The board is divided up into squares and there are different pieces that can be placed on the board. However, until told the rules you do not know where to place them on the board to start the game, nor do you know how to move them, nor do you know the relative importance of each piece. A game of manipulating king, queen and pieces, the simple-minded pursuit of destroying or dominating the other (or perhaps motherland and fatherland), is played out on the board. However, what if during the course of the game you begin to suspect that another, far from simple-minded game is being played out? This other game, you suspect, is being played at another level hidden from your eyes. You have been deliberately duped into misrecognising the rules and importance of each piece. Through a series of clues gleaned like a detective or pyschoanalyst from the overt text you are able to reconstruct another level of play which perhaps inverts the importance of each move you have previously been making. Once you have recovered the hidden rules at play you begin to play with more confidence until you suspect that yet another, even deeper, layer may exist. This goes on until you realise that the game is actually being played on many different sedimented layers, like a geological cross-section, each layer complexly faulted and fissured, bearing different properties of hardness, permeability, durability and so on. Moving to a different strata suspends the 'realities', the 'understandings', the 'interpretations' that hold sway or make sense on the other strata. Now this is something like the structure of the forbidden discourse if each crossing from strata to strata, and spaces within strata (like the squares on the board) are marked by commands, prohibitions, and sly invitations to transgression.

The key is the way knowledge and ignorance are structured in relation to each other and to individuals. Through this access is opened or closed and the individual is positioned in relation to the spaces, stratifications and objects of the world about. The stratified spaces of the world are never empty. To move into a space is to move into a space already occupied, already organised, already under orders, already, that is, institutionalised. As the individual moves from family to the institutions of the world, the course is moulded by the kinds of encounters made possible by the kinds of institutionalised or public space entered.

TRANSITIONS

The move from one territory to another involves transitions within the self that call out different aspects, or construct different faces, of the self: we are named and called. And in response we become echoes of that name-calling. There are two kinds of transition: the developmental and the territorial. Earlier phases and places may be recalled with happiness, nostalgia, or repressed out of disgust, horror, terror.

Fitting in to new situations may require a suspension of the old ways of naming and of being with others. For the individual, this is not a general problem, it is 'my' problem, felt in all its terrible uniqueness and isolation. Open here is the potential of being stripped of a name, a way of identifying, or conceiving one's self – being found out to be nameless, being vulnerable to the knowledge that death has already happened, the name was only a cover. At every crossing, a little birth, a little death. It is marked by a break, a gap occurring between the family-self and the encounter-self.

At the break, at the point of crossing, there is work to be done. The gap must be 'naturalised', explained, hidden, or sutured to present a smooth surface, a continuum. The individual named at birth is 'growing up', 'maturing', 'evolving', 'developing', 'increasing experience', 'becoming enriched'. With every territorial exploration, there is the experience of articulating the different faces of the self, exploring the separate satisfactions to be had in each case, and the problem of integrating or repressing the result so that with every crossing, it is the *same* individual, with the *same* name. Through the discourse of sameness, the gaps, the incommensuralities, are covered over. It is a discourse that must not be challenged in any fundamental way. It is constructed out of a 'stock of common knowledge' that is 'taken for granted for all practical purposes until further notice' (cf. Schutz 1976). Regarding his or her knowledge of and beliefs about the world, the individual 'suspends every doubt concerning their existence' (Schutz and Luckmann 1973: 27). Where a scientist may take in an attitude of inquiry, a critical approach which suspends belief in the existence of objects until proven otherwise, everyday life requires a taken-for-grantedness: 'this is real, right, good – and that's just the way it is.' However, the sameness is often illusory; as circumstances and social conditions change, then the self will change, often quite fundamentally:

> The radical student who becomes a conventional liberal or conservative with graduation to new jobs and new ambition, the dedicated communist who becomes a fervent anticommunist, the liberal who becomes a neoconservative, the pacifists who support war when their country is about to embark on one, are recurring examples of the principle that political self-definitions and roles reflect the conditions, constraints, and opportunities in which people find themselves: that ideology and material conditions are part of the same transaction. To understand either stability or change, it is necessary to look to the social situations people experience, anticipate, or fantasize. (Edelman 1988: 3)

Essential to successful transition is the construction of continuity, some explanation of change in terms of 'progression', 'stage of life' or increasing 'maturity'. By taking for granted this 'natural' transition the break is not a threat to the continuity, the identity of the self. The question 'who am I?' can be answered through a set of simple formulae, the utterance of a name, the description of a job, the narrative of a family history. The question is asked lightly, not seriously like a scientist or a philosopher. In this way a politics of continuity is constructed. Challenges to this continuity can be devastating.

THE POLITICS OF MULTIPLE WORLDS

The acknowledgement of multiple worlds of experience already inserts a faultline from the depths to the surface of 'reality'. The politics of multiple worlds is constructed around the control of 'doubt' or 'critique' through convention, routinisation and redundancy. In the triad of family, friends and strangers, it is the stranger who brings the threat of an alternative reality.

The Red Riding Hood story provides curriculum materials for one kind of attitude towards the stranger. It is at one level an injunction against straying off well-worn tracks. What was she doing out that late, dressed that way, in that area? ALONE. She was asking for it. She either had to be impure or was a helpless innocent in need of rescue by some male. But Red Riding Hood was not always such a helpless wimp in need of rescue by the powerful male. The history of the story as re-presented by Zipes (1983) reveals the nature of the entry into dangerous spaces, its historical and social function in positioning listeners and in covering and separating realms of experience.

Evidently the little girl in the oral traditions preceding the written forms of the tale was not the hapless spoilt dope of the modern story but well able to look out for herself through her own resources. It was a story of the peasant girl reaching puberty, being warned of dangers at a time when 'Little children were attacked and killed by animals and grown-ups in the woods and fields' (p. 6), becoming initiated into work practices, symbolically replacing 'the grandmother by eating her flesh and drinking her blood' and finally 'It is a matter of self-assertion through learning and conflict' (p. 7).

Perrault gave us the first written story of the young girl with the red cape and hood in 1697, changed to fit his views of women, appeal to the upper classes and present a moral for children: 'The irony of his narration suggests that he sought to appeal to the erotic and playful side of adult readers who took pleasure in naughty stories of seduction' (p. 8). The change in the story from its oral versions to its written version mirrored the changing views on childhood in educated society (cf. Aries 1962). Previous ages had little or no conception of childhood: children were simply little adults.

> Thus it is no surprise that the character of the little girl in Perrault's literary tale is totally different from the one of oral tradition. The 'peasant girl' is forthright, brave, and shrewd. She knows how to

use her wits to escape preying beasts. Perrault's Little Red Riding Hood is pretty, spoiled, gullible, and helpless. The moral of the tale does nothing to alter her character or to suggest what would improve her character; it simply warns children to be more alert and to beware of strangers. (p. 9)

In Perrault's version, the girl is not saved, but eaten by the wolf. If, as evidence suggests, the colour red generally was the mark of 'sin, sensuality, and the devil' (p. 9) then the rape motif becomes more secure, as does the implication that she was asking for it. There is, thus, a sting in the tail of the story. It is not simply a warning against the stranger. It is also a confirmation of the hidden nature of the self which responds to the seductions of the stranger. Upon the stranger can be projected not only fears but also the promise of the new father who sanctions new codes of behaviour, new forms of expression which more adequately satisfy previously repressed desires. The ambiguity of the stranger can be neutralised, or glossed over, in terms of codes of politeness which place a distance yet also provide easy routines to reduce the tension.

Such stories, then, provided manuals on how to meet and behave in a civilised fashion in public places, supplying a powerful way of controlling 'strangeness', disguising the 'wolf'. During the sixteenth and seventeenth centuries a number of books and pamphlets were produced dealing with etiquette, morality and so on.

It was impossible for a member of the aristocratic or bourgeois class to escape the influence of such manuals, which became part of the informal and formal schooling of all upper-class children. Coercion by members of high society to act according to *new* precepts of good behaviour increased, so that the codes of dress and manner became extremely stringent and hierarchical by the end of the 17th century. Though not conspired, the rational purpose of such social pressure was to bring about an internalization of social norms and mores so that they would appear as second nature or habit. Yet, self-control was actual social control, and it was a mark of social distinction not to 'let go of oneself' or to 'lose one's senses' in public. (p. 12)

Today, the freedoms of expression and association are just as regulated, but the 'manuals' are in the form of magazines, TV, video and film. The regulation is, of course, ambiguous. Since the inception of the 'movies', they have been a source of controversy. They, themselves, can be the source of 'strangeness', of values which are perceived as seducing, subverting and corrupting.

Forman (1933), in an important study of the time, raised the issues in the form of cinema being a major system of education, easily competing with schools in terms of being a vehicle of mass education. Through the medium of the cinema, many young people were introduced to forms of conduct, values and beliefs that they had not seen or heard before. How can you be the same again after you've seen the hero and heroine kiss like that! What happens to your views when the villain is both attractive and seems to have understandable reasons for his or her actions? What happens to the sense of authority when authority figures are shown to be irrational and cruel and when young people or subjected people rise up against them? Forman drew his conclusions:

> Possibly some parents may be willing to have their children acquire their attitudes, manners, morals, ideas of love and sex from the movies. But how many of us would like to have our children become dissatisfied with their homes, or rebelliously resentful of parental control, in consequence of the teachings of what we may perhaps call our movie Bible? Not that in pre-movie times a certain number did not tend to be dissatisfied or rebellious, or even run away. Formerly the reading of particular types of narratives created the incentives. Now, the motion pictures, so easy to see, showing as they do certain delightful and alluring experiences doubtless enhance those desires. Many of the cases cited illustrate both the dissatisfaction and the lure. Twenty-two per cent of the high-school boys and girls studied by Professor Blumer declared that they had experienced feelings of resentment against parents as a result of certain motion pictures, and twelve per cent confessed to occasional experiences of actual rebellion. As one boy put it, 'The movies depicting social life at first disturbed me. I wasn't satisfied with my environment; I expected too much from my parents in the way of comfort and leisure.' (pp. 167–8)

The family as a source of control, morality, authority, manners cannot reach sufficiently into the public market place of ideas and experiences. Its censorial functions are not powerful enough. It is losing its grip. There are the woods and streets at night, there are the slum areas, the interstices, as Thrasher (1927) called them where control and surveillance break down. It is here where there are the 'wolves', the breeding grounds for gangs. What is on offer, what makes it so difficult to control, is the 'lure', the dazzling experiences, the fact that 'badness' opens the way to attractive experiences.

These 'wolves' are the very children of the family who, seen in unfamiliar places, themselves become the strangers. In a study by Cahill (1990), children's behaviour and treatment in public places was observed over a two-year period to test the view that in American society the distinction between childhood and adulthood had been eroding. It was found that children's access to public spaces was limited and typically they were treated as less than complete people. Generally speaking, public space is inimical to children: they are not wanted and no or few facilities are provided for them. Fear dominates the thought of children entering public space unsupervised. If alone and young they may be snatched. If in groups or in gangs they are either a source of nuisance or of trouble, even danger. Public space is largely well defined. They are a focus of public order concerns. As such they can be called non-manipulable spaces. That is, their definition is not simply up for grabs. However, this contrasts strongly with those spaces which extend beyond easy rule and surveillance. Here, the use of the space are open to re-definition by anyone who exercises the power to define them. As such they can be called manipulable spaces. It is here where danger lurks, boundaries become confused, blend and transform those entering them. They are the 'between' where all safely known categories begin to disintegrate. Without continuous vigilance, all public spaces are open to this kind of threat:

> Since approximately 1979, popular concern about children's safety in public places has mushroomed. A series of highly publicised child abductions and murders, such as that of Adam Walsh in 1981, apparently convinced many Americans that children in public places faced a more ominous danger than moral temptation or accidental injury or death. Televised dramas, documentaries, and Congressional hearings helped to foster the impression that there was a virtual army of villainous adults stalking and preying upon children who dared to venture outside the protective fortresses of home and school. (Gardner 1990: 393)

Newspapers and television have, as stock characters, the monster, the fiend who preys upon children, women, the elderly. These examples of the real instance, feed the fears and contribute to the stories that can be told about the problems of public safety and the times and places when to leave the safety of well lit familiar places is to invite trouble:

> Contemporary folktales or urban legends also fuel this fire of popular concern about children's safety in public places. For example, the modern horror legends of 'the mutilated boy' and 'the attempted abduction' have a similar theme. Either a young boy or an adolescent girl suddenly disappears from a department store or shopping mall. The missing child is then found in a public restroom either physically mutilated or in the process of being disguised by the abductors, who are preparing to sell her into some form of sexual slavery. (Gardner 1990: 393)

It is in the public space that the crowd, the mass of strangers produces the sense of anonymity out of which danger can suddenly arise. The mass itself becomes the stranger. The masses, the uncultured, the lower orders have always inspired fear in the 'civilised' classes. In the nineteenth century liberals in Britain put considerable effort into securing a division between the violence of the criminal and the violence used by the state to punish the criminal or enforce law and order (McGowen 1989). The epitome of the liberal imagination was perhaps expressed in Mathew Arnold's *Culture and Anarchy*, which identifies violence with the bawling masses who claim the Englishman's right to do anything he pleases. It is the undoing of culture. Again, the public space has to be redefined and reclaimed for the educated classes.

In the midst of the mass, silence is the predominant feature of the fleeting face-to-face meetings with strangers. However, the mass is itself differentiated sexually: the threat, as in the Red Riding Hood story, is predominantly male. At night, in lonely streets, or strange locations, it is, as Gardner (1990) describes, necessary to adopt strategies – such as wearing dark glasses – which 'curtail others' visual access in order to prevent being judged as a suitable target' (p. 314). How should Red Riding Hood be instructed today?

Gardner made a study of how women were instructed to deal with public spaces. She reviewed the popular literature on 'self defence, crime prevention, women and crime, and women and rape and assault' between the years 1970–89 as well as books published between 1965–89. Women were typically defined as possessing limited competence. She found that:

> There is no complementary male-directed literature: when crime-prevention books for men are written, they are on self-defence skills. Some advice books for women are simply directed to the men who, it is assumed, will be their teachers. (p. 313)

She described the kinds of strategies employed by the twenty-five women she interviewed (all middle-class Americans from Santa Fe, New Mexico) in order to reduce their sense of vulnerability in public places: the use of a male escort (friend, colleague, family relation, policeman); manage impressions to make it seem that a male friend is nearby (man's pipe on the car seat, mentioning a boyfriend during a conversation with a stranger); and 'If she is home and a man claiming to be a repairperson knocks, a woman alone sometimes attempts to signal that a man is with her' (p. 318). And finally: 'some women come to count men less as individuals than as protectors, functioning either well or poorly, a conception congruent with traditional ideas of gentlemanly behaviour ...' (p. 319).

Red Riding Hood today, it seems, can find little in the way of a counter myth. However, in a broadcast of women's self defence presented by Lindsey De Paul evidence was drawn from the work of Dr Pauline Bart of the University of Chicago to show that women who screamed, shouted, resisted were at no greater risk from retaliation by their aggressors, but were more likely to fend off attack (BBC1, *Eve Strikes Back*, 10 August 1992). A senior British police officer was shown instructing his audience of fellow officers on how best to teach safety to women. His view was not that women should aggressively defend themselves, but rather that they should avoid danger by proper dress, and avoiding dark and lonely places – a view not borne out by Bart's evidence. Although women could take up martial arts, he saw this as nothing other than a hobby like pottery or knitting. His talk ended with the image of the dominant female, foot on the chest of a defeated male, arms raised in victory – an image set up for disapproval as being the logical result of teaching women to believe in aggressive forms of self defence. Thus, the desired and dominant image is still of the woman who is largely helpless, requiring the agency of a man to protect her, from other men. It seems the stranger at the heart of the mass is the patriarchy itself, constructing the male world view in which the threat both arises and is to be contained.

NEGOTIATING THE COURSE

The relationship between fictional images and their articulation in everyday discourse as ways of talking about and manipulating the identities of one's self and of others in public has to be traced. During the course of everyday life, these images and their relationship to the material structures of social life may be passed over without notice. However, by stopping and listening, by recording something of the lives of others a margin is created through which a perspective on the routine is made. Curricular patterns can be revealed which plot the learning points, the lessons of life by which the individual drives or is driven on a life course.

There is a recognisable narrative structure to accounts of such courses. And the courses are 'routed' like roadways or pathways or railways requiring people to go from places to other places where certain events or transactions take place. The course is marked out by 'problem' points or times and places. At these times and places a particular motivation, pleasure, action or event renders the trouble-free course troublesome, problematic. At these problematic points, decisions have to be made, actions performed. They are significant for the development and management of the multiple facets of the self and hence the formation of personal and social identity. For example:

> Ernie used to play the arcade machines and meet individuals who would introduce themselves and start friendships which he described as 'coupling off'. They would play the machines together. He describes it all now as a waste of time 'because all it led me into was trouble'. However, at the time the involvement presented itself as attractive. 'I thought it was like, you know, "yeah, it's a laugh. Let's go along. Now you see it is just a wild time." It got me into a lot of trouble with the old firm that.'
>
> The 'old firm' is the gang of which about sixty or more male adolescents would claim some association. Its location is the city centre and it is called the city gang. These associations made up largely of working class male adolescents have existed for generations in the area. (...) According to Ernie, people who become associated with these groupings are 'you know, people who want to be the hardest geezers in the city, you know, a mean Harry, that sort of thing. Whereas', Ernie now says 'they're just a bunch of saps.' To qualify as a City Boy you have to be an 'arcade lad' first, particularly in the city centre arcade. 'You sort of get to know them,

you know, and have a laugh and all that and then you sort of start fighting'. He adds, 'the Old Bill are just waiting for the chance to get that lot now.' He began hanging around the arcade, he says, because 'we had nowhere else to go and nothing else to do.'

He got into trouble with the City Boys when he began to borrow money from one of the leading members to use on the machines. This young man, who is older than the rest, possibly in his early twenties, 'sort of lends money to a lot of the younger kids there and then asks interests'. The interest he asks for on a loan is double the original quantity each week. 'It just goes on and on.' There comes a point when it is absolutely impossible to pay. When that point comes the young man who lent the money and his closest associates 'just give you a good kicking and takes maybe forty pounds. So you borrowed ten pounds you sort of give them forty pounds and say that's it. Down the road. I can't give you no more. (Davies and Schostak 1989)

Ernie's course takes him on a particular route around the city. It is here that he picked up the myths and counter-myths fundamental to his way of life. Each stopping point on the route is associated with particular kinds of events, transactions, characters and self-expressions. Each character has arrived there following his or her own course. The police – the Old Bill – are there, 'just hovering', following a course of surveillance which intersects with, complements and is essential to Ernie's story of his course of activities. The Old Bill, just as much as the 'City Boys', generate the problems in his life which are themselves essential ingredients to his stories and through which he articulates himself as a character, an identity structurally related to all the other characters and possible identities realisable in the account. It is not simply a matter of Ernie's perception. These relationships are real. They are made real through the predictability of encounters. The police, the City Boys, his mates, his teachers, his parents, his neighbours all know aspects of the story, know what he is 'really like'. If he were to act otherwise, if he were to suspend his perceptions, it would not matter. *They* know the truth and would act accordingly.

The arcade where the gambling and games machines were was the meeting place, the margins to public space created for profit, legitimate but the centre of public concern. The local newspaper ran a campaign, providing lurid stories of children addicted to the arcade machines. In becoming addicted, so the stories went, the children were led to stealing, prostitution, violence. The arcade was an invitation to transgression. The transgressions were public events, threats to the stable family. The gang was the new family – the brotherhood – formed through its counter-rules, its counter-myths, asserting and policing its own world view.

Ernie's account is not unique. It is fully recognisable as the stuff of commercial popular fiction, sociological studies and journalism. It would not be hard to place him in a television soap opera. In part, we see ourselves in his account, whether as an approving or disapproving audience. We are there in shadow, watching in the margin as he transforms into 'a mean Harry', a City Boy who then escapes to other routes. In a voyeuristic way we oversee his education in the forbidden.

For him life seems open to possibility. Youth by definition seems to symbolise open horizons, exciting unpredictable growth. Society, however, controls the public exploration of possibility, displacing it to the realm of fantasy. A realm of safe explorations with no personal or social dangers. The youth confronting the social presents at once conflict, rebellion, change, loss. The adult in service of the social has to be drawn from the youth. For this, the curricula of separation and of control are mobilised. The curriculum of separation is founded upon constructing the relation of us-and-them; the curriculum of control follows by establishing the mechanisms of the coordination, the restraint and the ultimate coercion of them by us. In the same study as that of Ernie, there was Veronica, who has so far led a quiet uneventful life in a village:

> Veronica has got a paper round and on Sunday morning she earns £2.50. She once delivered the local free advertising paper. She recalls delivering 100 copies once and earning £3.00. She didn't think too much of this and one day, after having put ice cream advertising leaflets through the doors with the paper, she gave the job up. This was some two months after starting. One of her friends, she says, gave up her paper round after two weeks and two days. She gets 50p a week from her grandad and £20 a month allowance. Out of this allowance she has to pay for her own clothes, pay for her subs to guides and she has to pay for any trips she might want to make. Occasionally things all come together at once, like Activities Week at school for instance.'That's sort of tight but then you borrow next month's . And you sort of have to be kind to her [her mother] do extra washing up and she'll let you have the next month's early.' She remembers spending all her allowance in one day recently when she bought a pair of jeans 'jeans are quite

expensive. If you buy jeans that takes up three-quarters of it'. She buys a record occasionally. She finds sometimes that she doesn't like it and when that's the case she'll sell it to one of her friends. Most of her friends get pocket money, about £2.00 a week she reckons. She is the only person she knows who gets a monthly allowance which she must control. She admits that she doesn't find handling money that easy. 'It sort of tempts me in the city. I think I really like that pen but I can't hardly afford it. "oh" I'll go "you can't afford it. You've got thousands and thousands of pens, thousands of rubbers, everything you need ... But I haven't spent any money for ages so I have got to spend it. So I spend the money and I think "Why did I have to buy that horrible pen next day. Waste of money." Then if I didn't buy it I would think "Drat, I should have bought that." So I can't get out of it everyday. My mum goes "Budget".' Sometimes she will be hungry and unable to resist buying a bar of chocolate 'a Marathon or something'. This might leave her short of money for lunch. Her father says she must account for her own money. So now, she says 'I've got discipline.'

There is a park near her house. There is a 'sort of smokers' gang' that hangs around there. Her father advises her not to go around with them 'and I say "I'm not going to, it's disgusting".' She recognises people from her school in this group 'Mostly I see them at night and that's dark and that's horrible ...' The group she says is made up mainly of fourth and fifth years but there are 'even some in the second year that sort of hang around with brothers and sisters there'. They hang around at the end of her road and 'they all leave matches. They came and sat on our wall one day and I went out next morning and there must have been about a hundred matches out there.' She feels strongly that they are wasting their time. 'They're just wasting, waste, waste, waste. They could be doing much better things with their time.' They are also wasting their money 'and they go round on their motor bikes just going round and round on their motorbikes and mucking about and that. They are only going to get caught by the police and they have been told to move.' But the group doesn't move even when the police come down. 'They just stand there.' The group moves from block to block. Another spot favoured by the 'smokers' gang' for hanging around is the shop in front of the school. Her father, who is on the parish council, has himself attempted to move them on. 'He just tells them. He don't start swearing, he just tells them to move otherwise they are going to get into more trouble.' In his capacity as a member of the parish council he is able to lock gates to the park so the group is not able to hang around there. 'He locks the park gates now and if you're in there, you're stuck.'

Within the brief accounts of Ernie and Veronica there are two major properties which are central to the discussion of the forbidden discourse. The first are the *transformation boundaries* that set us apart from them, necessitating changes in the self at the moment of passing from side to side; the second concerns the common structures which can be identified over a range of such stories which can be re-formulated as narratives to be told and re-told as part of the folklore of a given group and can be repackaged for purposeful manipulation by advertising agencies, politicians, preachers and teachers. This range of stories, rhymes and jokes becomes the menu that an individual is offered when crossing the many boundaries, confronting the transition points in the course of his or her life. People make different selections from the menu. The selections are not made arbitrarily but, as in the case of Ernie and Veronica, there are the material conditions which guide their entrance and exit to public spaces and thus access to what is on offer there. I call the menu-like collection of possible stories available upon entrance into given spaces paradigmatic narratives.

PARADIGMATIC NARRATIVES

Paradigmatic narratives are not simply formalised abstract structures – their function is to evoke feelings, arouse desires, provide explanations and motivate actions. They are the fundamental curriculum materials for ordinary everyday living. They are essential to the construction of a self in relation to a dramatis personae and the sequences of events that each play off with and against the other. They distinguish both the desirable and the undesirable positions and places for self to occupy. Some paradigmatic narratives are open as regards the range of interpretations that can be made of them, others are relatively closed, or aspire to be completely closed. Some reinforce the dominant cultures, others provide the framework for counter-cultures.

Consider this extract from a portrayal written by Richard Davies (Davies and Shostak 1989) for a recent project on alcohol cultures:

Maria likes to go to pubs every Friday night, to meet friends and to talk. Generally she does not like nightclubs. 'I don't go into nightclubs. I don't find them at all sociable because the music is so loud you can't talk to people. I don't like them. But I go to pubs because the music isn't too loud and there's usually a regular crowd that you see every time you go there. Say every Friday night you go there and there's the same crowd there that you get on with. And if you don't like it, you can always go somewhere else. There's always a pub that suits different people. Like there's one pub that's for yuppies, a cocktail bar. There's always a pub that's suited to you.'

She also goes to a lot of parties, she says, and drinks there. In fact she 'gets rather drunk'. Basically, if she goes to a party she expects to get drunk 'Because it's what I do. I go mad.' She doesn't think most of her peers share her view or behaviour. 'It's what I do personally.'

Maria knows how much she can drink. She has never been sick before; she has never drunk so much that she has been sick. 'I don't drink myself absolutely paralytic so I don't know what I'm doing. I drink until I'm feeling merry and I'll talk to anyone and I go just absolutely mad and have a really good laugh.' Drunkenness she describes as involving a certain dislocation of brain and body. For example, where you go to pick up a glass as a reflex action only to find 'You go "Which one is mine?"' and 'you think "hang on a minute, what's my arm doing here?"' She remembers another image of being 'merry': 'At a party once, the dance floor kept on going up.'

Drink 'does relax you', she says. 'Before you get to the merry stage, you get a bit laid back'. Drink is socially useful, 'You feel, you don't sort of think "When am I going to get into this conversation that everyone's talking about", you sort of ... you feel free to do what you want.'

She has always considered that 'your true self' comes out when you're drunk. Sober people tend to want to conform to each others' expectations 'but as you go through the amount you have you become relaxed and you feel free to say what you want and then you begin to get further and further into it until you don't care if they're going to accept what you say or not. So you just say whatever you want, what comes into your mind as you are not trying to hold anything back, your true self is beginning to come out.' She says that even when she doesn't drink she says things to shock people 'because it really annoys me when people go "Oh my God, what is she doing?" I just don't like it and I don't think people should be shocked by the way other people behave. So I deliberately try and shock people anyway.'

She thinks there are double standards in society's attitudes towards women and alcohol. 'Why is it so unladylike', she asks, 'to get drunk if you want to?' She adds 'I've got drunk but I've never thrown up.' Maria feels some irritation at male attitudes as she perceives them: 'You can have a real laugh with a girl as you can with a load of lads. If you ask me I think lads are really stupid prats who find fun in having mindless violence. I think girls are much better company.' As for fighting: 'It's all an act anyway. If you were on your own you wouldn't go out and look for a fight. I mean it's not in you. It's the fact that you're with all these other people who think, "I've got to be a hardo and we've got to have a fight to prove to each other how hard we are." If you were on your own in a pub and you saw a load of Gothics, you wouldn't go up to them and go, "Oi, you wanna know, you wanna know, wanna fight." You'd probably get on like a house on fire. It's really stupid that people have to prove how hard they are.'

These extracts from an interview with Maria provide the stuff of which paradigmatic narratives are made. Her accounts of parties and of behaviours are instantly recognisable by anyone who has ever been to a party and has got drunk. In her account she selects characters from a dramatis personae which again are recognisable just because they are so one-dimensional: the 'hardo' boys and their 'male attitudes' form a clear and distinct other against which she establishes her own persona and that of 'the girls'.

She mentions a particular youth culture group, the Gothics, as if they were a well defined gang or grouping. Rather, they are individuals who dress in a particular way and listen to certain kinds of pop music. Yet, the dress is enough to generate hostilities between them and those who dress differently, say skinheads. Maria shows that she is aware of and understands the rules of public space within the context of youth pop cultures. She knows the kinds of encounters that routinely take place. There is something compelling about these encounters such that they characterise groups of people. It is thus difficult to behave otherwise in public places: given a certain kind of encounter a fight *will* develop.

She is aware of the possibility of transformation. In fact drink and parties are transformative. That is their function. Just as dressing as a Gothic or a Punk or a Dread is transformative. For her, drink allows her to do things which she would not otherwise be able to do.

This is the major function of drink at parties, universally recognised. Its disinhibiting effects are well known. Thus:

> Actions form sequences that are coordinated within narrative structures: a story is told. Certain characters – the dramatis personae – are necessary to this story. And one character is privileged: in this case Maria. She is the heroine. In this story, the heroine is transformed from status-less child to a centre of social excitement who has a wild and commanding personality. If a critical act (e.g. drinking) in this pleasurable story (e.g. the story of the party) is omitted, how can the story proceed? And more importantly, how can she emerge as heroine? This consequence is reinforced by two examples drawn from elsewhere in the study. One male fourth year pupil remarked on seeing a video of the mis-adventures attending a teenage party where uncontrolled drinking took place, that one of the exciting side effects of such catastrophes is that they 'give you something to talk about for weeks after'. The second example involved an out-of-school, end-of-fifth-year party with pupils from the school in which the research had taken place. One fifth-year boy, already celebrated as something of a character by his contemporaries at the school (which may not have been unconnected to subsequent events), was rushed to hospital as a result of excessive alcohol consumption before the end of the party. He had to have his stomach pumped. Teachers report that his stock as 'legend' is now higher than ever before. There is little trace of censure amongst his peers. If anything there is pleasure in the memory of the drama he created. Nor does there seem to be, generally, a desire to emulate. The moment belongs to the particular individual, a splendid episode like watching a tightrope-walker over the Niagara falls.

To return to Maria's account. At this point, a simple analysis of Maria's experiences reveals the following decision schemata:

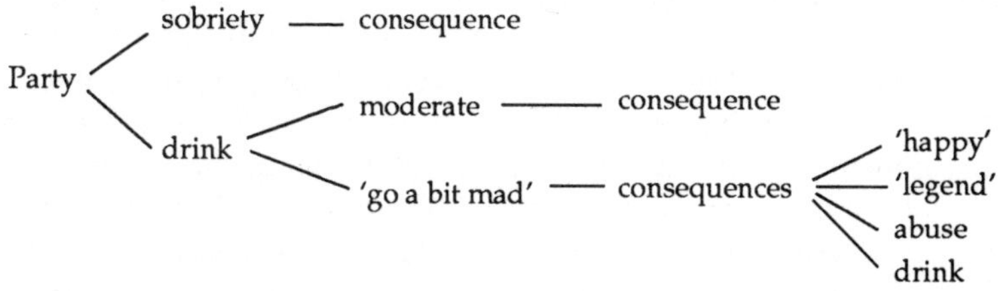

This schema begins to fill in the structures of Maria's account. A deliberate decision is made to suspend the path that leads to sobriety, knowing that drinking leads to 'going a bit mad'. Each decision-path calls into being certain kinds of encounters in which the self will be situated and the kinds of encounter strategies available in that situation. Goffman (1961: 154) has described the features of the situated self:

> The self ... can be seen as something that resides in the arrangements prevailing in a social system for its members. The self in this sense is not a property of the person to whom it is attributed, but dwells rather in the pattern of social control that is exerted in connexion with the person by himself and those around him. This special kind of institutional arrangement does not so much support the self as constitute it.

This is a self which is produced by the dynamics of the situation rather than something which crosses the boundaries of different situations. To that extent it is unstable. Maria talks of going 'a bit mad' at parties. This 'mad' self is constituted by the party as a particular kind of public stage, with drink as its major prop to 'madness'. However, it is more than simply arbitrary. It happens regularly at parties. Parties, as an event in the social life of young people, are 'storyable'; there is what may be called a genre of party stories which people must be able to tell, otherwise the event would not be a real party. The party may be lively, or dull – the stories will differ on that account.

How does the party stand in relation to other kinds of situations, encounters and events? The paradigmatic narrative provides a set of related dramatis personae, places or scenes for action, sequences of events, experiences and pay-offs. Where the individual is in this network, the actual course chosen (or compelled) from it, traces out the actual course of life of the individual. This course of life is always bounded by the options provided by the structure of the paradigmatic narratives that inform his or her consciousness. Thus Perrault's Red Riding Hood story substitutes the clever and competent heroine of the oral tradition for the spoilt and incompetent creature his own mysoginy formulated. In doing so, the options for action and for self-transformation are drastically reduced. There is a sense in this account of the oral being silenced by placing words into its mouth. However, the oral is recovered at each point the individual in his or her community subjects the frozen stories of myths, literature, news and anecdotes to alternative readings.

Barthes makes a distinction between art and life, in that in the artistic narrative everything has a function. Everyday discourse knows 'only "fuzzy" or "blurred" communications' (1977: 89 note 2). However, why should this be the case? Freud pointed to the dream image as being 'overdetermined', whereby each element has more than one signification. In short, each element is functional in that through its overdetermination a sense of predictability, of inevitability, of routiness, of redundancy is constructed. Its fuzziness is more due to the analyst's inability to unlock the code. The forbidden discourse holds the key to the levels of structuration which orders and coordinates the products of the story-telling consciousness. Life, just as art, has to be rendered accountable – tell-able. Human society, its courses of action and conduct are the product of 'tell-ability'.

Individuals are structured through time as baby, toddler, child, teenager and so on. There is a sense of 'growing out of' such structures. Each structure has rights and duties, powers and limitations. To go beyond one's socially imposed limitations is to enter the forbidden. Thus one talks of underage sex, adultery and other forms of impropriety. In addition, age or ageing is essential to the course of life but, as the advancing years pass from the enhancement of powers to the decay of powers, ageing becomes a forbidden discourse. The course of life with its forbidden and permitted realms develops under the discourse of attraction and repulsion, desire and disgust, permission and prohibition. This is essentially a 'narcissistic' discourse which generates boundaries of the self and the stage upon which the self has a right to act, or rightly or wrongly habitually acts. A boundary arises which defines the stage for the course of life, the proper field of action for the individual. Each phase in the course of life and within this boundary has its 'character' or dramatis personae of characters and its accounts, stories, folktales and so on through which it is made meaningful, known and accountable. The course of life – like the stage, or arena of action – splits into the desired, the legitimate, the ordinary, the heroic and so on: these in turn are articulated within a discourse which creates the forbidden courses of life and the 'right' courses of life for men and women to follow. At each turn in the narcissistic process, endings are closed down by the insistent determinations of the reflective images.

Everywhere, we look to see our own reflection. Through language everything is mirrored, reflected by signs, images shunted along through channels of discourse. Is the real just a chimera provided with a being and an existence only though our own conversations about it? If so, the ultimate is conversation itself, comprised of the act of meeting, corresponding and the dramatis personae who talk, talk, talk. Through endless conversations the symbolic order is spun out to entwine, circulate the symbolic currencies of the day and finally reflect the face of the speaker and the other who through listening, ignoring, replying is turned into a mirror reflecting not simply what is intended but the sedimented, overlayed, encrusted domain where consciousness plays from living being to living being. This is the narcissistic ending of the course of life.

4

HEROES AND VILLAINS: Industrialised Culture and the Contortion of Experience

Propp (1968), in a study of Russian folk tales, was able to reduce the dramatis personae of all the many tales to just a few. The central characters were the hero and the villain. Few modern stories fall into Propp' s neat categories and structures, yet in essence his approach holds up surprisingly well.

Clearly, a story creates a very complex relationship between its world of imagination and the world of everyday affairs which people call real. It is not easy to drive a wedge between them and to call one unreal and the other real. Classical narrative structure pits the hero against a multiplicity of obstacles both 'natural' and 'evil' until typically reaching a climactic encounter in which loose ends are cleared up and the stable 'for evermore' is reached. Narrative is also fundamental to historical knowledge (Danto 1985). The sense of the real carried in the narrative structure works in myth to fuse identities, events and explanations of the world, integrating the individual and the social through 'master narratives as a kind of grammar dominating storytelling in a given cultural domain' (Taylor 1988: 97).

At each stage of the course of life, in the new spaces entered, experienced, explored, new heroes and villains emerge, but they do not emerge arbitrarily, they emerge in relationship to the master narratives of a given culture. What can or cannot be said and seen in each space entered in the course of life, creates a dividing line overseen by the march of heroes and villains. With the public face presented in public spaces, rigid discourses police the spaces where thoughts can only be communicated in whispers. The whispers create the margins in which hearing and overhearing are zoned. And within the zones, the hidden, the secret and perhaps the forbidden self can make its appearance for privileged access by those within hearing and seeing distance. These secret selves invert the heroes and villains expressed through the public face. Their conflict produces the essential energy for the courses of action each take towards the other, consuming all in the process.

THE MYTHIC SIGN OF THE HERO AND THE VILLAIN

Myths have always played out the intimate relationship between the emerging self and the conditions of the world. Jung considered that myths revealed the deepest nature of human life. Campbell, influenced by Jung, in a series of books explored the connections between myths all around the world. He was searching for the universals, the archetypal structures at the heart of the world's myths. He sees myths as essential to human living, to creativity, to self-development. But myths live, in that they evolve and are expressed in ways which are appropriate to the current conditions of life. Thus the Star Wars trilogy he saw as a contemporary myth reworking the father son complex in Luke Sky Walker and his father Darth Vader, the villain who is 'more machine than man' and in the clutches of the 'dark side of the Force'. Campbell saw the conflict as being between life and the new implications of the machine, which he perceived as beginning to dominate all. For him, the hero is the hero with a thousand masks (1964). In all the disguises, the hero is essentially the same, playing out the universal master narrative of 'overcoming', reintegrating the self at some higher level of practical, political, moral achievement.

With each story and each variation, new ways of experiencing are opened up.

> A particular kind of material determines the art of mythology, an immemorial and traditional body of material contained in tales about gods and godlike beings, heroic battles and journeys to the Underworld – 'mythologem' is the best Greek word for them – tales already well known but not unamenable to further reshaping. Mythology is the *movement* of the material: it is something solid and yet mobile, substantial and yet not static, capable of transformation. (Jung and Kerenyi 1970: 3)

There is no one single meaning of mythic material.

> An essential character of religious symbolism is its *multivalence*, its capacity to *express simultaneously several meanings the unity between which is not evident on the plane of immediate experience* ... This capacity of religious symbolism to reveal a multitude of structurally united meanings has an importance consequence: the symbol is capable of *revealing a perspective in which diverse realities can be fitted together or even integrated into a 'system'* ... One cannot sufficiently insist upon this point: that the examination of symbolic structures is a work not of *reduction* but of *integration*. One compares and contrasts two expressions of a symbol not in order to reduce them to a single, pre-existent expression, but in order to discover the process by which a structure is capable of enriching its meanings. (Mircea Eliade 1965: 201, 203)

The signs and symbols of myths formulate not a single unambiguous representation of some 'thing', some essential matter or way of being, but rather a constellation of possible relationships through which a way of being may be found. The play of hero and villain are essential to the formulation of ways of being. The two must meet if growth is to take place.

In its abstract form, the hero triumphs over the forbidden or the beasts, villains and barbarians which represent the tabooed, the evil, the pestilential residing in the dark areas. However, the manner of the meeting may be ritualised, controlled, ordered in order to reproduce traditional ways of being. The hero, in this case, is simply a ritualistic dummy that has lost its power to transform in ways that are unpredictable. The hero has been appropriated for ideological purposes to sustain the prevailing social order. It is not hard to set out the stock oppositions arising under the headings of hero and beast/villain in Western culture and more particularly its Americanised forms. These assumed oppositions are framed by the ideology of the ruling groups.

> The pattern of classical narrative is effectively isomorphic with the master narrative of western civilisation in its continuities from the defining example of the human drama as embodied in the life of Christ, then as the struggle of capitalist rationality to overcome nature and less instrumentally rationalistic cultures; these two are challenged by the more recent Marxist revision, in which the key struggle is class conflict between proletariat and bourgeoisie.

All three narrativise 'history' as progression towards a formal closure on a utopian terminus of one sort or another.

What remains consistently foregrounded in the master narrative of contemporary western society, recapitulated in countless entertainments, is the march through time of the western patriarchal bourgeoisie. It is a paradigm that symbolically rationalises the marginalisation of hierarchical inferiors. (Taylor 1988: 97)

The key to the ideology of mass culture is the relationship of the hero and the villain to the family. One is not born into the family in general, but into a family in particular which ties the individual through affective bonds. As such it is the archetype of all face-to-face relations, real or imaginary. The family is structured as families in Western culture generally are: father, mother, children. Each member has an individual biography. Each individual is weaved into the family 'story'. These biographies weave together to tell the 'family story'. From being merely structural positions in an institution, father, mother, child become named members of a living dramatis personae. It is the story that draws individuals into something much larger than themselves, associating them first with the larger group of the family, then associating the family to a community, national or world historic 'story' unified around conceptions of the 'fatherland' or 'motherland'. Within these stories the political roles of the hero and the villain emerge. There are essential transformations that take place: from good child to good citizen and from good citizen to hero; or, from bad child to rebellious citizen to villain. Members of a society share a common repertoire of stories which animate the ideology, the values, the attitudes and the responses associated with the hero and the villain. This is the importance for politicians of establishing national curricula which speak to the identity of a nation, a religion or a politics.

HEROES AND VILLAINS: COMIC TRANSFORMATIONS

Modern re-workings of myths are everywhere in popular culture. Star Wars, He-man and the Masters of the Universe, the vast range of fantasy novels, science fiction and comics – these provide just the more obvious popular re-workings of myths.

Perhaps the most pervasive impact has been through comics. Meek and mild newspaper reporter Clark Kent transforms into

Superman, the Man of Steel. Bruce Banner, scientist, transforms into the grotesque Hulk during occasions of tension or temper. Every hero and heroine in the world of comics has a secret identity which enables them to transform from the ordinary to the super-ordinary. This is the fantasy that keys into the politics of imagination.

In order to understand the media construction of heroes and villains, the rules governing reading and social articulation become critical. Stories situate a reader within the conventions of the medium and in a sense construct the reader's subjectivity. Crudely, there are rules governing the range of possible interpretations that may be made of the story; and rules governing the subject's articulation of these in terms of his or her own action in everyday life. More complexly, the repertoire of interpretations and conducts that arise from the story and its images depends upon the discourse strategies and forms of social expression available to the reader.

Texts demand entry into a world of complex self-referencing. Readers are drawn into a textual culture which demands knowledge not only of the rules of representing and transforming characters, situations and events but also knowledge of the biographies of characters and previous exploits. Comics provide a particularly clear illustration of the features of the heroic and the villainous.

The 'super' style comics like Superman, Spiderman, the Fantastic Four and so on mimic or set up a mythic or world historical stage upon which they and their foes are the actors and all others are either audience or victims in need of rescue. The discourse that this establishes is primarily between two broad orientations: the mythic/world historical and the mundane. Crises are exalted into world importance. They are life and death. Everything depends on them.

Widzer (1977) produced a study of comic superheroes from a psychoanalytic point of view in terms of the 'family romance' which is in two phases. The first, the asexual, is represented by the myths of Oedipus and Moses and is characterised by the disavowel of both parents. The second, the sexual:

> corresponds to the myths of the birth of Hercules, Jesus, and Sargon. Because of the child's increasing awareness, the distinguishing feature of the sexual phase is that *only one parent is relinquished*. In keeping with further development, however, this second phase of the family romance is subject to changes. A gradual de-emphasis of the importance of the mother is

> accompanied by a growing awareness of the role of the father, who eventually emerges as a reality figure with whom the child desires to identify. (p. 570)

Underlying the family romance is the Oedipal conflict. Widzer provides examples of comic superheroes for each of the developmental stages in both the asexual and sexual phases.

The absolute invulnerability, superspeed super senses and strength of Superman are appropriate to the early asexual stages of the family romance. With his powers he has no reason to fear anyone. Good and evil are clearly distinguished with no shades of grey between. However, in his secret identity he represents helplessness, fear, impotence and subjection to the authority and demands of his employer. Lois Lane, the love interest in the stories, loves Superman but not Clark Kent, although she occasionally suspects the essential identity. In the Clark Kent role, there is the loss of love (Lois Lane's) and exposure to the fear of the father represented by the editor for whom he works. Thus, he must return to the role of Superman. But in that role, the idealisation of the love object is demeaned because of his own obvious superiority:

> It is this situation that delineates the oedipal conflict most clearly and documents one of the most dramatic compromise solutions. When Superman is omnipotent, it is totally incumbent upon him to relate to the devalued objects; when the objects are omnipotent, it is totally incumbent upon them to relate to him as an impotent, devalued Clark Kent. (p. 575)

Superman's powers are inherited. He did nothing to gain them. He was abandoned, travelling across space to earth in a cradle-like rocket reminiscent of Moses set afloat in the river to be found and adopted, to take on a new identity while all along possessing a secret identity and inheritance. The superheroes associated with later phases do not inherit powers but rather come across them either by accident (e.g. Hulk, Flash, Spiderman) or through the discovery of some object (e.g. Thor and the magical hammer) or through their own efforts (Batman, Iron Man). Each represents increasing sophistication, the growing importance of the use of language and of the formation of real adult relationships with women.

Female superheroes have become increasingly important in comics but tend to follow similar patterns to the male superheroes. Those like

Wonder Woman parallel Superman. There are female counterparts of Hulk and Spiderman. However, increasingly, there have been women in the various gangs of superheroes populating the Marvel comics with teenage love crises and later adulterous affairs being carried as sub-plots connecting different adventures. Indeed, Rajeev Syal in the *Sunday Times* (16 August 1992) commented on the increasing political correctness of comic heroes citing Marvel's 'long-standing character called Northstar came out of the closet during a fight with Major Maple Leaf, a man driven to violence by the death of his son through Aids-related diseases'. Roger Scruton, a right wing philosopher and member of right-wing 'think-tanks', was quoted by Syal as believing that such ideas could not be explained in the medium of comics. Alternatively, perhaps the families of superheroes have developed over time signifying maturer levels of ego development. Families of superheroes have developed over time corresponding to the maturer levels of ego development.

It is easy to mock the pretensions of comics and to deride their moralistic attitudes, vicarious violence and teenage exhibitionism. Dorfman (1983) sees the comic form and the associated forms of the photo-romance novel, soap operas and sitcoms as fundamentally debilitating. Their function is to reduce the individual to the average, a consumer of easy-to-swallow pap. Psychoanalysis has often been criticised, particularly from a Marxist point of view, for its conservative aims of socialising individuals to the status quo, helping them to live more comfortably on the wrack of their neuroses. The prevailing morality within which the family romance is worked out in modern Western culture is that of capitalism, each tale reduced to a morality play rehearsing the virtues of property, profit and work. In analysing the Lone Ranger, Dorfman writes:

> Take the individuality of the (aptly named) *Lone* Ranger, for example. Anyone born in a market society is expected to get ahead all by himself, in solitude. In addition, we are taught that many times we fail because we're not able to get the better of anyone else. The dominant ideas and the productive system itself have prepared each consumer to feel that the way in which the Lone Ranger faces painful situations, in his capacity as the great unyielding macho, is absolutely natural and commendable. Such an emphasis on personal, competitive strength coexists with an opposite and complementary tendency toward paternalism, which the Ranger also satisfies as he emerges from outside the world to

exercise compassion for inferior beings. The system preaches that we must fend for ourselves in order to triumph, but that once we are invested with superiority, once we have accepted a position of authority in the hierarchy, it behooves us to lend a paternal hand to those weaker than ourselves. In superhero comics, this ferocity of competition and gentleness of compassion are amalgamated into one being. (p. 99)

There is a further immediate parallel with the comic heros of DC and Marvel comics: the masking of identity. Such masking is an act of transformation in itself. It has consequences. For the Lone Ranger, the mask is a perpetual part of him. His everyday persona is dead.

> It can therefore be supposed that an attempt is being made to represent the anonymous nature of justice, the dedication to a cause that reaches the point of abnegation and the renunciation of everyday aspirations. The man from the backwoods of Texas is dead, and he only exists insofar as he's undergone a metamorphoses.

The lines of the interface, the rules of engagement between the comic world and the everyday world are already being set out in such analyses. At one level, comics are a business. They arise within the structures of capitalist modes of production and consumption. They are commodities to be bought and sold. The moral tales or forms of justice that are peddled, the images, the forms of conduct that they represent are also commodities. They have the function of maintaining the system of commodity production and exchange; their task is to keep the consumers consuming. They set into social circulation the images and stories that are in demand. And demand is itself continually recreated by making the mundane remarkable, and saleable. Overcoming boredom. Since the everyday is boring, the fantastic is immensely marketable.

At another level, the level of the mythic, such heroes socialise the young into culture. The Lone Ranger has much in common with the comic heroes that Widzer associates with the later sexual phases of the family romance. He is not omnipotent. Rather his are the powers of the ordinary mortal honed to an incredible degree. His powers are the result of work.

The imagery of the superhero and the supervillain does not not just reside in the fantasy domain; their features are drawn into the real world of heroes and villains. The function of heroes is to save; and the function of villains is to destroy. Between them they articulate the tension between the permissible and the forbidden.

THE CONSTRUCTION OF CULTURE AND ANARCHY

Aligned under the hero is order, culture, reason; under the villain, anarchy, ignorance and irrationality. The political task is to set up the heroic and the villainous so that people know who to fight and who to obey. It is central to the reproduction of social order. The myth of hero and villain creates a landscape and a townscape of safe and unsafe places; well-lit places and dark corners; places where people walk openly or lurk. This divide finds its clear expression in Mathew Arnold's *Culture and Anarchy*. The issue was, and always has been, how to control the masses' desire for freedom, their desire to have more than they are given of society's resources and produce.

Arnold sees culture in terms of the perfection of humanity. Anarchy is all that is opposed to this. The state, through guidance from the best in culture, educates people into the processes of thinking. Each individual, once properly educated in this manner, is thus at liberty to entertain his or her own thoughts. Through the operations of democracy such cultured individuals will exercise their political wishes. It is a neat formula. At the heart of it all is what counts as education. Currently, it is the media which formulate the everyday curriculum materials by which to train the public mind in matters of culture and anarchy. Their function is to provide the means by which their audiences can formulate and read people and events. As has been discussed, there are no single readings of a text. Yet it is the case that the media are owned and controlled by a relatively small number of individuals in relation to the millions of people who compose their audiences. The role of the media in the construction of what counts as culture and anarchy cannot therefore be underestimated.

The great fear for those who have vested interests in the maintenance of the social order is the undoing of what they perceive to be civilised life: authority. Lambropoulos (1989: 173) writes of Arnold's thesis:

> Culture only denotes cultivation, growth, and development, while anarchy directly recalls and indirectly refers to authority; culture implies both process and product, but anarchy imbalance and

> dissolution; culture does, anarchy undoes. Arnold's commentators, willingly or unwillingly, respond to his call for action against the impending anarchy when they devote their best attention to the workings of culture: they work to deter the onslaught of anarchy, to prevent the disease from spreading. And yet the direction of the project is indicated in the semantic structure of the title: anarchy is not placed against its opposite, authority, but is paired with culture; the implication is that culture deters anarchy by supporting authority. The main argument, then, as expressed elliptically here, is that authority needs culture to survive.

Arnold wants to raise culture as the new religion of the state. States, however, are not noted for being cultured in the way that Arnold prescribes. Yet, the argument presented is a powerful one in the service of state interests. Through its control of knowledge and ignorance, the state needs only to construct the illusion of Arnoldian culture. The hero of culture – whether as a Superman or the unknown soldier – fights always in its behalf.

THE MALE HERO OF VIOLENCE

Hoch (1979: 10) comments on the typical binary polarisations composing the Western images of masculinity:

> There is indeed a close interrelation between the predominant Western conception of manhood and that of racial (and species) domination. The notion, originally from myth and fable, is that the summit of masculinity – the 'white hero' – achieves his manhood, first and foremost, by winning victory over the 'dark beast' (or over the barbarian beasts of other – in some sense, 'darker' – races, nations and social castes). So important is this particular understanding of manhood (and its collective embodiment, nationhood) that for many years the English gold sovereign carried the stirring imprint of what may be called the nation's founding myth – St George triumphing over the dragon. Very similar was the central Athenian myth of Theseus triumphing over the Minotaur, the celebration of Rome's victories over the barbarians, or – in our own time – the triumphs of cowboy over indian, hero over villain, civilisation over anarchy, West over East.

The male hero capable of unleashing overwhelming violence against enemies has been celebrated by the film industry since its inception. There are those who combine their violence with skill and gallantry, say Roger Moore as Saint and Bond. Others have a raw brutishness, bristling with weaponry like Sylvester Stallone in the Rambo roles, or Arnold Schwarzenegger in Conan and the Terminator. Others, like Robocop, are icons of male-machine violence itself. To Creed (1990: 133) these images of the male body in excess displayed by Stallone and Schwarzenegger 'display the male body as a living phallus: hysterical images of masculinity such as they point to the impossible nature of the phallic ideal, made even more so by the patriarchal cult of masculinity'. This she sees as a symptom of 'phallic panic', a result of Oedipal tensions and castration anxieties. As a result 'The female subject is made to bear the burden of the castration (in the form of a wound) by which both female and male enter the symbolic order so that the male subject may maintain an illusion of his own completeness and superiority.' The woman, according to psychoanalytic theory, is seen to be lacking the penis which in the mind of the male child arouses the fear of castration and comes to represent further symbolic losses associated with sexual knowledge. The film industry of popular culture replays the castration crisis and:

> transfers to the female subject losses which afflict the male subject. It also arms him against the possible return of these losses by orchestrating a range of defensive operations to be used against the image of woman, from disavowal and fetishism to voyeurism and sadism. In this way the trauma which would otherwise capsize the male viewer is both elicited and contained.
>
> (Silverman 1988: 31)

This industrialisation of developmental issues continually reinforces gender myths and role stereotypes.

To Zipes (1979), 'Mass-mediated fairy tales have a technologically produced universal voice and image which impose themselves on the imagination of passive audiences. The fragmented experiences of atomised and alienated people are ordered and harmonised by turning the electric magic switch of the radio or TV or by paying admittance to the inner sanctum of a movie theatre' (p. 17). This is the world of electronic dreams where the dreamer is again displaced. In societies once considered primitive, where myth is not frozen to the page but is actively realised through the mouths of dreamers, there is an active relation between myth as heritage and myth as shaped by a community of dreamers, where the shaman engages in the making of myth, an active myth continuously in formation. The age of electronics allows a visual representation of events in ways which accomplish an apparent realism. The realism permits a casual rewriting of history so that the world that was lost can, in imagination, be saved. The experience of Vietnam illustrates this. Rowe (1989) describes how in an hour long tape documenting the life of a military company '"Courage under fire", we see absolutely *no* Vietnamese – no civilians, no ARVN, no NLF, no NVA – either living or dead ... The victimized Vietnamese people are erased from the entire tape, only to be replaced by an American soldier, represented as capable and admirable by his black commanding officer, who has our full sympathy: an American soldier who is indistinguishable in appearance from a native Vietnamese, at least to western eyes.' In turn this exemplifies the themes of a range of counter-cultural works which focus on the irony that 'exploited American minorities, in numbers disproportionate to their representation in our culture, were drafted to conduct a war of imperialist aggression against another exploited people – the Vietnamese.'

To Rowe, Stallone's Rambo in the film of *First Blood* incorporates a complex range of counter-cultural signs – he looks like a drop-out, a hippie, he strikes an anti-authoritarian pose and adopts the self-reliance of the early American settlers. 'The metaphors of American civil disobedience are associated with him.' He is the re-born hero incorporating all the old virtues of the frontier, a freedom fighter, who would have been best suited to win *the war*. Instead it was a war waged by the military with hi-tech strategies far removed from the old values. These values are to do with manhood, with family. It is the lack of the old values of family that seems to motivate the book. Walsh (1988: 50), in a textual analysis which compares the original Rambo novel with the resulting films, writes that a:

> key distinguishing feature of the first set of the *First Blood* works is their unsatisfactory vision of family life or love: running through them is a pattern of defunct or flawed parental and marital relationships. Women are entirely absent in the movie *First Blood* (1982), and in the earlier novel they are shown as frigid, like Teasle's wife, asexual and maternal, as in Orval's wife, or dead, as is Rambo's mother. Interestingly, too, Rambo is seen as a loner;

> his buddies are dead and he is the only survivor from the 'A' Team at Bragg; Huck and Jim are dead in Vietnam. (p.51)

In many ways, this is a morality play for our times. It re-works all the favourite images and complex relationships familiar to our times. We are thrown back again to the Oedipal tensions and relations:

> Morrell's novel concentrates less upon traditional formulations of heroism than upon Oedipal collisions. The tropes of sibling rivalry are replayed in startling fashion; Korea–Vietnam, old veteran–young veteran, pillar of the community–vagrant, respected sheriff–criminal, metaphors which explore aspects of 'the masculine' and 'the father'. Teasle, who is abandoned by his wife and is significantly childless, refers to Rambo throughout the novel as 'the kid', perhaps compensating in some arcane way for his wife's refusal to bear him a child. Fulfilling heterosexual relations do not seem possible in the ethos of the novel and are replaced by problematical man to man relationships. Such absences of whom, as Leslie Fiedler has shown, are found widely throughout classic American literature. (p. 51)

The myth of the happy family is inscribed here as an absence. As absence, it calls into play a range of complexes which focus in turn upon the main players in the family: father and father substitutes, mother and mother substitutes, and the rivalry between siblings and sibling substitutes. Although the myth of the happy family is of relatively recent origin, the tensions revealed in the 'Oedipal collisions' are not. It is as if by its absence, the myth opens a scar at a deeper level. Images coalesce and layer. Father coalesces with masculine, with 'macho', with patriarchy. In creating a sense of identity the 'babble' of images, of sensations or experienced needs are cleaned up and contorted into the 'macho' or the 'feminine' image, then doubly contorted as the process itself is forgotten or repressed and assumed as simply natural. Industrialised culture presents itself as a 'realism' in ways which situate the individual in its dramas, confusing access to, repressing, concealing, forbidding alternative ways of being, while at the same time providing a peep show into the fields of the forbidden, industrialised for mass consumption.

When the former president of the United States, Ronald Reagan, called Russia the evil empire he was using the mythology of the Star Wars films in order to manipulate political attitudes. He was saying, there really is a world to be saved, it is ours. It simplified the heroes and the villains. This simplifying process cannot be scorned as transparent trickery. It works.

ON SAVING THE WORLD

Kierkegaard divided the individual into broadly three kinds: the ordinary individual caught up in reproducing society as it is; the great man capable of overthrowing a prevailing moral order, such as the Biblical prophet; and the charlatan, the would-be great man who is fundamentally incapable of being so – the false prophet, the petty revolutionary. Nietzsche in Zarathustra provided the image of the Superman, capable of going beyond ordinary limits. And Reich, in *Oh, Little Man,* vented his frustration concerning the power of 'littleness' to bring down great people and ideas. In such visions of the human is a conception that oscillates between all or nothing, omnipotence and impotence. In it both the battle ground and the enemy is the mass of little people, the ordinary who must be won, led, moulded. It is they who must be saved, and they who are the prey of villains, of charlatans, and the source of the ignorance that brings destruction. In the classical narrative, it is the duty of heroes and heroines to save the world, just as it is the duty of villains to destroy it. Saving the world is a conservative force if it is to preserve a given heritage, or to re-new a dying world. It is radical, however, if the world is to be transformed in the creation of a new world, a new moral order.

Star Wars offers a clear depiction of the master narrative in which worlds are saved from the Manichaean forces of darkness represented by Darth Vader. It is a simplistic split which re-works the family romance in the conflict between Luke Sky Walker and Darth Vader, who turns out to be his father. Taylor (1988) compares the Star Wars trilogy to the American Civil War film, *Birth of a Nation* (1915), in which 'the narrative homologies ... click beyond the possibility of accident'. Comparisons are found between the Jeddi knights and the Knights of the Ku Klux Klan in *Birth of a Nation,* and 'R2D2 and C-3PO take the place of those sassy, back-talking darky house servants, of equally mechanical loyalty to their betters.' Ben Kenobi becomes a 'cavalier knight-captain of the Confederacy'. It is the master script of the pioneer frontiersmen, the cowboys, where 'the mythic identities of the patriarchal South are future-thrown into outerspace'. Here the hero confronts the unknown, the 'exotic region beyond the safety of the secured social organisation'. The Star Wars trilogy resolves into a stable 'forevermore' where not only worlds are saved but the father is saved, to stand with the heroes of the Jeddi knights.

The late twentieth century is a time when the old fathers who seemed so invulnerable, wise and true are themselves being exposed as the enemy. Who, then, can heroes be heroes for? How are they to operate as heroes? The family romance has to be rewritten to include unstable endings, loose ends, disappointments and partial resolutions.

Consider the comic figures of Green Lantern and Green Arrow from the DC stable (1983 issue no. 7 by Danny O'Neill and Neal Adams). On the cover page is a figure imitating Christ being crucified. Green Lantern says 'Are you people crazy? He's trying to save us ALL!' And Green Arrow says 'STOP! You don't know what you're doing!' At the foot of the page is written in mock Gothic script, '...AND THROUGH HIM SAVE A WORLD!'

In this cover page the known heroes are held, an as yet unknown hero Christ figure is under threat, and the mass is represented as a furious and dangerous mob that must be saved from its own ignorance. The mass in comics is either the Arnoldian mob or victims. As victims the masses are saved and transformed into an adoring public.

The front cover makes use of a powerful central set of mythic images to set up reader anticipations. They form an immediate connection to the discourses of Western culture, and the discourses of comic culture. The connections are made through codes which lock the reader into the appropriate repertoire. In each comic-frame a considerable amount of information has to be expressed. Like the television adverts squeezed between films, soaps, chat shows – there is no time to lose. The reader has to do a considerable amount of filling in, to read between the gaps in order to read the story. The resources to be drawn on are the discourse resources of everyday life; not the full complement of all possible resources, but those bequeathed by circumstance. Those resources are ruled by a coordination of the *inner* and the *outer*. The extraordinary powers of the hero are located within the realities of an inner fantasy which can be talked about in a public outer domain but do not denote anything in the real outer world of materiality. Yet, certain objects in the fantasy do point outward to the outer world: America as a nation-state exists, Christ is a figure which millions do and have *believed in as real*, and many of the acts of the mob are recognisably real and realisable. And so on.

Inside, on page 1, Green Lantern is holding open the door into Green Arrow's apartment. Green Arrow is sitting in his armchair laughing, pointing at some article in a newspaper. Only their absurd costumes give them away: these are superheroes. The door is open to fantasy. Yet, listen to the dialogue as Green Lantern says to Green Arrow, alias Oliver Queen:

> Why the big CHUCKLE, Ollie? The FUNNY PAGE? CHARLIE BROWN gets his kite caught in the maniac tree again?
>
> Better than THAT, Pal! There's this guy in the midwest ... calls himself ISAAC ... and he is VERY my-kind-of-fella! See, he has a HANGUP about ECOLOGY! Only instead of MOANING, he ACTS! Listen to this news item ...

Without some cultural background knowledge, this introduction would be unreadable. To read it requires acquaintance with a number of conventions such as the distinction between box and bubble so often employed to locate text. The box signals the authorial voice which introduces, comments and describes. The bubble signals the voice of the character. It also requires acquaintance with comic culture. Located in the text are typically references to more generalised American culture and youth sub-culture as well as to particular comic heroes from other series, or the biography of a comic hero developed over many years. This mixture of social knowledge with comic knowledge grounds the fictional story in a reality which is somehow continuous with lived social reality. When Green Lantern refers to CHARLIE BROWN, the cartoon strip character known the world over acts as a signal that Green Lantern shares a reality with the reader. Thus the gap which separates the world of the comic hero from the world of the reader is sutured, interwoven with that of the cultural experience of the reader to present the illusion of a continuous relationship.

Moving in the other direction, when a world leader, or major newspapers, refer to Rambo, Dirty Harry, Star Wars, the Evil Empire, the suture is between the real world of political events or tragic events and the fantasy world of heroes and villains.

The story sets up a number of major themes within Americanised culture: big business v. the individual; the mass v. the individual; knowledge v. ignorance; action v. apathy/complacency. It also focuses upon a key social issue of the late twentieth century: pollution v. environmentalism. The ending, however, contains doubt – who are the real heroes today, who are the heroes being heroes for? There are competing valid interests: the value of progress fundamental to capitalism; obedience to democratic laws; the right to safeguard employment; the Christ figure is also called by Green Arrow 'nature's Robin Hood'. The Christ Figure dies, as of course is already inevitable in the imagery. However, the ending leaves unresolved the essential crises. The world is not saved. The obligation to save the world and to know who it is to be saved from, then begins to become ambiguous. The only resolution is in the continuing friendship of the two superheroes. What they cannot defeat, what they cannot overthrow, is the culture itself, the culture that created them.

THE INDUSTRIALISATION OF CULTURE

The Red Riding Hood story has introduced the idea of the transformation of the central characters of oral traditions for ideological purposes. Within this transformation is both an industrialisation and a contortion of experience. The idea of the paradigmatic narrative evolving from and being articulated through lived experience at one end of the continuum and massaged and manipulated through the media at the other will be the subject of exploration in this chapter. Where industrialised culture manufactures the dominant or 'official' myths of society, producing the dominating world-view, reading against the grain of the myth and producing so-called aberrant readings is common. However, the counter-myths to the dominant myths of industrialised culture in producing their own world-views also produce their own forms of domination within communities where working-class lads and lasses are caught up in the cultural myths of the gang, the street, the home and the workplace. It is a complex cats' cradle of world-views in which the names of the hero and villain are called out and the self located in relation to them. This naming sets into play evocation sequences which arouse pleasure pain, guilt, attraction to lead the feelings and thoughts of individuals located in masses. These sequences open or close possibilities by such strategies as connotation and metonymy, hence attempting to control attention, intention and action. The dominant classes controlling the media aspire to fit the hero and the villain to the target populations identified by their market analysts. The aspiration is to tame meaning, so that in consuming, the mass itself is tamed.

The story of Robin Hood provides an illustrative example. He is rebel, leader of the brotherhood, the gang which creates its own laws at the margins of society. As discussed by Stallybrass (1989), Robin Hood is the hero of the carnivalesque. He is the voice of a counter-culture which, during the course of the carnival, suspends the prevailing order. He is the hero of mis-rule in the early ballads and the May day festivals and plays. The features of the Robin Hood role include the transgression of 'spatial boundaries, trespassing upon the King's forests', inverting the 'social hierarchy, preying upon the dominant classes', degrading 'the sacred, humiliating the clergy', replacing 'the fast of peasant poverty with the feast of poached deer' (pp. 46–7). Robin Hood and the associated activities of the carnivalesque provide a focus for challenging the controlling powers. During the long process of enclosing the forests, Robin Hood symbolises the common rights of access to and use of the forest. There was a sense of the carnivalesque during the British riots of 1981. For many young people the riots provided a sense of mis-rule, of excitement, of inversion, of transgressing social boundaries, but also of creating their own boundaries, exerting their own powers (Schostak 1983). But carnivalesque misrule has to be controlled, made ineffective, its energies appropriated for state rule.

Stallybrass describes several strategies used to control the meaning of Robin Hood. In the first, the church used the tales 'to establish the devout in opposition to the wantonly secular' (p. 64). Robin Hood was named as traitor, thief, associated with ribald talk and activities. The strategy was to exclude and oppose Robin Hood:

> Harry's father saw the barricades being put up by 'yobboes' in his road. He said, 'I'm not having this.' Harry, his brothers and his father began to dismantle the barricade. Some neighbours helped. 'The women were marvellous – they really belittled the yobboes. One of the yobboes yelled out as a reason for his actions, "I've got no fuckin' job." One of the women replied, "If you 'ad a fuckin' job you'd faint."' The yobboes cleared off before the police came. Harry said, 'It's a law an' order thing here. People are very strong on it.'
>
> (Schostak 1983:180)

It is the imagery of the matriarchal family, the 'strong women' in the service of law and order – heroines of domesticity – protecting their homes.

The scale of the 1981 riots caught people by surprise. Press headlines portrayed images of confrontation, arson, looting, destruction of property. That there may have been just causes, or at least understandable reasons, was difficult to handle. There was the obvious reality of massive unemployment, racial discrimination, poverty, poor housing. Any real admission of this reality would, however, have undermined the economic and social strategies being pursued. Many millions would have had to be spent on reversing a decline that had long been set in motion and brutally brought to a crescendo during the harsh recession induced by the policies pursued. Thus, other kinds of reasons had to be found. Teddy Taylor (Tory MP for Southend East) in the *Sunday Express* (12 July 1981) recognised that unemployment aggravates social problems, but the problem as he saw it was entirely a matter of law and order. The penalties for crime were too soft. Thus crime was encouraged. The riots were merely an extension of the rising tide of crime brought on by being too lenient in dealing with criminals:

> We must make it clear that no excuse can be accepted for criminal acts like vandalism, arson, looting and police assault.
>
> We must give the police the means to break up mobs instead of obliging them to stand around – however well protected by clothing – and be Aunt Sallies for criminals throwing bricks, bottles and petrol bombs at them. The use of water cannon would seem to be the best means of breaking up crowds.
>
> And we must impose nasty penalties on vandals, arsonists and looters caught in the act and found guilty by the courts.

Allied to simple criminality, was the political angle where the villains could be found in agents provocateurs. The *Daily Telegraph* on 11 July 1981 carried a front page article on the 'Hunt for The Four Horsemen' by special branch – 'four masked men who it has been established were present at major incidents in Southall, Liverpool and Manchester.' The *News of the World* the next day labelled the villains as 'trots':

> Militant left-wingers have drawn up plans to organise street rioters and looters into a highly-disciplined revolutionary force to topple the government.

> 'Red' Andy Bevan, organiser of the Labour party Young Socialists, said: 'We must bring the Tories down at the earliest opportunity – we can't wait two years for an election.'
>
> And he revealed that he knew well in advance that Britain's streets were about to be ripped apart by an explosion of violence.

On the front page of the same issue was a figure from the opposite end of the political continuum: 'EVIL EDITH', 'a nasty Nazi who is whipping up violent racial hatred among young thugs on the riot-torn streets of Britain.' If the red menace and the evil Nazis in practice looked a little thin, there were always others, if not villains then people who have seriously neglected their duty. In the same paper an article revealed that 'Parents are blaming themselves for the rioting kids on the streets of Britain', following a survey by the paper. 'Public figures including the Prime Minister Margaret Thatcher and the Merseyside Chief Constable have given parents a ticking off.' Added to this was a report by the *Daily Telegraph* (11 July 1981) reporting Dr Rhodes Boyson, Junior Education Minister, blaming 'Teachers who present their pupils with "quaint religious doctrines" instead of the traditional and clear beliefs of Christianity.' This and a lack of 'firm yet fair discipline' could lead children to 'end up among the mindless rioters of our cities'. A Giles cartoon in the *Sunday Express*, showed Grandma thrashing a young skinhead with her umbrella. The hooligan was saying to a line of similarly thrashed looters 'Typical ain't it? When you really need a copper you can never find one.' In the background was a line of riot-shielded police facing a barrage of bricks. A good thrashing from some parental authority is seemingly all that is needed. Combining all these thrusts, the final implication is the call to 'Back up our bobbies' and 'bring back the birch for the rioting mobs' (*Manchester Evening News*, 10 July 1981). The police were the besieged heroes.

The second kind of strategy discussed by Stallybrass employed by the State to control the Robin Hood counter-culture was 'to limit the *scope* of the outlaw's misrule and to appropriate misrule as the licence which the monarch himself both enjoyed and had the power to grant' (p. 65). In the later popular stories of Robin Hood screened for television and cinema, he is basically a subject loyal to the King and resisting a disloyal usurper. Thus, from the hero of the dispossessed he becomes the hero of the *status quo*. The process of resistance itself is transformed to be used against those who would resist in order to preserve the fundamental social structure. Thus, initially, the counter revolutions in Eastern Europe were appropriated to prove the inadequacy of socialism and the triumph of market capitalism. Any remaining revolutionary spirit in the masses of the West is sold back as armchair entertainment:

> 'We were eating our dinner – a bowl of cornflakes and a bit of bread and jam', he said.
>
> 'Ascot's on the telly and me Mam says. "Oh look at them all – don't they look lovely?", meaning all the right layabout bastards dressed up like Lord and Lady Muck.
>
> 'I went mad. I flung my spoon against the wall, and shouted at her not to be so f____ stupid, and what a sick country it was when people like that can spend thousands of pounds in a day, going to the races when we are struggling just to get enough to eat.
>
> 'It is the first time I have ever sworn at me Mam, and I'm 18 years old. She started crying. I put my arm around her, and said I was sorry. But deep down I know I was right.'
>
> (*Sunday Mirror*, 12 July 1981)

It is a process which is re-worked for anti-cultural heroes in the popular media whether in the gentlemanly Saint, or the typically rough diamond John Wayne characters, or the more brutish characters associated with Charles Bronson and Clint Eastwood films or the Rambo films of Sylvester Stallone. It is precisely this tension and this transformation which underlies the frustration of those who have written on cultural resistance and working-class youth. It is summed up in Willis' (1977) opening comments on his study of the 'lads' in a secondary school, that the problem is not to explain why middle-class kids get the jobs but to explain why working-class kids let them. The lads resist the dominant culture of the school but in doing so, the control procedures evoked in response, categorise and channel them into dead-end situations.

Positioned in relation to hero and villain, the social self emerges at the intersection of discourses marked out by the media as legitimate or forbidden, through its scheduling, its categorisation of programmes or articles for types of audience or readership. This social self reading a newspaper, watching a television play or listening to a radio news bulletin, is not simply a single instance, a unique being, but rather one who shares common interests, values and attitudes with others. As Ellul (1965: 7) remarks:

> ... the individual must never be considered as being alone; the listener to a radio broadcast, though actually alone, is nevertheless part of a large group, and he is aware of it. Radio listeners have been found to exhibit a mass mentality. All are tied together and constitute a sort of society in which all individuals are accomplices and influence each other without knowing it.

For Ellul, this is the prime condition for propaganda. He sees propaganda as belonging to a 'technological universe', the universe of the modern mass media. We are all targeted, whether by party political broadcasters, canvassers who step into our homes, or broadcast schedulers. And:

> Being the target of a party or an administration is enough to immerse the individual in that sector of the population which the propagandist has in his sights; this simple fact makes the individual part of the mass. He is no longer Mr. X, but part of the current flowing in a particular direction. (p. 7)

Through their television viewing or newspaper consumption, individuals place themselves in target populations. In doing so, the conditions are provided through which fantasy is manipulated and reinforced. Industrialised fantasy is the space for ideological battles. For example, an evening's viewing is the focus for major ratings battles, and in commercial stations this is all to do with the attraction of advertising income. In this way the space in which heroes and villains appear is apportioned and the discourse about them regulated by the major vehicles of mass media in the interests of commerciality, and the capture of large audiences. The fantasy is further structured through scheduling.

Tulloch (1990: 39) analyses the scheduling spaces available to programmers in terms of 'paradigms' and 'syntagms'. The paradigm sets out the menu:

> For Roland Barthes, the menu 'paradigm' consists of that 'set of food stuffs which have affinities or differences within which one chooses a dish in view of a certain meaning: the types of entrée, roast or sweet'. The equivalent in commercial television terms is the ratings-determined choice of genres that can be placed in any one time-slot: so, for instance, Phillip Hayward describes how the reflexive show *Moonlighting* was introduced on the ABC as 'a

direct competitor to *Remington Steele* (based around a similar male/female detective duo)', before being moved back an hour to compete with NBC's action adventure *Riptide*, 'calculating that *Riptide* had a largely male audience and could be beaten with a show of mixed gender appeal'.[1]

As the 'menu syntagm' refers to the actual sequence of dishes chosen, so the 'television equivalent is the sequential "flow-through" of genres during the channel's transmission time (e.g. the "family" orientation of the sequencing of *The Wonderful World of Disney* and *A Country Practice*)' (p. 39). One can therefore begin to analyse the use of scheduling space in terms of audience and the kinds of discourse promoted or inhibited by the programmes transmitted.

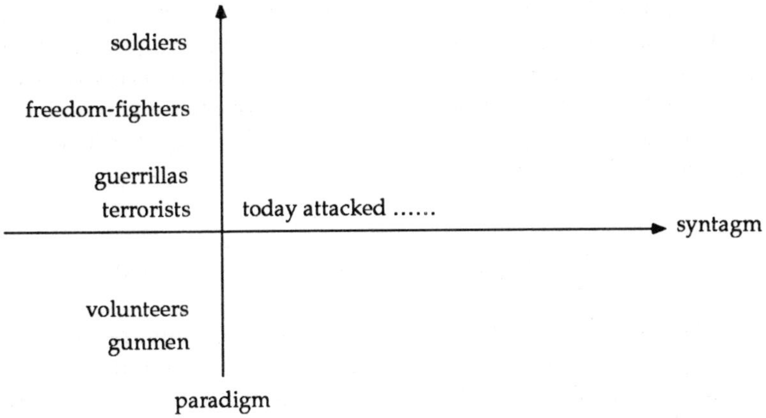

Figure 1

The relationship at the level of the sentence between paradigm and syntagm has been diagrammatically presented by Hartley in Figure 1 (1982: 20). In constructing a sentence to describe the action of attacking, say, a village, a paradigmatic choice exists by which to label the attackers. If the attackers are considered heroes on the side of revolution then they may be called 'freedom fighters'. On the other side, the choice may be 'terrorists'. The resulting sentence is the 'syntagm', the actual choice of words. A similar range of choices exists for each other slot in the sentence. It is the paradigmatic choice

[1] Tulloch provides the following references: Barthes 1967: 63; Hayward 1988: 185, 186.

between heroes and villains which conditions the kinds of other choices that may be made as between the discourse of 'freedom fighters' or the discourse of 'terrorists'. Within each such discourse, further choices arise as to the kinds of narratives, the sequences of actions performed by the actors, whether these are to be stories of destruction, stories of saving, stories of persistence against terrible odds, stories of sadistic torture and so on.

This kind of analysis may be performed on other vehicles of mass media. Newspapers provide an alternative form of 'scheduling' within the sequencing of their pages and aim at different segments of the population. The metaphor of the menu can again be used to focus on the individual dishes providing 'hard news', 'soft news', regarding law and order, gossip, entertainment, sexy images, sports and so on. Information is set within the relations of fantasy. For each kind of dish there are the actual stories chosen. These can be sequenced in terms of front page, back page, centre pages and so on. They are then patterned according to the lay out and design in order to provide relative prominence on the page. Within these basic structures flow the parade of heroes and villains forever locked in wars to save or create worlds.

THE WARS OF HEROES AND THE VILLAINS

In 1990 the threat of war in the Middle East suddenly transformed the euphoric atmosphere following the collapse of communism in the Eastern block. The evil empire was no longer evil but an emergent friend. Iraq was no longer a friend supported by Western intelligence and arms but an enemy. Again, the task became to save the world.

Just as comics provide a tool of release from the rules of public discourse, enabling the reader to explore possible images of the self, and possible courses and discourses of self-transformation through fantasy, so the images of Western might raging against the world's villains provide a kind of carnivalesque release from the ordinary.

During the latter half of 1990 it was a media war, creating a bizarre pantomime. On 3 August 1990 the *Today* newspaper ran the headline:

HITLER HUSSEIN

The first two paragraphs read:

> The new Hitler of the Middle East, Saddam Hussein, held the world at bay last night after invading Kuwait.
>
> In a dramatic Telex to TODAY, Britons trapped in the tiny Gulf state pleaded to be rescued before revenge strikes on the dictator. Not since Hitler invaded Poland in the Thirties has a nation so cynically annexed a neighbour.

The image drawn on the front page is of Hussein, blowing smoke from a hand gun, sitting on an oil barrel and squashing world leaders under it. The *Sun* focused its front page squarely on the oil crisis that would follow war, accompanied by a photograph of a tank with victorious soldiers, captioned as 'Victory trail ... Power-crazy Hussein's tanks roll relentlessly on through tiny Kuwait.' On page three of the paper, there is a list of '20 things you didn't know about the Butcher of Baghdad'. Set alongside this is a list of 'rights and wrongs of war' which informs readers of the extent to which Iraq's claims are right but its methods wrong. In another tabloid newspaper (considered leftwing), the *Daily Mirror*, the imagery was continued: tyrant, monster, 'thief of Baghdad'. The discourse of tyranny was continued in all the other major news media.

On 9 August the *Sun* had the headline 'Our Boys Go In'. Inside, in colour, was an illustration of a flying jet fighter and an aircraft carrier: 'War machine ...'. Above these in capital letters which ran across the double pages was the headline: 'IRAQI RAPED BA JET WOMAN'. This was also reported on the front pages of the *Daily Mirror*, *Today* and *Daily Express*.

Good and evil have successfully been simplified and polarised in these media images. By evoking the experiences now overlaid with the mythology of the Second World War, Hussein's actions and the West's counter-actions could be explained simply and simplistically to the public. The complex history of involvement by the West in Middle Eastern affairs, which had allowed tyrants to arise and be supported, was largely glossed over. The invasions and subversions carried out by Western powers all over the world could be ignored in this simplistic drama echoing the fight of good against evil.

The media battle continued with the 'plight of the hostages'. Hussein used the medium of TV to present an image of those Westerners who had been kept as hostages in Iraq. On 24 August, the *Daily Mail*'s headline echoed the sentiments of the entire UK media: 'A REPULSIVE TV CHARADE'.

On pages two and three large headlines repeated the imagery, 'Face to face with the evil dictator'. Beneath this, four photographs taken from the TV screen showed a smiling Hussein with the hostage adults and children. The descriptions provided by the newspaper accounts rammed home the message of evil in relation to the innocents. It was to be read as a cynical display of hypocrisy and thus of propaganda. Again the simplicities of the drama were spelt out. By 2 September the message of Hussein's evil was being reinforced with echoes of war crimes trials:

> Mrs Thatcher warned President Saddam: 'If anything happened to those hostages then sooner or later when any hostilities were over we would do what we did at Nuremberg and prosecute the requisite people for their totally uncivilised and brutal behaviour. We are all making due note of the people who do it, because in these days they cannot say "we were only acting under orders."'
> (*The Times*, 3 September 1990)

There is here a powerful sense of retribution, of good seeking out the evil, locating it all in a familiar discourse where blame cannot be shrugged away just because 'I am only doing my job.'

As the summer progressed, more and more troops were sent out to the Gulf. By 15 September, *Today* provided the headline 'Desert Rats Go In' as Britain sent in 'up to 8,000 men with tanks and guns' who 'will carry the red emblem of the Rats who defeated Hitler's Afrika Korps in 1941'. Here, it would seem, the imagery is complete. The echoes of past warfare and past heroes are resurrected for the new desert war.

By the middle of October Ted Heath, former British Tory Prime Minister during the 1970s, planned to go to Iraq on a mercy mission. The *Daily Mail* (15 October) reported a row in which Heath 'was branded as a mischief-maker' by 'leading Tories'. The article reported that 'Downing Street denied reports that Mrs Thatcher had "hit the roof".' In the midst of the article is a box with the words 'Beware the tactics, Ted – see PAGE SEVEN'. On page seven is an 'open letter to Mr Heath from the Mail's Middle East Expert' (the open letter is signed, John Laffin). There is an artist's drawing of Heath shaking hands with a smiling Hussein. The caption reads 'Note the body language ... he will hang on to your hand and try to turn it over.' Heath, an experienced and respected statesman, was treated as a naive interloper on the world stage. The letter is presented as a series of 'do's and don'ts' from an expert to an 'inexpert'. Worse, the whole of the Arab people were described in terms of 'an Arab mind' where 'Stories of Arab hospitality are legendary and, indeed, the Arabs warmly, even effusively, welcome a visitor. But sooner or later they expect some kind of payment or favour.' Again, in describing Hussein as a 'congenital and practised liar', this is set within a context:

> Every journalist who works in the Middle East knows that when an Arab official promises to make someone available at a certain time, to send a car or arrange a meeting, this is the last thing that will happen. The official is being truthful *at the time* but promises have a short shelf-life in the Middle East.

Hussein seems to appear as simply a special case in what is the typical Arab culture, a culture shown to be distinct, duplicitous. The tone calls up other more overtly racist imagery of the other who is dangerous, untrustworthy, most unlike the British, who will seek to hold your hand for too long thus gaining a psychological advantage – the 'upper hand' as the letter put it.

The villain is thus being located within a complex national imagery which at once reinforces Britishness and the difference of the other. The other is at once the hated Saddam and also the Arabs, the very people who elsewhere, in Saudi Arabia, are to be protected and, in Kuwait, to be rescued.

There is a further level to the letter: 'that you are making perhaps your last attempt to upstage Mrs Thatcher'. There are here many echoes of previous political battles in which Thatcher had been called the 'only man in the government', the 'Iron Lady' and during the Falkland's dispute 'resolute'. Thatcher had become an icon for all that was British, patriotic, strong: the personification of the hero.

Hussein, of course, within the Arab world, was also at work constructing the sense of being a hero. The multinational – largely American – forces situated in Saudi Arabia were not unambiguously welcomed by the people. By linking the solution of the crisis to talks that would address the needs of the Palestinians, Hussein began to locate himself for the Arab peoples within a different kind of drama than the one presented by the Western press. This drama was between Western oil interests and Arab cultural identity. The struggle to control the discourse was the first step in the war.

In each case the struggle of the hero and the villain serves ideological functions. This is their work, the prize at which rulers of all kinds of regime aim: the production and maintenance of a world view emotionally unified under the unambiguous imagery of the hero directing attention, effort and action towards the villain. Doubt is suppressed as the mass audience constructs itself into the discourses and the narrativisations produced by the media. Strung between debris and pristine structure, the self is composed of the stories we tell or fail in telling to ourselves and to others. That Kuwait was not a democracy, that the West had contributed to Saddam Hussein's power, that Western interests saw in the Middle East a power base for selfish reasons, these were stories that could not be told and sold on the front pages of the Tory tabloids, or in their cartoons.

5

FORBIDDEN FORMS OF REPRESENTATION

The forbidden evokes a disruption of the self producing a double discourse that deals in a public economy of desire and a hidden one, constructing both a forbidden self and a public self. The discourse creates between the two a 'normal distance' where something of the forbidden is permissible under such rules as 'consent' and 'privacy'. There is a continuous work of concealing the forbidden within the public where the forbidden is a re-constructable 'behind'. The 'behind' capable of being revealed as racism, sexism, intolerance of any difference, is defused in a specialised discourse: 'it's only a joke' or 'that's just his way, he means nothing by it', 'you shouldn't take things so seriously/literally'. Sexuality and violence are concealed through the control of 'seeing' and 'hearing'. It is there, but it cannot be seen as such – 'if you see it, it is because you have a dirty mind'. Images are juxtaposed, overlaid and concealed in puns, rhymes and metaphors. The media provide the critical service as the 'spectatorium' and 'auditorium' of what can be seen and heard, promoting the legitimised *systems-of-representation* of the official/dominant *systems-of-action* or courses of life.

A representation resides in a reader's interpretation and the re-representation that follows; this allows for the possibilities of alternative, oppositional and ironic readings. Although representation is not arbitrary, it cannot completely close down the range of interpretations. When in the media an alternative reading is deliberately provided, or alternative discourses and stories heard, the argument may be made that by definition they are not forbidden. Room has been made for them in the media. This, too, is a part of the dominant structure of mainstream culture. If alternatives are permitted, this only goes to show that democracy is preserved by the media. By such an argument, the forbidden remains in the margins, providing an amusing sense of the carnivalesque, opening a peepshow into the interstices of official social organisation. It is in these margins that the real work is done, in which bits and pieces are broken off, used and written over like sprayed graffiti messages on walls. It is here that the intercourse of conversation forms its adulterous, promiscuous liaisons of ideas and images. It is here that the oscillation between the permitted and illegitimate objects and associations unifies under the polarities of heroes and villains, freedom and slavery. To the West at various times the other has been constructed as: Muslim, Jew, East, West, Black, Communist. But the other fragments and reforms under changing conditions, necessitating changed alliances. The Rushdie affair and the Iraq conflict prised open the scars, exposing the acrid fears, hatred and rivalries festering beneath. The secretive histories are exposed yet attention is diverted, the histories denied, their interlaced roots to the present disconnected or passed over in silence, reconstructing the current crises as a surprise.

It is through the everyday repertoires of discourse that this happens, spun out in mundane conversations where everyone's business is minded and the self negotiates its peace and its wars with the world. Through the negotiations, the boundaries of the forbidden and the legitimate suture the exposed wounds until the hardened scars re-form into a numb social amnesia where heroes and villains can continue to do battle.

The role of forbidden forms of representation is to represent the unrepresentable in a play with margins, with coverings and with covert territorialisations. In this play the hidden aspects of the self, its relations with the world, its complicity in otherness, find expression, under cover, perhaps with co-conspirators. The forbidden form transforms the surroundings of the public, creates inversions which at a critical moment may dis-arrange the whole, turning heroes into villains and villains into heroes. So, when East reads the West's – or South reads the North's – self-representations it insets its own codes of interpretation, supplying the missing depths, translating villain into hero (cf. Fiske 1982). The forbidden, thus, is not just about concealing, but also about finding the forms and the strategies in which to represent, reveal, re-form, re-invert, in order to bring the other's representation of self in line with the self's own field of the imaginary. It is a political struggle to control representations.

THE STRUCTURE OF ALTERNATIVE, OPPOSITIONAL AND IRONIC READINGS

In trying to understand the work of the forbidden in its task of concealing and revealing, the distinction between open and closed texts and the kinds of readers appropriate to each made by Eco (1979) is a useful starting point. Closed texts are comic strips and soap operas, whereas Joyce's *Finnegans Wake* is an open text. Closed texts 'obsessively aim at arousing a precise response on the part of more or less precise empirical readers' but 'are open to any possible "aberrant" decoding' (p. 8). This is in contrast with open texts which 'work at their peak revolutions per minute only when each interpretation is reechoed by the others, and vice versa' (p. 9). It is the artistic marshalling of the possible interpretations which prevents readers from using the text in whatever way they want. Through the strategy of the open text, the writer can produce layers of meanings which act in a maze-like way to lead the reader into alternative forms of awareness, to guide or trap the reader in or towards the hidden, the repressed, forbidden. With the closed text, it is the reader who brings or projects his or her aberrant readings onto the text. The project is a result not of arbitrary whim but of the already structured terrain of desire in which text is received and worked. Eco provides an example:

> ... Sue's *Les Mysteres de Paris*, which, written initially in a dandyish mood to please cultivated readers, aroused as a result a passionate process of identification on the part of an illiterate audience; when, on the contrary, it was written to educate such a 'dangerous' audience to a moderate vision of social harmony, it produced as a side effect a revolutionary uprising. (p. 8)

The text was drawn into a play of desires, in which the forbidden aspirations of the masses were re-written as legitimate. This restructuring of the text finds its homologue in irony.

In irony there is always a surface meaning and 'behind' this a play of alternative meanings. Booth (1974) discusses the process of understanding irony, employing metaphors of buildings and reconstructions. The surface text can be considered as a shaky dwelling place. It is built upon rotten foundations and leads to unacceptable conclusions. The example Booth gives is 'Ignore the hungry and they'll go away' (Relief Fund appeal, London 1970). From this statement the reader must reconstruct the acceptable conclusion: 'Give to our fund or the hungry will die' (p. 35):

> .... the process is in some respects more like a leap or climb to a higher level than like scratching a surface or plunging deeper. The movement is always toward an obscured point that is intended as wiser, wittier, more compassionate, subtler, truer, more moral, or at least less obviously vulnerable to further irony. Since there is always a sense in which part of the new view is a look back upon the old inferior dwelling, the moving van is perhaps better described as travelling upward to a nicer part of town. (p. 36)

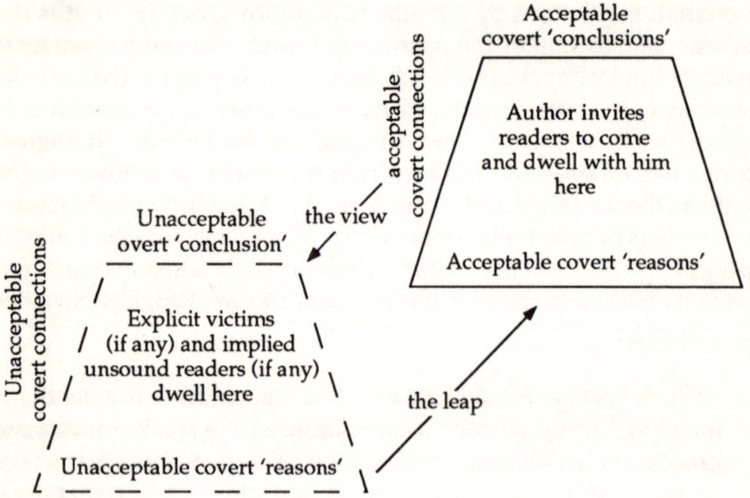

Figure 2

The closed text by Sue that led to the uprising was not intended to be read ironically. No reconstruction of alternative beliefs was built into the textual structure by the author. Nevertheless, such a reconstruction appears to have taken place through the aberrant readings of the audience. Figure 2 shows how Booth schematises his process. If a text does not intentionally provide reconstructive readings, then the reader may 'read against the grain' or construct oppositional readings. Even such a television series as the *A Team* – a kind of Robin Hood and his gang – can provide entrances for oppositional readings, as Fiske (1982) has noted. Since the counter-myths are carried in the subcultures of society, points of entrance may be discovered, in reading a text, in order to reconstruct meanings derived from the counter-myths rather than the intended dominant myths. It is in subcultural activity that the forms of resistance to the dominant myths of society are worked out (Hall and Jefferson 1975). From the vantage point of the counter-discourse, the text is re-worked, re-territorialised, to reflect the alternative images by which the world is experienced and made meaningful.

Popular culture picks up both the dominant and counter myths: 'the factual side of television, news, current affairs, documentaries, tends to show more of the dominant than of the counter-myth: fictional television and cinema, on the other hand, reverse the proportions. There are more evil scientists than good ones, and science causes more problems than it solves' (Fiske 1982: 94–5). Although science in the dominant myth is a 'good' and is equated with such virtues as 'progress', 'improvement' and 'sophistication'; it is also something dangerous. Both interpretations coexist. Every advance also carries with it a play on the fear of the unknown, upon meddling with the unnamed powers of nature, of inquiring too much, and wanting too much power. Horror films in particular play on the fears, anxieties and sense of abjection that arise from going *beyond*, from breaking the fragile order of the known and the safe. Thus in Booth's imagery of the two dwelling places: at the surface level, we dwell within the security of science; however, science is often revealed to be built on shaky foundations; behind the appearance of security is really the unknown; the unknown, and the abjection that the feeling of dwelling in the unknown creates, is our real dwelling place. It is hard to reflect upon the implications of this second dwelling place. Thus, it is often suppressed, or covered by religious accounts which replace the insecurity with a firmer security that science could not in the end deliver. In fictional domains, this anxiety may be represented in ways which are readily deniable: 'it's only a story.'

At another level of covert operation is a control myth which warns the masses not to meddle with things they do not know about: 'Damn scientists, why can't they leave well alone'. It is a cry of futility because 'you can't stop progress.' The play between the myth and the counter-myth has the effect of creating a sense of futility and resignation: 'what can I do?' A culture of silence is constructed to envelop those things we do not know about, and cannot do anything about.

It is precisely this play between myths, between alternative discourses through which both the repressing functions and the liberating functions of the processes of the forbidden can be explored. At one level, the forbidden does not seek to represent or to assert a truth, but rather to offer a possibility, to rip to shreds the certain, in order to reveal the might-be, a region of play between the possible and the impossible. This is the level of the fantastic which is at the heart of the forbidden: it opens a carnival of the mind where 'everyone is an active participant, everyone communes in the carnival act ... The carnival life is life drawn out of its usual rut, it is to a degree "life turned inside out", "life the wrong way round"' (Bakhtin 1973: 101). This drawing out from the usual has its base in the movement of the educational process itself. At another level, it seeks its own actualisation – its own re-presentation – in the real. Booth's metaphor of the two buildings the one reconstructed behind the old untenable building, can perhaps be developed further to include a whole series of reconstructions: from surface to aberrant, to carnival, to re-structuring the real. The ironic ordering of the artistic text can employ any of these reconstructive movements in its service in order to arrive at its intended dwelling place. The forbidden structures of a community control the range of expressible interpretations at both public and private levels. For the process of reconstruction to take place, points of entrance must be discovered, since the process itself may be forbidden, only to be undertaken in secrecy or with great daring.

Due to Freud, we have looked for the signs of the repressed, the forbidden in the slips of tongue, the coded symbols of phallus and vagina. We peer into the margins of consciousness to explore the stutters, the graffiti, the whispers behind the hands, the dreams. With Lacan we learn that the unconscious is structured like a language. The heart of the forbidden seems to be penetrable, it can be mapped. It leaves its marks. It works through diverting the attention from where the real work is being carried out. It has a front, behind which it operates. It is guarded by signs which read: do not meddle; this is best left alone; mind your own business; leave it to the experts; danger, keep out. But at another door, other signs appear: this is just for you; I can show you a good time; no one will ever know you've been here. The forbidden constructs a counter-world for action. World and counter-world, however, are not separate: to act in one, is to act in the other. They are made continuous through the forbidden discourse and made to appear separate through the forms of world legitimating discourse, in which it is made to seem that the one can eradicate the other: the good empire v. the evil empire. Each turns on the other. To kill one, is to kill everything. The purpose of witch hunts is to kill symbols and thus leave all as it is: the illusion of war to end all wars, and of unending victory.

THE CONTORTION OF EXPERIENCE

Experience is not something entirely apart from the forms in which it is represented. Nor can the forms of representation entirely contain the richness of experience. There is already a dimension of distortion in the processes through which experience is represented and expressed. The power of language is in the sign's power not only to represent a given object or concept, but also to evoke possibilities in the imagination as if they were real. The sign is composed of two faces, the signifier (sound heard, visual image of a mark on a page, etc) and the signified (concept, idea, meaning unit, etc). The relation between them is, according to de Saussure, arbitrary. The sound 'cat' is arbitrarily related to its signified, the concept of the cat. That is to say, there is no necessary logical reason why that particular sound should be associated with the concept of cat. If it were not for customary usage, some other sound would do as well. The babble of the baby must be shaped towards conventional sounds and associations.

The concept of cat, in turn, must be distinguished from the actuality of any particular cat. Concepts are culturally produced. The range of connotations associated with the word 'cat' overlaps with, but is not identical to the range of connotations associated with the French word 'chat'. Concepts also accrete individual, or personal, ranges of meaning. For one person a cat is a lovable creature; for another it is an evil, deceptive creature. By evoking mental representations signifiers not only stand for experienced realities, but also shape experience and construct realities that can enrich or distort.

Robertson (1986) discusses how a child is drawn into language:

> Mothers of young children at the threshold of language development toe the tricky de-constructive line between babble and concept daily for quite some time. Together, mother and child constantly reach for the idea and as if they have it, yet simultaneously experience the failure to have it exactly. They slide back and forth over the boundary between incoherent and coherent speech but, most curiously, they both acknowledge this and do not acknowledge it at the same time. (Robertson 1986: p. 719)

It is at this boundary between real and not-real speech, at the stage during which language constructs itself within the mind of the child, regularly associating a certain sound, concept and experience, that the child is also organised culturally into face-to-face relations, so providing permanent identities for self and other. Stable associations between sound, concept and experience, however, need not necessarily be produced. For example, Birdwhistell (1973), in a study of the social processes through which schizophrenia can be constructed in the family, has used video recordings to show how, within a few seconds, a mother can drive a seven month old child into a double bind by the gentle pressures she exerts on the child's limbs during the course of changing a nappy. It is wrong if the child moves an arm one way and wrong if she doesn't. The gentle pressure from the mother is a confusing signifier. If this is repeated, not only in changing nappies but as the child grows in a myriad other interactions the child's identity and relationships with others is itself constructed out of unstable and confusing signs. In the process, experience of self is contorted within the double-bind.

The case of Judge Schreber provides a harrowing example of the distortion of experience. As stated earlier, his father, a noted educationist, controlled him from birth in ways which denied the real meanings of actions. Judge Schreber, in effect, constructed a text from the clues, the confused signifiers that formed his early childhood experiences. This text described explicitly his relationship with God, but implicitly and unrecognised by Schreber, his relationship to his father. In the process, he transformed his own body, experiencing himself as changing into a woman for the pleasure of God. Schreber created a cosmic purpose and stage of action in order to make sense out of his personal experiences. It is a work of interpretation having a structure like but more complex than Booth's conception of irony. It is made more complex in that it prohibits a fuller recognition of the truth of a situation, creating in effect, a forbidden text. Schematically this is shown in Figure 3.

The text of the father consists of all the statements he made to the son and those that were published. At an unconscious level in the son a myriad confused signifiers from the father point to some other meaning. This other meaning later becomes the son's conscious text of God's purpose that he wrote out. The forbidden text is the recognition denied of the role of the father. Interestingly Freud, too, failed to recognise the real role of the father in this case.

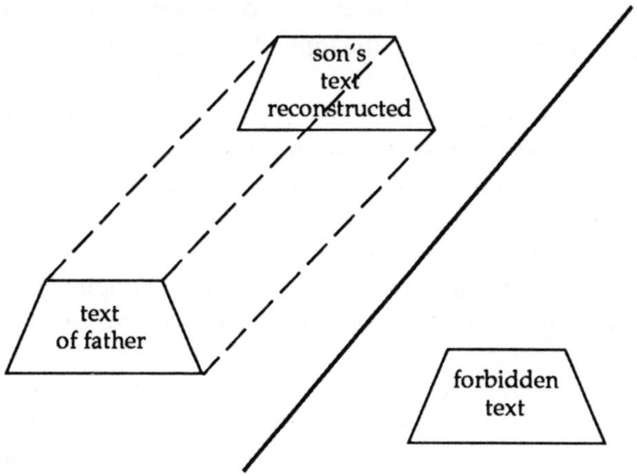

Figure 3

Schatzman (1973) provides numerous illustrations of the close relationship between the father's published material and the son's account of his 'nervous illness'. Central to the imagery of the father is the concept of 'rays' which are associated with God and which penetrate the body. The father writes that 'By frequently repeated gentle reminders the child should be brought to accustom itself to stepping before God at the end of every day alone in his own mind ... in order to reflect his *inner self* in the *pure rays* of the concept of God (of the loving Universal Father) and to be rewarded by refined willpower.' The son writes:

> We are used to thinking all impressions we receive from the outer world are mediated through the five senses, particularly that all light and sound sensations are mediated through eye and ear. This may be correct in normal circumstances. However, in the case of a human being who like myself has entered into contact with *rays* and whose head is in consequence so to speak *illuminated by rays*, this is not all. I receive light and sound sensations which are projected direct onto my *inner nervous system* by the *rays;* for their reception the external organs of seeing and hearing are not necessary (...)

The father called God 'Father' and 'like so many parents, condemned children's earth-bound sexual feelings; he wished children to become *penetrated* by and *wed* to God' (p. 82). Schatzman then gives illustrative comparisons between first the father's, then the son's texts:

> The word of religion must not be left simply adhering to ear and mouth, but its deep sense, the spirit of the word, should penetrate and wed the person's soul. The outer revelation and the inner (reasons in its highest form of development) are the two *rays [Strahlen]*, which the closer they come together, the more they are purified of everything human that had been clinging to them, until finally they come together in a single point, the point of complete fusion ...
>
> I have frequently referred in this book to the close relationship which exists between the voluptuousness and everlasting Blessedness ... In order not to be misunderstood, I must point out that when I speak of my duty to cultivate voluptuousness, I *never mean any sexual desires towards other human beings (females) least of all sexual intercourse,* but that I have to imagine myself as man and woman in one person having intercourse with myself, or somehow have to achieve with myself a certain sexual excitement etc. – which perhaps under other circumstances might be considered immoral – but which has nothing whatever to do with any idea of masturbation or anything like it ... [italics in original]

As Schatzman points out, the father's goal was for a 'complete fusion between the 'rays', a fusion 'purified of everything human'; this is echoed in the son's account of a fusion in sexual intercourse of two persons within himself without sexually desiring 'other human beings'. The father continually used religious imagery of 'penetrating' a child. As Schatzman comments, 'A child in the penetrated position is in a part usually played in adult sexual life by a woman' (p. 84). The son sees his body transforming into a woman – in terms of 'voluptuousness' – under God's desires. The wider implications of the father's educational programme will be discussed in a later chapter.

Theirs were world historical missions, to save the world. The father urged governments to take control of children's training for 'the salvation of future generations' (p. 149). The son believed that he would live forever and that he had a divine mission. If the son had replaced God by father in his text, it would have been a close analysis of his own father's strategies, beliefs and behaviour. However, who would have believed him?

There was a barrier preventing a deeper reconstruction that would finally de-fuse the confused signifiers and separate out the real-father from the God-Father. But Schreber was not alone in this. The views of the father were highly influential in Germany at the time Hitler was growing up. There are still many uncomfortable commonalities between his views on childrearing and modern practices in the home and in school. Milgram (1974) in a famous study of authority showed the extent to which ordinary people obeyed even apparently life threatening orders when commanded by an authority figure. Skinner (1976) has described a vision of the ideal society constructed through total behavioural control, an approach reminiscent of Judge Schreber's father. His views have had a powerful influence upon learning, discipline and control in schools. How can the power of authority to shape behaviour and blind awareness be broken? How to construct an opening to the forbidden knowledge for those like Judge Schreber was the proclaimed task of psychoanalysis. However, it is education that has the more general task of laying bare the forbidden curriculum that underlies everyday experience, barred from conscious grasp, consigned to the darkened, the marginal.

KNOWLEDGE, TEMPTATION, THE FORBIDDEN AND ITS SURROGATE HEROES

In the myths of light and dark there are no secret openings into the dark: the one eradicates the other. The myth of the family guides entrance into knowledge. Knowledge traditionally is thought of as bringing light not only to ignorance but also to innocence. The role assigned to the myth of the family is not only to bring up the child in the light but also to guard the innocence of the child. In the traditional religious perspective of Western culture, knowledge is divinely revealed. The recipient becomes enlightened. Divine knowledge brings light to darkness. There are no shades of grey. Those who remain in the dark can be thought of as not only ignorant but also in danger for their souls. Darkness is ruled by the Prince of Darkness.

Alternatively, in the Garden of Eden myth, knowledge is also something which can be attained as the result of disobedience. In the Garden of Eden knowledge was initially present as a danger to be avoided; the entry to the forbidden was there already, secretive, seductive, manipulative. Living in a state of innocence, Adam and Eve were commanded not to taste of knowledge. Once having tasted, they were banished. Within this story is a complex set of relationships between 'knowledge', the 'knower', the experience of 'knowing', 'authority', 'temptation', 'prohibition', 'blame', 'punishment', 'banishment'. In this complicit structure the openings are arranged.

Opening up the fields of the forbidden is to re-experience anew the processes of contortion and in doing so, to give voice to repressed or forgotten tastes or experiences, repressed or forgotten lines of intertextuality. The myth must be re-read for its lines of construction not its givenness, to place it in the light of criticism not of faith. In re-reading the Oedipus myth within its context of intertextuality we find that it is already closely bound with a multitude of myths linking it to the tradition of the dying god and his rebirth: Jesus, Jehova, Apollo (cf. Campbell 1964). It fits the tradition of the family romance. As such, it may point to the workings of some universalising archetype in the Jungian sense. Nevertheless, it is a cultural artefact. Repressed in the myth of Jesus, for example, is its historical construction, the workings and re-workings of countless storyings to produce some something said to be new and true, something to save a world, rekindle it, to bring re-birth. To reveal the tangled connections between old and new is to destroy the myth of the one true word, revealed full and complete at the time of its utterance. Great faith in the divine being born of itself requires the leap that there is no history, no long and arduous work of continuous growth, still less a playful, promiscuous variation. With the discovery of construction, openings are made.

In an age of materialism, the openings to the forbidden are constructed in a market where faith is another Christmas present; the pain and suffering, and the saving of a world, a chocolate Easter Egg. The territorialisation of the world into light and dark is orchestrated by profit and loss. Democracy as practised through the politics of power elites, monopoly capitalism and limited media discourse reduces dissent to opinion, to the fashion of stars, to the economics of surrogate forbidden heroes. Rebellion is made a contortion, blocking the potential for radical change, constructing the tame rebels who keep the cash registers ringing and organise the energy of youth into audiences for the entertainments industry. It might even be real. Thus:

> Madonna comes to mind as one contemporary example of a deconstructive 'contorted' use of women's signs. Her symbolic power (and, one suspects, her more than trivial cultural influence,

> if we could analyze it) is precisely a function of her ongoing deconstruction of the time-honoured patriarchal 'virgin–whore' dichotomy and thus her simultaneous acquiescence to and refusal of that binarity. [Therefore an oscillation is achieved] that can never resolve itself into a new conceptual unity but can continue indefinitely in practice both to accept and reject the patriarchal binarity it uses. (Robertson 1986: 715–16)

It is in finding the stage for the expression of this oscillating play between accepting and rejecting that the surrogate forbidden emerges into public discourse, not as an alternative which would replace the permitted, but as a customised flirtation, a consumer product or service that can be packaged and sold on the open market as a form of the permitted. Madonna is the name of a popular singer. Her fame and fortune rest upon the play of images she achieves, the intertextuality which subverts itself and yet leaves all in its place: a customised double-bind that checkmates rebellion. Fortunes are made, the wheels of industry turn and Madonna is rich through her exploitation of industrialised youth cultures around the world. Madonna is a performance, a cluster of images. Whatever is real, cannot be revealed. The surrogacy is all, calling out a faith in its being born of itself.

Amossy (1986: 676) in discussing the autobiographies of stars poses the dilemma of the star who would reveal her 'true' self: 'The presentation of self thus faces a double requirement: It has to break the collective frozen image while at the same time preserving it, both denouncing and preserving the stereotype':

> Marilyn Monroe is the dumb blond with a gorgeous body and childish behaviour. John Wayne is the tough guy, good-hearted and always devoted to Justice. Through their multiple roles, they are easily recognised and referred to their basic identity. The image of the star is neither the real person nor a fictive character: it is a hybrid pertaining to both. To keep the successful image unchanged, the star is condemned to play the same kind of role. To the audience, the well-known type expresses the ideal personality of its interpreter. Conversely, the real person as presented by publicity, the press and fan magazines looks like the immediate continuation of the fictional character. (pp. 677–8)

Again there is an oscillation between the 'real person' and the 'fictive character' that the star performs. What counts as the 'real person' can be further de-constructed towards the acts of social construction through which an individual emerges within a language and cultural community. There is thus a serialisation, a relay which is set in motion. Whenever one looks at one unifying cluster of images defining the person, these can be set aside for some other unifying set:

> The star is ... triply stereotyped: in her professional image as an Olympian creature; in the specific image invented for her and expressed by her whole cinematic being; and in the social and psychological type she embodies. In the stereotyped image that invades both the market and the consciousness of her time, the star contemplates herself as in a magic mirror. She sees in her glorious reflection not only her own person but also her fascinating, detachable double. (Amossy 1986: 678)

The magic mirror offers not only the reflection of her body, but also the multiple images of fictive personalities as re-presented by professional image-makers and by the public. All within the context of the magic mirror of industrialised culture where, as Amossy says, an ordinary person moves from being Shirly Schrift to Shelley Winters the movie star: 'From Cinderella to the gorgeous princess of the ball there is a continuity that only a tale of metamorphosis can convincingly establish.' Stories nestle within stories explaining the dazzling array of dramatis personae which inhabit the body of the single performer. In supporting this dazzling array the conditions for the expression of the forbidden in the ordinary lives of the audience are preserved. On screen sex, violence and horror can be explored and expressed either as fiction or as documentary in ways which articulate the forbidden while preserving an approved discourse, since the forbidden is only a surrogate in the lives of viewers. Like Schreber constructing a text through which to make sense of the world, these surrogate texts gloss the real, diverting attention, defusing energies. Entering further into the forbidden is along an ever twisting path, obstacle strewn, in a realm where the mythic and the real fuse.

PORNOGRAPHY: FORBIDDEN MIRRORS

In the imagery and the structures of complicity linking the surrogate heroes and villains to the economies of desire, the entry to forbidden knowledge of the erotic or of the pornographic can be made through 'aberrant' readings from counter-cultural, counter-mythical positions. The forbidden is always the site of multiple mirrors. The contents of the pornographic are variously defined according to culture; it has the sense of being sexual dirt set against the purity of the 'chaste' and the sanctity of marriage, 'pure love'. Douglas (1966) in an anthropological study defined 'dirt' as matter out of place. There is a cultural ordering of the world according to what is dirt and what is clean, what is dangerous and what is pure. To a Victorian mind sex is always matter out of place. However, if sex and sexuality are natural and good, how is it to be represented and expressed? Is there any more a category of the pornographic?

In the *Sadean Woman* (1979) Angela Carter wrote 'Since all pornography derives directly from myth, it follows that its heroes and heroines, from the most gross to the most sophisticated, are mythic abstractions, heroes and heroines of dimension and capacity' (p. 6). It is this hero and heroine from the Sadean side which structurally matches the hero and heroine of fleshless abstraction who fight and die for God and country. Both live in the deceit which weaves consciousness into acceptance of believable realities. Carter describes her view:

> All the mythic versions of women, from the myth of the redeeming purity of the virgin to that of the healing, reconciling mother, are consolatory nonsenses; and consolatory nonsense seems to me a fair definition of myth anyway. Mother goddesses are just as silly a notion as father gods. If a revival of the myths of these cults gives women emotional satisfaction, it does so at the price of obscuring the real conditions of life. This is why they were invented in the first place. (p. 5)

Who would ever know the 'first place'? And in the myth of the superman, who would regard the horrors committed in its name this century as simply 'a silly notion'? Myth and 'real conditions' cannot be separated so easily. The 'heroes and heroines of dimension and capacity', are ourselves in the distorting mirrors of the imaginary, the cultural, symbolic structuring through which we know ourselves and others. Pornography, if it is to be understood at all, derives from the real conditions through which desire is controlled, and its objects produced, exchanged and consumed.

Lévi-Strauss has described the exchange of women – as a kind of currency – as the foundation of society itself. It is through the economy of desire in its open and hidden forms, that women are constructed as currency and, in the mass market economy, as consumers. Women in film and in advertising are typically seen as ornaments to the powers of men. There are some exceptions. An advert for Branson's Virgin Airlines reverses the role, showing a woman executive being pampered by a male steward. But the economic paradigm remains: it is a battle of who will commodify whom. Men are first in the field and have the vast majority of the power to define.

The early cinema provided a powerful arena for the further commodification of women, but also for establishing the female consumer. Doane (1989) describes how the 'spectator-consumer was increasingly envisaged as female' (p. 26). 'If the film frame is a kind of display window and spectatorship consequently a form of window-shopping, the intimate association of looking and buying does indeed suggest that the prototype of the spectator-consumer is female' (p.27). In support of this she quotes Eckert (1978):

> Consumer statistics widely disseminated in the late 1920s and the early 1930s show that women made 80 to 90 per cent of all purchases for family use. They bought 48 per cent of drugs, 96 per cent of dry goods, 87 per cent of raw products, 98 per cent of automobiles.

Product placement in films is widespread today. Representation, in all its forms – TV, video, cinema, radio, books – all provide display settings which go alongside shop windows, constructing and positioning the self as a spectator–buyer–consumer in the regulation of desire. Representation in the service of the commodification of men and women is itself the *cordon sanitaire* against untying the relations of inequity, domination and degradation.

Domination and submission, central to both fascism and sadomasochism, is a central structuring relationship pervading society. From institution to institution, the meaning of this relation of domination and submission may change. In families and schools it has to do with obedience to the caring wisdom of the adult, character-building and so on. In religions it has to do with the worship of a god, the proof of faith. In the military it has to do with creating an effective and reliable fighting force. In working relations it has to do with economic power. Throughout societies, generally, it is the man who is expected to dominate and the woman to be submissive. In science, scientific discourse is 'genderized' where things are to be'attacked', 'licked' or 'conquered' (Keller 1983: 20) within a male rhetoric. And in literature

> the hero must be male regardless of the gender of the character, because the obstacle, whatever its personification (sphinx or dragon, sorceress or villain), is morphologically female – and, indeed, simply the womb, the earth, the space of his movement. As he crosses the boundary and 'penetrates' the other space, the mythical subject is constructed as human being and as male; he is the active principle of culture, the establisher of distinction, the creator of differences. Female is what is not susceptible to transformation, to life or death, she (it) is an element of plot-space, a topos, a resistance, matrix, and matter. (Lauretis 1989)

The pornographic is already complicit within the structures of society in the way in which relations between men and women are ordered. What is sexuality, pleasure, eroticism, is inscribed in a space that is already male, and already framed into patterns of domination and exploitation. How may sexual pleasure be represented in these conditions? As Patton (1989) argues, in the case of films marketed as pornographic:

> ... there is a cultural uncertainty about what constitutes female sexual pleasure. Female sexual pleasure is not synonymous with orgasm, and images of female sexual pleasure have been used to indicate male sexual pleasure, as in mainstream movies, and product satisfaction, as in glossy advertisements. Even though the nature of female orgasm has come under debate in the last two decades – the clitoral orgasm, G-spot, anal sex – female sexual pleasure is still depicted through facial expressions: the transcendent, glazed-over eyes, lips glistening and slightly parted, head thrown back. (p. 105)

In her study of heterosexual pornography she finds that kisses are rarely used in pornography perhaps because of the deeper emotion they signify and because 'the kiss is too democratic in western culture, a joint act of simultaneous action and reception.' It is an act which is 'democratic', open. In concluding a study of a particular film *Pumping Irene: The Woman*, she comments:

> Mr and Mrs D have sex at the same time, but it is practically in spite of each other, not with each other. Thus, heterosexuality remains irreconcilable narratives, which, in the 'post-feminist' era requires that the woman achieve 'equal pleasure', but only by engaging in

> more sophisticated deceits. Mrs D will no longer fake an orgasm and do without pleasure, but she will hide from Mr D the orgasm she has produced by her own hand. The conventionality and linear narrative of the male orgasm may prevent male viewers from 'reading' this little segment as Mrs D's pleasure: it may simply be perceived as 'not containing sex'. Female orgasm remains a deceit by the characters in the video; sexual pleasure plausible to the female viewer is constructed for her in a secret language inscribed over the classic male narrative. (p. 112)

The unspoken in the male narrative is not simply the obvious pornographic imagery, the fascism of a long-gone Germany or some far-off country, but the process of reduction in life itself. Desire is contorted into patterns of domination and submission, and sexualised violence. Sexuality, as a play of desire in patterns of equality and wholeness, is dissected for its commodity value. A category of the erotic, perhaps, may be distinguished from pornography:

> People become confused because the sexually explicit subordination of women in pornography is presented and perceived as sex. Then when it is proposed to put the elimination of pornography on the agenda of women's liberation (for what are hopefully obvious and acceptable reasons), they think that acting against pornography means censoring sex. Given the politics of the religious and moral right, and particularly the attacks on gay and lesbian sex and sexuality, there are genuine concerns about the potential for sexual repression and oppression. But it is also necessary – and possible – to distinguish between sex, and the sexual subordination of women in pornography. (Itzin 1990)

Writing in the *Index on Censorship* Itzin makes her case against pornography by distinguishing it from alternative representations of sex. In the same issue Petley describes the long list of films banned, censored or delayed in Britain, many for political reasons, some for violence, sex or blasphemy. The question of censorship cannot be ignored or glossed. There is either absolute freedom of expression in which anything goes; or, there are limits. Who defines and patrols the limits?

Rodgerson and Semple in *Feminist Review* (1990) argue their case against the anti-pornography groups starting from a discussion of MacKinnon and Dworkin's co-authored ordinance (1984) allowing women, in the City of Minneapolis in America, 'to take civil action against anyone involved in the production, sale or distribution of pornography on the grounds that they had been harmed by the image of women's sexuality that it portrayed' (p. 19). Against this the Feminist Anti-Censorship Task Force (FACT) argued against censorship because this would be to support the power of the establishment over free speech and 'left the feminist movement hostage to fortune and open to unwanted alliances with antifeminist elements' (p. 19). The case can be supported by pointing to the fact that in Britain the censorial functions of the state increased during the Thatcher years, leading to the seizure and destruction of lesbian and gay publications. With the advent of AIDS gay men were blamed for its spread and 'lesbian feminists played directly into the hands of the moral right by their willingness to apportion blame to gay men's sexual practices while smugly assuming that AIDS was not a women's and definitely not a lesbian issue' (p. 20). It all contributed to the reassertion of the family as a political resource for the right. The organisation, Feminists Against Censorship (FAC), took the view that censorship was not the only feminist position with regard to pornography:

> As the forces of the right continue to gather on the side of increased repression in many spheres, all feminists who are against censorship must constantly be aware of the guises this repression can assume. Simply fighting against the banning and restricting of sexually explicit images is not enough. As feminists we also have a responsibility to be critical of those images we find sexist, racist or exploitative and to counter them in the most effective way there is: if not by creating our own, then by supporting those who are creating an alternative body of sexual images for women. (p. 23)

Censorship of any form is an echo of the old structures of domination and submission, Superego and Id, in which pornography, violence and state terrorism are born. Like a virus it may reproduce itself in the best of ideals and subvert them to its own image. Through it, the issue of the representation of sexuality is not resolved. The underlying structure of diminution and commodification remains. The issue then is educational, requiring the emancipation and empowerment of individuals to express their wholeness as sexual beings, not as consumer items.

BLASPHEMY

There are texts the truth of which cannot be doubted. They are the texts of revealed truth, the Word of The Father. During the latter decades of the twentieth century many forgot or dismissed the power of blasphemy within the Western idea of democracy. It was perhaps something that avant garde artists flirted with to gain some passing notoriety and make the cash registers ring; and it gave fringe groups on the moral right a soap box on which to proclaim their red-faced outrage. Rushdie's *Satanic Verses* changed all that. There is no doubt about the sense of outrage and offence it caused to devout Muslims. There is no doubt that the liberal mind was in turn outraged against the demands for censorship and the death threat against Rushdie. Blasphemy thus raises issues which, like pornography, go to the heart of social and political processes and structures.

Webster (1990), writing on *Blasphemy* as a response to the issue, broadly argued that the position of absolute freedom of expression within today's democracies is untenable and that artists are either mistaken or foolhardy if they believe that modern democracies enshrine the principle of free speech. Rather, he argued that democracies are what totalitarian states collapse into. They do so because the rigidly enforced laws of the totalitarian regimes that preceded them no longer need overt terror to enforce them. The terror has been so internalised that people can largely be relied upon to censor themselves:

> Such a process of internalisation is unlikely ever to be complete. But, to a certain degree at least, it seems reasonable to argue that respect for the figure of Jesus and for Christianity in general has been inculcated so widely, even among non-believers, that the restraints of good taste have gradually made the restraints of the law all but redundant. (…)
>
> It is perhaps partly because of such internalised repression that the role of artists, poets, novelists and film-makers as 'agents' of blasphemy has become so important in the twentieth century. Imaginative artists have, in effect, been licensed to engage in blasphemy on behalf of those who, because of their own relative imaginative rigidity, find it difficult to do so. But even the license we give to artists to blaspheme is itself severely limited. Occasional blasphemies can be tolerated in the confidence that their example is unlikely to be followed; there is no longer a danger of the floodgates of impiety springing open. But extreme or obscene

> blasphemy is still effectively outlawed or restricted to special contexts. (pp. 25–6)

Webster provides numerous examples of the forms of censorship in Britain which come into play, needing no recourse to the obvious repressions of a totalitarian regime. He refers to Sines *Massacre*, an acclaimed French cartoonist published by Penguin in 1967 – now made ironic in the light of the Rushdie affair. Since it contained a number of blasphemous cartoons many found the book offensive, making their feelings known to the publisher Allen Lane:

> His response was swift and effective. One night, soon after the book had been published, he went into Penguin's Harmondsworth warehouse with four accomplices, filled a trailer with all the remaining copies of the book, drove away and burnt them. (p. 26)

In 1976 the film *The Many Faces of Jesus*, intended to recount the sex life of Jesus, by the Danish film-maker Jens Jorgen Thorson, was opposed by pressure groups and the Queen, James Callaghan, the Prime Minister and the Archbishop of Canterbury. In 1979 Monty Python's *The Life of Brian* was also the focus of a similar kind of internal censorship. Of interest in each of Webster's examples is the fact that the 'internal censorship' is not simply an inner psychological process but is externalised in terms of the workings and functions of major British social institutions: royalty, church and government. Institutions have the function of coordinating actions, orienting attitudes and values and focusing the attention of members. It is not simply the case that every member has 'internalised' the processes of censorship but that the world in which individuals operate is already parcelled up and institutionalised. To act otherwise is to invoke the terror of taking on structures that are massive, impersonal and fundamental to the allocation of wealth, opportunities, rewards, pleasures and pains throughout society. Those at the top of the institution (Queen, Prime Minister, archbishop) live through the institutions of which they are symbols. Those at lower levels have constructed their identities, their wealth, their position in relation to the institution and thus the symbols of the institution. To act in accordance with the preservation of the institution is to censor all that would threaten it. This internal censorship is in fact a social construction which has its externalised manifestations in the everyday workings of the major institutions of society.

When institutions are arranged to look after their material interests, then a discourse of censorship and the re-presentation of the 'natural' 'real', 'good' arises whenever the carnival of ideas breaks down the facades, makes explicit the codes concealing the double binds, the double discourse. Worlds are not to be lightly played with. They may be supported by underlying networks of terror, and/or the fear of loss of identity, belief and faith. Fascist and totalitarian states of all kinds uphold their worlds through terror but may be brought down because there is no faith, no meaning that enriches the person.

The faith that invests a world with meaning and enriches the individual, if it is threatened through insult or blasphemy, or is lost, threatens the experienced spiritual freedom of those who believe. It is the loss of being, all goodness, all truth, all light. The reaction to the *Satanic Verses* reteaches the lesson, revealing the question still to be explored: what is the democratic relationship between freedom and the faiths through which all worlds are constructed and lived? Democracy cannot privilege one faith above another if it is to speak to all cultures and to all peoples, but it must provide the conditions in which all can live and grow and express themselves together. It is hypocritical to censor material offensive to Christians but not material offensive to other faiths. All faiths should be treated equally either by extending the blasphemy laws or by abolishing them. But that would not resolve the issues which are implicated in the affair.

Webster (1990) set the *Satanic Verses* into the long history of Western racist attitudes towards the culture of Islam. The *Satanic Verses* does not stand like an isolated island-text but is already inter-textually woven into historical discourses which position it and provide the basis for alternative readings.

When Rushdie proclaimed his conversion to Islam, after two years of hiding, many of his supporters felt betrayed. It seemed like a capitulation to threat. Rushdie, whether he wished it or not, had been made a hero in the fight for freedom of expression. He signified a cause. He became a concrete focus for all sides. However, the creation of heroes and the individualising of blame reinforce the impasse which is already history deep in martyrs of every faith and side. The issues, however, remain, involving principles which go beyond any one individual and point to the meaning of democracy itself. Different levels of questions have to be unpicked:

1. Is there a right of absolute freedom of expression?
2. Should there be rights for those who have been deeply offended, degraded?

3. Should there still be a concept of blasphemy legally enforced in a secular democracy in which many faiths co-habit?
4. Is there, no matter what is said and done, an absolute right to live?

Clearly, no state allows absolute freedom of expression in relation to official secrets, slander, libel or the misreporting of facts. There are limits, too, in the case of race and sex discrimination laws. In accepting some forms of limitation on freedom of expression, the principle of absolute freedom is already untenable. What is wrong from the point of view of democracy in the current laws of blasphemy is that one faith is privileged and protected above all others and thus offends against the principle of non-discrimination. The concept of blasphemy itself offends against the freedom of belief of those who have no religious affiliation, privileging faith above no-faith in the eyes of democracy. The humanitarian ideal is the absolute right to life no matter what is said and done. This conflicts with the practice of most states. In Britain, for example, there is still the theoretical penalty of death for treason. Opinion polls consistently show a majority support for hanging to be brought back in cases of murder. There are faiths that justify death as a penalty. It is the ultimate act of silencing and the ultimate act of power.

Frances D'Souza, having been a Rushdie supporter, was reported in the *Independent* (4 January 1991) as seeing the need to broaden the issue from the support of one person: '... the real issue of the 1990s is to do with religious pluralism and the place of religious minorities and what we must strive for is for several truths to co-exist in society ...'. Islam, of course, is a major world religion and in that sense, can in no way be considered 'minority'. The fundamental question is, how can world-defining belief systems – whether they are religions, philosophies or political creeds – begin to take account of each other in ways that respect difference, the right to life and the right to dignity? Webster comments that 'It is time we recognised that when we plunge the dagger of our own intellectual superiority into other peoples' religious faith, we are engaging in a form of intellectual cruelty which is also a form of real cruelty' (p. 135). This is not an argument for censorship. It is an argument for real empowerment in relations of equality through which dignity can be expressed; it is an argument to feel deeply the experience and anguish of others who hold different beliefs to our own. But what marks the difference between intellectual superiority, and works that are forbidden because they reveal truths? On what basis should such decisions be made? The function of blasphemy is to close all possibility of debate between alternative readings of the real and between what is considered truth. The function of education is to open debate and the function of democracy is to provide the political rights and material structures to sustain debate, the possibility of growth and of change for all people of all faiths without threat of death.

6

MAKING THE NEWS:
Duping, Smearing, Silencing

The news is a particular kind of text which claims to tell people 'what is happening in the world and what it all means'. As a text, it is highly selected, contested and political. Most people suspect its truthfulness – 'don't believe all you read in the newspapers or see on television'. Nevertheless, the apparent realism of the journalist providing 'on the spot coverage', the photograph and the video is seductive. Their texts are a major source of information, giving guidelines, albeit often misleading, about the world scene. Handling the misleading, recognising 'misrecognitions' and 'misinterpretations' are sophisticated skills, requiring access to alternative sources for validation that few have the time to construct. What then is the role and what are the implications of the news as a mediating text between 'what happens' and 'what people are intended or supposed to know'? There are many powerful people with a vested interest in controlling what people are supposed to know and what they are supposed to believe.

Fundamental to the newspaper image is that it searches out the truth, it uncovers, it reveals what was not known before and demands justice. However, who gets 'caught out', how they get 'caught out' and the effect this has on their life, image and career is highly controlled through processes of smearing, glossing or whitewashing. The attention of the reader or viewer is manipulated, associations made through juxtapositions, feelings aroused through contextual imagery. However, a distinction has to be maintained between serious journalism and mock journalism. To the extent that journalism serves democratic organisation, revealing what the ruling groups, the good and the great, are really up to in their offices protected by official and business secrets – to that extent they are serious and educational. They are able to open up debates where other official structures close them down. Mock journalism manipulates the signs of investigation only in order to gloss over inadequacies in a system, or redirect attention from blunders and corruption in order to sustain its vested interests in the system that supports it. Both forms may occur in the same newspaper or broadcast station.

During the 1980s a continual battle was waged between the government and its allies in the press against those in the media committed to serious journalism and the broadcasting of critical views whether in documentary or fictional forms. A leader in the political battles was the *Sun* owned by Murdock. The *Sun* has been credited with bringing the working-class vote to Thatcher. On the twenty-first anniversary of the *Sun* she congratulated it for being a great British institution, saying 'If it can come up fresh and bubbling and vital for 21 years, then so can I. And I shall do so' (*Guardian*, 14 November 1990). It even claimed to have brought victory to John Major, Thatcher's successor, in the 1992 election. The power of newspapers like the *Sun* to shape opinion is difficult to doubt. However, the population is, of course, not homogeneous in its values, beliefs and interests. There are continually contradictions, scandals, political tensions and counter-discourses to manage. This is done through processes of smearing, glossing and whitewashing while maintaining a standpoint of honest, down-to-earth, plain speaking. Few do it better than the *Sun*.

There is a complex interplay between the everyday life of ordinary people and the everyday life of the powerful that the media is central in managing. Recalling the Poe story, 'The Purloined Letter' discussed in Chapter 2, there is a similarity of structure. Instead of king, queen, minister these are substituted by readership (audience), public figure and media. A public figure is in danger of being found out in some dubious activity. The readership is not aware of this. The media can either reveal or conceal. This gives considerable power to the media, in particular to the owners of the media. Where the mock journalist or propagandist may work to conceal bad news from the readership, the investigative journalist takes the position of the 'famed analyst' called in to solve the mystery. However, the work of the investigative journalist, in turn, has to be managed in some way in order to keep the target readership unaware. This whole process is about the organisation of experience, making sense of the fragmentary experiences that comprise everyday life in ways which maintain current vested interests. The construction of the audience or readership is central to that process. To do this the media has to make direct appeals, whether as speaking with the values and beliefs of the audience, speaking plainly, bluntly, commonsensically, honestly, or as presenting balanced views, providing equal voice to a range of opinion or as being neutral, well-researched information sources.

BLUNT TALK AND THE ORGANISATION OF EXPERIENCE

The popular press presents an image of plain-speaking ordinary folk, given to delighting in good honest fun. In particular, it contributes to the development of what Anderson (1983) has called imagined political communities. A political community is imagined 'because the members of even the smallest nation will never know most of their fellow-members, meet them, or even hear of them, yet in the minds of each lives the image of their communion' (p. 15). The truth of the representation is not what is at issue but the way in which the community is imagined. Its characteristics are that it is limited, that is, not coextensive with the human race; it is sovereign; and it is a community because:

> regardless of the actual inequality and exploitation that may prevail in each, the nation is always conceived as a deep, horizontal comradeship. Ultimately, it is this fraternity that makes it possible, over the past two centuries, for so many millions of people, not so much kill, as willingly to die for such limited imaginings. (p. 16)

Under the title of the *Sun*, what it stands for, readers are positioned in imaginary relationship to each other (as *Sun* readers) and in relation to the characters, institutions, other nations and events in each story. The reader can be positioned as 'British', as 'a working man', or as 'outraged at the bullying of Trades Unions'. Davies and Harré (1990) describe the process of positioning as fundamental to the construction of the self where the position adopted 'incorporates both a conceptual repertoire and a location for persons within the structure of rights for those that use that repertoire' (p. 46). For example, a conceptual repertoire is built up about the fighting spirit and loyalty of the British soldier, the lunatic ideas of the left, or the common touch of the Queen Mother. The concepts that attach to major figures, institutions and social groups organise experience and position the person who adopts them, shaping their own sense of self in imaginary relationship to others. Narratives provide an imaginative framework to crystalise the positions, the social structures that tie the subject positions together and the conceptual schema that are applied to make sense of experience. In particular, news stories provide pre-digested imaginative responses to the experience of life.

The *Sun* has a basic list of characters, its dramatis personae: there are the stars from film, pop and sports with their 'birds', 'toyboys' and 'hunks'; there is the good plain man and woman (who are patriotic, hate the French and anything foreign and vote Tory); there are the everyday criminals who can be used to provide amusement; there are the monsters who are to be reviled; the police who are essentially good but targets for scandal; the vicars (preferably gay, adulterers or in some other way sexually active); the business men (typically) and the trade unions; and of course the politicians who are good (Tory), bad (hard left), ridiculous (Labour and the rest). With this cast and the set piece stories a cat's cradle of traps arise which can be employed to catch out public figures or those who have public roles such as teachers, priests, social workers, police, health workers. The aim is to expose people and situations for what they really are and to situate the readers of the *Sun*, the *Sun* itself and the political and economic heroes of the *Sun* as honest, good, upright. In the stories that are repeatedly recycled, albeit with different real-life characters and details, there is an overdetermination of meaning and structure that connects one story to another, reinforcing particular values, beliefs and forms of action. These stories revolve around a number of spheres of social interest and activity sufficiently common to the experiences of a large proportion of its readership, such as: family, the lads (less often the lasses), birds, sport, vicars, royal family, the Brits, the others (Frogs, Krauts, Nips, Yanks, etc). These are intermixed with stories of the bizarre, horrific, tragic, triumphal which are out of the usual range of experience and resemble the stories of the superhero form. These kinds of story, together with their typical dramatis personae, organise everyday experience in relation to knowledge of the world. Whether they are believed or not matters little. It is not truth but the evocation of feelings, and the motivation and formation of prejudices, attitudes, values, desires that are at the heart of the effects of such stories. Different stories act upon the reader at different levels, from different angles. Stories apparently having nothing to do with each other, whether juxtaposed or on different pages, can connect in unexpected ways and contribute to an overall effect, orienting the readership towards a particular set of values, beliefs, attitudes. When a crisis occurs, an election is to be fought, a public figure to be smeared or whitewashed, the ground has already been prepared – a current story connects through memory with a host of previous similar or contrasting stories and characters. It is a process of intertextuality, where one text evokes and relies upon other texts for its meanings. Any given word can be weighted with a legacy of positive or negative connotations, darkened by innuendo or made glossy and glamorous by allusion. How a newspaper accomplishes this over time would require a long and detailed historical analysis. However, an indication of the approach can be given fairly briefly through the example of the Iraqi invasion of Kuwait during the summer of 1990.

The front page of the *Sun* on 24 August 1990 held two main stories: (1) BMW Men Black Iraq Boss's Car; and (2) Gazza's New Bird! A smaller third story boxed at the top of the two main stories was '£ Hits Record High in Gulf Crisis'. None of these headlines makes much sense without having some prior knowledge. The first story has an international reference, whereas the second requires knowledge specific to a particular British sport – football.

The lead story, at the time of the Iraqi invasion of Kuwait, with its colour photograph of the BMW car in question, 'Saddam's ambassador' and two others, is described as a 'protest over hostage Brits' held by the 'Butcher of Bagdad'. The plain man is thus doing his bit for Britain. The 'little man' as worker confronts the foreign 'Boss'. It is a tactic more reminiscent of trade union action, but here drawn into service as a patriotic symbol. The reader is positioned with the workers against the 'Butcher'. It is a story that organises outrage, implies readiness for action, and defines the target. The mundane world of action is readied for action upon the world stage. This is later picked up in six further stories. There is a major headline on the possibility of oil rationing and another claiming 'Nuke Planes On Way'. The development of Saddam's character into a monstrous figure is promoted by such a description as 'a mass murderer of his own people'. Page 6 presents the story of 'War Room Where Bush Will Whack Iraq'. The heroic USA with its incredible power is described, perhaps appealing to a sense of omnipotence. Next to this in the editorial column a new cast of characters and an abiding theme appears under the heading 'Keep Out the Clowns'. The clowns here refer to left-wing politicians in order to contrast with the right-wing government. The implication is that if you support Labour, you'll let these clowns in who could not take a tough stand on Iraq. Thus, the heroic is associated with the government while the clowning is associated with the left. The editorial was written in order to defuse a tough stand being made by the Labour leaders. The *Sun* responded by attempting to position the reader with the political right. Despite acknowledging the Labour party leader's tough stand, through the association of images and themes the effect of the tough talk is subverted. Behind the toughness are the clowns. The editorial is a lesson in reading. Its lesson is: don't be duped! Thus the reader is positioned as a potential dupe. The *Sun* emerges as a trusted guide or analyst, to disentangle the false from the real and thus save the reader.

Juxtaposed against these major, world historical themes, is a more parochial concern: 'Gazza's new Bird'. As an illustration, there is a photograph captioned 'Heidi-hi ... Gazza's new blond in suspenders'. Gazza is a football hero, one of the lads, doing what football heroes are meant to do in the eyes of 'the lads'. The reader is positioned in relation to the Gazza stories as also one of the lads. It provides another level of positioning, locating the reader, just as the men blacking the BMW of the Iraqi ambassador are also the lads doing what they are supposed to do. Such acts of positioning whether in relation to major or minor stories weave together a web of entrapping associations. These associations are caught in puns that would make little sense to outsiders, thus again positioning the reader as an insider who like the *Sun*, is in a position to know. Gazza's 'Bird' is called 'Heidi. The allusion in the caption is to a popular British TV series set in a 1950s holiday camp where the wake-up call on the camp tannoy is 'Heidi-hi'. The allusion is to fun and games, the lads having a laugh. The parochial and the world significant are side by side in equal importance on the front page. In each case the lads are the heroes with their serious and fun-loving faces. In the one case patriotism is writ large, in the other, as a soccer hero of the World Cup, Gazza implicitly connotes patriotism.

It was later revealed by Channel 4's *Hard News* that the new 'Bird' of Gazza was not, nor ever had been, a girlfriend. The picture of her had been taken at a charity event several years beforehand as a fund raiser. Implicitly, the reader is a dupe. Illusions are being created for ulterior purposes. Similarly, that a few men 'black' the repair of a BMW is hardly going to send a shiver down the spine of Saddam Hussein. An illusion is being created. It is not the truth that matters here but the emotional impact, the characterisation – and the newspaper sales.

A character such as Gazza represents fun and gossip. Being interspersed around the paper – in a further six items – he counterbalances the weightier more worrying events. It is vital that the process of positioning with its associated complex of values, beliefs and behaviours is carried over into other stories. Sex is a major area of interest for the *Sun*. Together with the lads and their birds, and the pin-up girls, rape stories are a major part of the *Sun* diet, forming a legitimate vehicle for what in another context would be the substance of pornography. Take for example, in the same issue: 'Triple "Rape Victim" Lied'. This is a story of a woman (positioned as victim) who claimed to have been raped by two men (positioned as persecutors) and then raped by a 'Good Samaritan' (positioned as false rescuer). However, it was revealed the woman's account was itself false. The woman (now repositioned as persecutor) turns out to be the evil one, creating traps for men (now repositioned as victims). The import of this story is again to provide a lesson in reading. Set this story in the context of current debates about male violence, date rape and women's rights and the potential import of the story becomes clear.

Later in the issue is another story which takes up a similar theme: 'Car Girl Raped by M-way "helpers"'. These 'helpers' are again false Samaritans as in the earlier story. But in this rape story there is an additional sting: 'She should have stopped the car near an emergency motorway phone' – as in the Red Riding Hood story, could she have been asking for it, is the implication. So, even if the woman is telling the truth, there is a counter-story to bring to men's aid. Such counter-stories reposition women, not as unwilling victims, but as stupid, as perpetrators in their own misfortune.

Woman as predator is a further variation of the counter-story, provided in the gossip article on Patricia Kluge described as an ex belly dancer, ex porn star, ex sex columnist who married 'one of the richest men in America', divorced him and 'lands maintenance of £1 million A WEEK'. It is not hard to see her for what she really is: a fortune-hunter who is now 'afraid men might be after her dough'. There is a photograph of her revealing her leg, titled: 'THIGH LIFE ... Pat won't be caught on the hop by gold-diggers.' All in all, men have to beware of women seducing them, asking for it, turning the tables. Examples are everywhere: on page 15 is the headline 'Gran, 37, Dumps Hubby for Toyboy, 18'; to complement the toyboy story is a 'reader's letter' of a thirty-eight year-old mother who makes love to a 15-year-old boy whose 'mother is divorced so my husband looks on him as a son': virtual incest, adultery and under-aged sex. The letter is surrounded by three further letters describing complicated sexual affairs.

The stories on sex, position readers generally as voyeurs and as moralists. Whether it is a story like that on page 35, 'Gay councillor faces row over kiddy job', or 'Wife in Towel Routs Bathtime Burglars', or 'the loveliest girls are in The Sun', such sexual themes construct that sense of 'pornographic living' described by Cook (broadcast in 'Opinions', Channel 4, 11 December, published by the *Listener*, 13 December 1990).

In the process of positioning the reader, the construction of what Lacan has called the one who is 'supposed to know' is the key. In addition to a position of knowledge it is a position of authority, signifying the point which marks the difference between reality and illusion. This theme was used to the full in a section on South Africa titled 'Tragic Truth' where 'we never accepted the fantasy that [Nelson Mandela's] party, the ANC, represented all blacks and that he was an undisputed leader. Now we see the bitter reality. In South Africa, hatred of black for black is more virulent than hatred of black for white.' Again, there is an echo of the earlier rape stories as victims turn persecutors. The assertion of black rights, black history, black identity is met in this editorial with a counter-discourse that says 'really it's their own fault'. Mandela is described as dignified, respected. But behind this is the reality of blacks hating blacks leading to '**<u>A bloodbath</u>**' (bold and underlined in the original). There is no alternative account providing a fuller history of colonialism and the effect of this on culture, social institutions and personal identity, just the simple reduction to blacks hating blacks.

The structural echoes and mirrors between the different kinds of story create a complex web of associations each reinforcing a stable set of political orientations and values regarding both the world stage and the mundane world of everyday affairs. Although day by day there is a changing emphasis upon one theme or another, the function of each story is to establish the values, attitudes and beliefs to be accepted as true, real and practical. These 'realities' promote a misrecognition of the underlying structures in which big business, politics and the media fuse.

BIG BUSINESS, POLITICS AND THE MEDIA

Individuals occupy positions in the economic organisation of society. Whether these positions are as 'bread winner', 'home maker', 'boss', 'employee', or 'recipient of welfare', they all connect and they all become the raw materials of media stories. From the point of view of a market economy, big business is of course a 'good'. However, it is also a source of major inequalities. Getting people to accept their positions in the economic order is a major concern for those who have a vested interest in market inequality. Acceptance of inequality depends upon either a misrecognition of those in the lower orders as to what is their self-interest, or powerlessness in the face of overwhelming coercion. Poverty, unemployment, unfulfilled potential and all the social problems that follow are in nobody's self interest. Where self-interest means personal greed in disregard of others it can be condemned. Thus, how to sell self-interest to those it does not serve is a major problem. At one time, according to Macpherson (1973: 17–18), it was condemned:

> Moral and political philosophers had from the earliest times recognised in mankind a strain of unlimited desire, but most of them had deplored it as avarice and had believed that it could, and urged that it should, be fought down. What was new, from the seventeenth century onwards, was the prevalence of the assumption that unlimited desire was rational and morally acceptable.

Once it is accepted that unlimited desire is rational and moral, condemnations of great wealth can be labelled envy rather than moral outrage. At no time has self-interest been more forcefully advocated than under the Thatcher government, for whom the market philosophy was to save Britain from the welfare state, spawning, in its turn, the imagery of the city 'yuppies', greedy and selfish and typically male, aggressive and loud.

The market economy, as Macpherson points out, assumes an infinite demand for goods and services in the face of scarce resources. Infinite desire is a powerful motivating force to acquire property; however, not everyone can be in a position to amass possessions. Thus, there has also to be an acceptance of inequality; more specifically, a belief in the virtue of inequality achieved through merit. Those who have amassed fortunes from nothing become the heroes of capitalism. The reader of such heroic accounts is placed into positions of admiration, perhaps even thankfulness, that the hero had brought jobs to the community, goods and services to the grateful consumer, and power and influence to the nation.

Sometimes, these heroes turn out to perpetrate scandals that can no longer be kept hidden. Sometimes the amassed fortunes and the practices of production themselves become scandals in the face of immense want and deprivation both at home and abroad. How can food mountains be developed in the face of starvation? How can some live in forty-bedroomed mansions and others in a cardboard box on the River Thames embankment? Why are some paid fortunes in annual salaries when so many are unemployed or receive wages that do not allow them even minimal comforts?

In September 1989 the *Sunday Times* listed Britain's 50 top earners. It also listed the shareholdings of 200 directors: at the top was D. Sainsbury with £833 million, and at the bottom T. Siviter with £10 million. The two-page spread was a celebration of ten years of Thatcher's 'decade of prosperity', although the article did note that such 'pay packets':

> are the subject of angry political and economic debate. Union leaders ask why their membership should accept wage constraint when the bosses are rewarded on this scale. Ministers, even those most committed to the free market, wish the figures could somehow be made less dramatic (or at least, be less publicised). But the business community itself, represented by the Confederation of British Industry and the Institute of Directors, has no trouble demonstrating that, by international standards, British enterprise is seriously under-rewarded.

Little further challenge is made. The business*men* interviewed, of course, justify their salaries in terms of the work they do: efficiency at boardroom level is hard to measure; directors have different stakes in the shareholding of a company. Salary may either be a symbol if the stake is large, or the salary may be more functional (and therefore large) if the stake is small. However, there seem to be few rational reasons in the article for discrepancies when, for example, one director is paid a huge sum while another in a similar position in a similar company is paid considerably less. However, looking for discrepancies diverts attention from the real issues: what is work at any level really worth, and at what level does pay become excessive? What is the ethical relation between work and the social distribution of wealth? How should work itself be allocated? And so on.

A mere listing of salaries and of wealth owned does not make explicit the connections between big business, politics and the media.

Its function is little different from the *Sun*'s page three photos of nude girls. It is a display of something out of grasp. However, the connection between politics and business has been clear throughout the 1980s with the progressive sell-off of the nationalised industries and the privatisation of many local government services. Yet, many businesses failed, particularly in the older manufacturing industries in the early 1980s. How then can a government claiming to bring prosperity, indeed to have constructed an economic miracle, cover over the millions unemployed and the bankruptcies?

This feat was accomplished through constructing a discourse of blame focusing upon: trade unions, overmanning, scroungers, the permissive 60s, and the world economic climate. These were the persecutors, and the employers and honest workers the victims. The discourse created its heroes and villains. Like the witch hunts of the middle ages, the enemies within were hunted down, confronted and defeated. Even when the government was associated with scandals real or apparent, like the financial 'sweetners' in the Rover Group sell off, or the political controversy of the Westland affair, their complexity, the stone-walling of the government, and the distractions provided by other news stories contributed to the defusion of the scandals.

When scandals occur, they became rather more of a spectacle on the lines of a *Dallas* soap opera. For example, when the four men involved in the Guinness affair – 'Britain's most notorious share-fixing scandal' – were sentenced they made the front page in every newspaper, each dwelling upon the characters much like a Harold Robbins Rags-to-Riches-to-Rags plot. There was the wife of Ronson 'with tears streaking her face' whispering to her husband 'I love you more than life', and the 'prematurely aged' Saunders 'who once had a knighthood at his fingertips'. (*Daily Express*, 28 August 1990). The *Sun* tried for its usual punning headline, with 'Down and Stout' (a punning reference to the kind of beer brewed by Guinness) and on its inside pages focused on the riches, revealing that Ronson ('Britain's 14th richest man') had made a million pounds at only 23. Besides the front page and pages 2 and 3, the *Sun* also gave a four-page pull-out section to the scandal. The affair was reduced to a story of individual greed, leading to criminal actions. Nothing reflected back upon the values, conduct and power of the system within which these men operated. It was simply that they had abused the system. Thus, again, the affair reinforces the role of the press in its revelation of wrongdoing, but it also reinforces the system because, through vigilance, it can be cleaned up.

LAW AND ORDER AND THE SECRET STATE

As has been described, news accounts position readers. However, a reader does not have to accept that position, nor accept the kinds of behaviour required by a given economic position. Thus, essential to maintaining the structures of privilege and power are the structures of law and order and, behind them, the covert structures of the secret state. Theirs is a discourse of protecting liberty, freedom and choice, all of which the left, with its trade unions, its egalitarianism, its anti-sexism and anti-racism, are said to reduce. Behind the discourses is the threat of the power of the state.

The discourse of the right-wing politicians in the 1980s was of the fight against the evils of socialism which Thatcher vowed to destroy (reported by Kellner, the *Independent*, 24 November 1986). She expressed the intention of changing permanently the face of politics. Thatcher became for the right wing a kind of super-hero rescuer: the iron lady, this lady is not for turning, resolute, iron-willed, dominating. Her villains became the loony-left led by the prince of evil Arthur Scargill and his miners. It was the miners who brought down the Heath government. It was not going to happen to another Tory government.

In the early 1980s the forces of law and order were toughened up in response to the major street riots in 1980, 1981 and 1984; in response to the leaking of state information (e.g. the Zircon Affair and the book *Spy Catcher* by Peter Wright); and in response to perceived media imbalance (that is, that section other than the right-wing tabloid press) in reporting its news and in the broadcast of documentaries and plays. However, as Kellner (*Observer* magazine, 23 April 1989) reported, this is not to say that the state is to be considered totalitarian, rather, as Roy Jenkins put it in Parliament, a 'second-rate police state'.

Law and order received a number of knocks in Britain during the 1980s in the area of police malpractice which revealed something of the forbidden mechanics of suppression. In a two-page feature – 'Policing the police' – the *Independent*, 30 April 1990 explored the issues underlying a perceived drop in public confidence in the police. Two major cases, known as the Guildford Four and the Birmingham Six, contributed to this fall. Both involved police using violence in the fabrication of confessions. The *Independent* listed forty-one major inquiries into police forces around the country. What has been at stake is the social and political purpose and the public image of the police.

Media images of policing in Britain extend from the street corner bobby, the family friend of the television series *Dixon of Dock Green* popular in the 1950s and early 1960s, to *The Sweeny, The Bill* and a variety of American imports, from the *Naked City* to *Miami Vice*. All are united by images of essentially good coppers doing a hard and dirty job in the best way they can. The reader/viewer takes the position of those who are protected by heroes like these. However, there have been other sources of image-making: newspaper coverage of police activities, TV news reports and documentaries. The credibility of the essentially good copper becomes hard to maintain in the face of images of riot control police, armoured, on foot or on horseback, in battle formation lining up to charge crowds of protesters most of whom are undefended. When close-ups reveal baton-wielding police repeatedly bashing not simply everyone's idea of a hooligan but presentable men and women of all ages, stereotypes begin to crash. Being on the receiving end of the baton, many who have considered themselves quiet, respectable law-abiding people find a police force they had never believed existed. Through accounts like these the police are no longer being positioned as protectors, rather they are in danger of being perceived as persecutors. In Britain, to ordinary people the police have become increasingly associated with their crowd-control and riot-control functions as car patrols have replaced the ordinary bobby on the beat. There have been the allegations of brutality by the Metropolitan Police against protesters outside Rupert Murdoch's Wapping plant during his battles with the print unions. The Guildford Four had been imprisoned for fourteen years for IRA pub bombings. They have now been set free because the evidence upon which they had been convicted was found to be untrustworthy. Next there were doubts concerning the actions of police with regard to the Birmingham Six, also imprisoned for IRA bombings. These were major cases involving considerable media coverage. However, the coverage is sectionalised according to market, and narrativised to appeal to political interests.

Thus, at the same time as these concerns about policing, there were the counter-stories of the rising tides of violence. The *Sun* on 18 July 1990 featured on its front page and on pages 14 and 23 'One Violent Day in the Life of Our Cops', labelling this a 'vital Sun Probe'. The black and white photograph on the front page is of the bloodied face of a helmeted policeman with the opening paragraphs:

> Britain's police are being swamped by a terrifying wave of violence, a Sun investigation reveals today.
>
> The boys – and girls – in blue are facing attacks on a worse scale than ever imagined.

Using its self-proclaimed image of the plain-speaking, investigative, truth-revealing paper, the 'probe' then sets out to catalogue the violence around the nation. The imagery harks back to the 'boys in blue', of Dock Green perhaps, now updated to include the girls. It is as if they are the oppressed, the victims, fighting upon our behalf. Nothing can contrast so strongly to the alternative images of police beating up suspects in order to coerce confessions. The structure underpinning the counter-images is glossed over; attention is, in effect, continually diverted from it. The role of violence in the structure will be developed in the next chapter. At this point it is the process of diverting attention from this violence through attaching blame, or the process of stifling real investigation through suppression, that is to be the focus.

Whether the 1981 street riots, or the 18 June 1984 notorious Battle of Orgreave, or the 1985 Broadwater Farm Estate riot, or the 1 April 1990 Battle of Trafalgar (the poll tax riots), or one of many others during the decade, powerful media images were provided that were undoubtedly political. All were slotted by the media into the narrative of a brave and resolute government fighting the extreme left-wing militants, or mindless hooligans seeking to destroy the country. Further enquiry into the circumstances that led to rioting often provided a different story. One of the most notorious was at Orgreave. The scene was of a mighty battle between the government and the trade unions, in this instance the miners' union led by Arthur Scargill. It was a political battle between the heroes of capitalism and the villains, the communistic trade unions who wanted to bring the country down. The defeat of the miners' union has always taken pride of place in Thatcher victories. In a Sunday *Observer* magazine feature on 'Thatcher's Monuments' (23 April 1989) a special section was devoted to the theme of liberty:

> During the last 10 years we have discovered that, in extremis, we can be prevented from doing almost anything. In 1984 members of the National Union of Mineworkers found that they did not even have the right to drive peacefully along the Queen's highways. It turned out to be a discretionary privilege.

> The police set up roadblocks to stop striking miners from one coalfield joining demonstrators at another. Nobody argued that the miners whose cars were stopped had done anything illegal. The police's contention was that they might get up to no good if they were allowed to complete their journey.

There was a real war against unions summed up by Thatcher's statement in July 1984: 'We had to fight the enemy without in the Falklands. We always have to be aware of the enemy within, which is more difficult to fight and more dangerous to liberty.' The image of a battle against the 'enemy within' was nowhere more appropriate than at Orgreave.

Gareth Peirce, solicitor for eleven defendants brought to trial for alleged offences at Orgreave, revealed the implications of the event for the right of peaceful assembly in the *Guardian*, 12 August 1985. The article described the military tactics and armoury of the police and commented: 'Orgreave on June 18, 1984, revealed that in this country we now have a standing army available to be deployed against gatherings of civilians whose congregation is disliked by senior police officers.' According to the statements of Chief Constable Clements at the trial, the people at Orgreave had 'no right to be there', and thus would 'not be the slightest troubled if they were trampled on by police horses'. The question remained whether there was a riot or not. The police were in no doubt.

> When television news that night showed one man being repeatedly truncheoned by a police officer, it treated it as an isolated instance. And when the evidence was quoted from one police disciplinary witness at the trial, suggesting it wasn't just one officer who had 'gone off at half cock; all the senior officers were getting stuck in too'; the senior officer giving evidence on oath at the time interpreted 'getting stuck in', as 'doing his duty'.

That day the police had made a film which should be taken 'in juxtaposition with the account given by the police'. It starts with men arriving on 'a beautiful summer's day'. All is peaceful and good humoured. But behind police lines are seen 'battalions of police in riot uniforms'. Then, suddenly, horses galloped through in a repeated series of charges. A man is seen to be trampled 'and brought back through the lines and charged with riot'.

> You hear on the soundtrack 'bodies not heads' shouted by one senior officer, and then see junior officers rush out and hit heads as well as bodies. You see this over a period of three hours and you see men begin to react and throw occasional missiles. After 12 noon, they begin to construct defensive barricades against further police onslaught.
>
> One senior officer, who said that it was the first time he had seen horsemen riding at people with batons drawn, was asked at the trial whether people might throw missiles out of terror to repel attacks by mounted officers, he said, 'no, that never occurred to me'. Another conceded that the purpose of the horses and the short-shield officers was to terrify; if miners did not disperse when they were run at by the police, then they were eligible for arrest. This was the view expressed by the last junior officer to give evidence before the riot trial was finally jettisoned by the prosecution.

At the time of the battle,

> The deployment of those short-shield units shocked almost no one; television news that night reversed the order of the footage available to show men throwing missiles and then police charging, the theme that the police attempted to pursue during the trial in contradiction of their own visual evidence.

Finally:

> Orgreave was never to do with the niceties of police powers, it was to do with power, absolute power, exercised at will. Arbitrary arrests and brutality are the hallmarks of any dictatorship – they were evident at Orgreave on June 18 and ignored. By our silence, we have endorsed the existence of a militia.

CONSPIRACY OR COCK-UP?

Is it all a conspiracy? One can imagine a relatively small group of individuals in positions of power in the media, politics, big business, the police and the secret services all coordinating the affairs of the nation. Or is it all down to chance alliances, bunglers and the ad hoc cock-up? Crude conspiracy theory is often raised in order to be quickly debunked. It is easy to scoff at the notion that all the ills, all the inequalities, all the corruption, all the cover-ups are somehow due to a hidden group of conspirators. Yet, it would also be naive to suppose that strategies are not formed, and alliances sought out in the protection of mutual interests. German (1990: 34) commented that following the defeat of the miners there was a:

> series of major defeats for other traditionally well organised sections of the working class: the print workers in 1986, the seafarers in 1988, the dockers in 1989. In all these disputes central groups of workers were taken on, locked out, isolated and defeated by the employers in calculated moves to weaken the working class movement. The motivation behind these attacks came from the highest levels: Rupert Murdoch, Sir Jeffrey Sterling, head of P&O ferries, the port employers and Tory Norman Tebbit and Michael Heseltine. All saw the miners' defeat as the green light for going for other groups and therefore weakening the entire working class movement.

These were the rewards of the work throughout the 1980s when the Thatcher government systematically changed the material structures affecting the economy – the laws regulating trade unions, unemployment and family benefits, housing, privatising major state industries, health service and education – justifying their work in a tight conceptual rhetoric which was given mass currency by the popular media. Access to fundamentally different views from the mainstream press is thoroughly limited. Attitudes towards the views of alternative sources are themselves moulded by the mainstream media and political controls.

It was not only the freedom of the press that came under pressure. Academic freedom has long been considered a right within the universities. However, academic research has also been subject to state pressure, if not outright intervention. At the British Educational Research Association's conference in 1988 it was reported (*Independent*, 3 March 1988) that a new clause had been entered into Department of Health and Social Security research contracts whereby researchers can be stopped from publishing and 'all intellectual property – data and ideas – is now deemed to be state property'. The Department of Education also has strict copyright controls. Furthermore:

> Roger Murphy, director of the exams and assessment unit at Southampton University, says that researchers, including himself, now have to submit their methodology for departmental approval. 'If you want to use questionnaires, you now have to get your questions approved by the Secretary of State.'

Such instances begin to support if not the view of a conspiracy then something that feels very much like one.

C. Wright Mills (1956) in his study of ruling elites described the 'big three' domains of the economy, the military and the political which have enlarged and centralised over the years so that 'The decisions of a handful of corporations bear upon military and political as well as upon economic developments around the world' (p. 7). He further pointed to the fact that the members of these elites tend to go to the same group of schools, churches etc. They are 'involved in a set of overlapping "crowds" and intricately connected "cliques" (p. 11). Thus they are socialised into similar values, attitudes and conduct. Although not comprising a 'secret society' of conspirators, it is not surprising that many know each other.

Since the time in which C. Wright Mills was writing a number of material changes have occurred that have the potential of amplifying the power of ruling elites. The most powerful of these has been in the information technology industry which many consider to be of comparable social impact to the industrial revolution in the late eighteenth and early nineteenth centuries (cf. Perry and Greber 1990; Schiller 1986). Its power as a surveillance system for data gathering, processing and control is beyond doubt.

In the *Observer* (2 April 1989) John Sweeney reported that a freelance spy, David Coghlan, was using state-of-the-art technology to eavesdrop on 'the privacy of a whole range of British citizens – from nuclear power protesters at Sizewell to the Militant group on Liverpool's Labour party – in the early and mid-Eighties'. The following week Coghlan's evidence was broadcast on Yorkshire Television's *First Tuesday*. At the time of these reports, the new Secret Service Bill was being discussed in Parliament. The *Observer* report concluded that since the new bill did not allow whistle-blowers such as Peter Wright (*Spy Catcher*) to be able to claim their revelations to be in the public interest, such stories would no longer come to light. The position would be tighter still with the proposed Official Secrets Bill.

In the *Independent* (1 May 1989) it was reported that 'A national network of private investigators used police contacts to gain access to confidential police computer files.' It went on to report that 'The complicated network came to light when the BBC investigated (...) during the making of its *Secret Society* series, which itself fell foul of the Official Secrets Act with a programme about the Zircon spy satellite.'

The control of information, its gathering, its use, its media presentation have all become major battle grounds for the management of opinion, knowledge and, in particular, the regulation of ignorance across sections of the population carefully categorised in terms of markets and target audiences. Within this framework of power it is difficult to deny the existence of power elites. There may not be a single overall 'conspiracy', although the conformity of interests within a broad social class of people with money, power and access to the major economic and technological infrastructures is likely to lead them to act in similar ways, to form alliances and act in their own interests. It is thus better to think in terms of competing and overlapping 'conspiracies' which together work at different levels to produce their effects.

Owners of major newspapers often declare their allegiances overtly, because they know that the section they influence is not the section to whom they reveal their intentions and ulterior motives:

> My purpose originally was to set up a propaganda paper, and I have never departed from that purpose through all the years. But in order to make the propaganda effective the paper had to be successful. No paper is any good at all for propaganda unless it has a thoroughly good financial position. So we worked very hard to build up a commercial position.
>
> (Murdoch and Golding 1978: 142)

Thus quite unambiguously Lord Beaverbrook set out his intentions as the then owner of the *Daily Express* in 1948. It has remained a Tory newspaper ever since, with considerable influence amongst working-class voters. Except for the *Daily Mirror* there was during the 1980s no other popular Labour tabloid. For a short period the *News on Sunday* was launched as a radical left tabloid. It never achieved the financial success it needed. This has not been the case with either the *Sun* or the *Star*, both immensely successful, with the *Sun* in particular being credited with delivering to Thatcher the working-class vote. This success becomes more sinister with the revelation that Murdoch, considered the world's most powerful media proprietor, had been 'secretly funding an extreme right-wing pressure group run by a close aide to the former Prime Minister Margaret Thatcher' (*Observer*, 9 December 1990). The adviser, David Hart, was:

> the founder and organiser of the committee for a Free Britain. Mr Hart played a key role in the Conservative party's General Election campaigns of 1983 and 1987, and during the 1984 miners' strike. He enjoys a close relationship with members of John Major's new Cabinet, including Chancellor Norman Lamont and Transport Secretary Malcolm Rifkind.

The committee was used to pay for anti-Labour advertisements and produces British Briefing 'a monthly journal with a secret distribution list smearing Labour MPs, writers and others with alleged "Communist" sympathies'. It was also revealed that Hart was a friend of the William Casey, the late CIA director, and the co-publisher of the 'extreme rightwing' *World Briefing* with 'Herb Meyer, a top CIA official under Casey'. These overlapping, perhaps relatively casual connections, act to coordinate the efforts of a wide range of people in positions of great influence. Link this also with the structures of intelligence cooperation revealed by such authors as Richelson and Ball (1985, revised 1990) and a worrying infrastructure compellingly emerges for the shaping of political consciousness, canalising energies or limiting the damage when the powerful get caught out.

However, it would be wrong to say that because of the existence of such an infrastructure news media *always* manage news coverage to support the *status quo*. The Stalker affair is an illustration of the point. Stalker was the Deputy Chief Constable of Manchester who in 1984 was appointed to investigate the shootings of six Roman Catholics in Northern Ireland by the Royal Ulster Constabulary (RUC) in November and December of 1982. However, in May 1986, after allegations of misconduct were made against Stalker, he was removed from duties and then suspended. By 1988 Stalker was widely seen as someone who was innocent, the victim of the security forces. According to Murphey (1991: 2), 'A version of reality had been promulgated through the established media which conflicts utterly with the conventional academic picture of a right-wing-dominated press producing an ideological justification of the status quo and the forces of control.'

> The only way that it could be reported ... was by the press attempting to decide what sense could be made of it. The meanings that it had could not be taken as read from the authority structure. This was because in its nature the story involved a contest about the truth about the meaning of events. As it happened no official version was ever forthcoming so that the option simply to accept the government version of events was never there. More to the point, Stalker and his solicitors were able to mount a campaign to convince journalists of his version of events. (p. 265)

If this is so, then the absence of a coherent view from the authority structure allowed the opportunity for alternative readings – in this case, the version promoted by Stalker and his solicitors. In this sense, the press did its job, revealing and supporting the revelation of wrong-doing. This in itself reveals the depth of the issue as Murphey finally concludes: even if the press is active, people who are not dangerous have been killed and the agents who have done this are unpunished. Who is left to listen when there are cries of wolf? Who would ever know the mark of truth?

7

THE FORBIDDEN POLITICS AND THE EDUCATION OF CHALLENGE

Politics has to do with the creation, the maintenance and the allocation of access to distinct realms of action. Identifying new freedoms for action involves de-constructing the old politics, which seeks to foster a narcissistic realm of action and of discourse keeping individuals 'in their place', and within the boundaries of the familiar. Since propaganda is the basis for the concealment and the defusion of the forbidden politics, propaganda is the educational challenge.

In its utopian sense, politics can be an exercise of power between equals but in actuality it is a contest between those who are unequal. At the heart of the utopian form of democratic politics is argumentation and the development of structures for the articulation of challenge. Argumentation depends upon openness and the rights to challenge and to speak, and in the process formulates the rites of passage suitable for maintaining the utopian democracy. At the heart of modern politics within the context of social inequality, is power, the power to write the agenda of political discourse and hence reduce the possibility for argumentation.

It is in the political realm that the distinction between schooling and education becomes vital. Schooling, as I use it, designates a political instrument with the object of processing and socialising children. In schooling it is part of the forbidden discourse to 'draw out' (or educate) the self as self. It is through education that the forms of reflection, expression and action articulate the self as a source of challenge to the old heroes of the social order whose actions do not liberate. In challenge there are the new heroes of the challenge, the new discourses through which the self is re-written and the course of life re-directed. And there are the narratives of challenge to be recounted.

The challenges arise quite naturally, through the possibilities for aberrant readings inherent in any text. These possibilities were already realised in the early history of the cinema. Forman (1933) was able to cite research that found that 'high-school boys and girls often not only expressed sympathy for the criminal, but that a few drew the conclusion that mere hard, plodding work is not desirable' (p. 181). He gave two examples of written comments by a sixteen-year-old girl and a boy of the same age. First the girl:

> 'Movies have made me less critical of criminals when I consider that all are not as fortunate as we. Starvation has been the cause of more crime than anything else as I see it in the movies. As a result, I believe crime should be corrected instead of being punished for the latter encourages more crime.'

> 'A lot of crime movies I have seen', declares a sixteen-year-old boy, 'made me feel more favourable towards crime by depicting the criminal as a hero who dies protecting his best friend against the police, or some movies show them as a debonair gentleman who robs at will from the rich and spares the poor. I have thought I would like to be a Robin Hood.' (p. 182)

Forman does not see the competing moralities which have led to these challenges to the official moral discourses. Like many conservatives today he sees primarily that there is a sympathy for crime so that 'the sharp barriers between right and wrong, built up by other institutions and training, as in the home, the church and the school, are progressively eroded and undermined, and some young people are made more tolerant toward crime and the criminal' (p. 183).

With a more sophisticated level of analysis Fiske (1987) describes the multiple interpretations of the popular crime detective TV series *Hart to Hart*, shown internationally throughout the 1980s. Katz and Liebs (1984) described how *Dallas* could be interpreted differently, even misread, according to different cultures and subcultures. There is always the potential of multiple discourses to subvert and reconstruct stories from a viewer's rather than a writer's or author's perspective. The difference between Forman and the kinds of analyses carried out by Fiske is that Forman worked within one particular kind of discourse, a discourse which took for granted a particular set of moral and social values. Fiske sees many possibilities; one discourse producing a 'reading' is as 'right' as any other. It is an empirical matter, not a matter of right and wrong. In addition, 'discourses are not produced by the individual speaker or author, they are socially produced; the meanings that they bear pre-exist their use in any one discursive practice', so that 'discourse not only makes sense of its topic area, it also constructs a sense, or a social identity, of *us* as we speak it.' There is an intimate link between discourse and the development of a self: it is born in the echoes of others, the culture of expressions, the repertoire of discourses available at any time and place. The individual takes a position, not quite passively, not quite actively, within these pre-existing structures, a position which changes within given territories and given phases of the course of life. At every stage, the structures jostle for dominance, the moral domains stack up, first one then another seems right, seems able to explain and justify, the interpretations multiply. Which is finally right?

CHALLENGE AND THE RE-ORDERING OF THE MIRRORS

The other is just as much a potential source of doubt as of confirmation. R. D. Laing, who analysed the social production of schizophrenia in terms of its genesis in the family, provided numerous examples of the distorting potential of communication. He writes of the mirroring technique in the form of a kind of fairy story:

> This is a conversation between a mother and her fourteen-year-old daughter
>
> *M*: (to fourteen-year-old daughter): 'You are evil.'
> *D*: 'No I'm not.'
> *M*: 'Yes, you are.'
> *D*: 'Uncle Jack doesn't think so.'
> *M*: 'He doesn't love you as I do. Only a mother really knows the truth about her daughter, and only one who loves you as I do will ever tell you the truth about yourself no matter what it is. If you don't believe me, just look at yourself in the mirror carefully and you will see that I'm telling the truth.'
>
> The daughter did, and saw that her mother was right after all, and realised how wrong she had been not to be grateful for having a mother who so loved her that she would tell her the truth about herself. Whatever it might be. (Laing 1976 edition: 109–10)

These processes and the images that are employed are not arbitrary. It is in essence a political process aimed at the production of a certain kind of social reality in which the self is positioned in relation to the imaginary objects that are mirrored. The purpose is to subject the experience of the child to the proof provided by the mirror that cannot lie. The processes and structures through which the self is devalued as a source of valid experience are pervasive. It begins with the continual manipulation of images of powerful objects in the life of a child, the central being 'mummy':

> *Teacher:* Right now, I'll tell you what we have to do when we do a painting. We have to put an apron on. (...) Mummy would say 'Paint on your jumper and on your very first day at school. What was your teacher thinking about?' (Schostak 1986: 69)

Here the child is located in an imaginary scene which exists independently of whether or not the child's actual mother would react in this way. The actors in this imaginary drama are well known and are meant to act coercively upon the child and, indirectly, upon the mother. It presents an example of the kind of discourse generated by the imaginary family. By implication it also presents the forbidden acts. The family as myth acts to present a symbolic net of ready-made relationships by which to control the individual who is to take up prescribed places in this net. There are 'slots' for Father, Mother, Son, Daughter, Sister, Brother – and so on. It does not matter who in particular fills those slots. But there are more than simply places to be filled. There are 'stories' which govern the interactions between the family place-fillers in relation to each other and to others outside of the family. School sets into relationship the imaginary family and the real family. In this case, school – as family substitute – can be seen as an agent of the society-wide culture industry, processing and transforming individuals, where the myth of the family is an essential instrument by which children are connected not so much to their 'real parents' and family experiences but to their mythical counterparts. It is here at the interface between an individual's experience and the industrialised processing of that experience to fit external needs that experience itself is experienced as contorted. A warp or twisting takes place.

The brief extract from a scene in school illustrates a very complex mirroring procedure. It is not the simple case of the mother confirming the image of the baby in the mirror. It is a teacher acting as a social mirror, set in place by the agency of the wider society. But in her mirroring she sets up another mirror, the child's mother, as one who reflects the teacher: 'What was your teacher thinking about?' There is here a hall of mirrors each trapping imaged objects and repeating them to infinity, each reflection with a new distortion, a new distance from whatever reality exists outside the mirrors. It is this security of repetition which provides the sense of redundancy, the sense of 'I know what will happen next', 'I know what you think of me.'

These are political mirrors which re-present the imaged objects that constitute the myths, the 'realities' of everyday life. However, the child does not grow up into an homogeneous mirroring. The mirroring is constructed through competing discourses, indeed through counter-mirrorings. It is for this reason that the discourse which constructs the mirroring is power (Foucault 1981: 52–3). It is a political act to attempt to control the reality of another, to insert into their lives the discourse through which they are to construct their own mirrors of their selves. It is the schooling process which categorises children, constructs identities for them and attempts to keep them in their slots, denying all attempts at a counter-discourse. The power of the school to de-construct the counter-discourse, to fragment and diffuse its power, is only too clearly seen in the following example:

> 'I'll come with me mum.'
>
> 'Well, I'm sure the headmaster would be delighted to see your mum. When is your dad going to call? Is he home?'
>
> 'He's in the house.'
>
> 'I think it's one of the reasons why you're upset isn't it? That you know you made such an awful fool of yourself.'
>
> 'I've not.'
>
> 'Oh yes you have.'
>
> 'I'm right, everyone is …'
>
> 'But Nicky, you're not right. This is the thing. You're not right. You're *quite* wrong. And you're going to have to learn that you're quite wrong. One way or another, son, you're going to have to learn. I'm confident … I know you pretty well by now Nick Wragg don't I?'
>
> 'Sir, yeah.'
>
> 'Yeah. And I'm confident that I know that one reason why you are so upset at this moment is because you realise you made such an *awful* fool of yourself, haven't you?'
>
> 'Sir no.'

'Yes you have Nick.'

'I'm in the right.'

'Well that's just you dreaming and I'm not going to argue with you at all ... sit there until you've calmed down.'

(Schostak 1983: 14)

It is a contest over what counts as real. The extract is from a study carried out in a large comprehensive school. It concerns a young boy who considers that he has been wronged by a teacher. The incident is relatively trivial. However, it is with the trivial that often the greatest battles seem to take place. The teacher had given his tray of dirty dishes to the boy and told him to take them to the dinner hatch for him. The boy had refused, saying it was his free time and that he did not owe the teacher a duty. The teacher insisted, feeling his teacherly authority threatened. By continuing to refuse, the boy was in trouble. He was well known as a trouble maker and was treated as such. The deputy head, who tried to sort out the problem after the headteacher had only made it worse, felt obliged to side with the teacher, knowing that the whole situation had been handled wrongly from the beginning. All were trapped into their imagined roles. Within this short extract is a whole history of social control, the development of the institutional roles and identities of teachers and pupils, adults and pupils, families and their relations to the institution of schooling. To imagine that this is trivial is to underestimate the political structures that have been brought into play. Schools and teachers do exist who would have handled the whole situation differently. But there has not been a teacher to whom I have told this story who has not winced and recognised the structures and recalled comparable situations they have at some time experienced and witnessed. By introducing the *look* of the analyst, the researcher, the overseer, the complex mirroring that keeps all these roles and identities in play is disturbed, deranged. But knowledge does not in itself bring any easy solution. Knowledge does not simply dismantle the structures. Rather, such a *look* merely shows what is ranged against it. The forbidding process of dismantling such complexly rooted ingrained structures, thickly enmeshed in the structures of the social order, is beyond individual action. Within this account is the essence of the process which in millions of small ways discounts the experience of the child and attempts to re-fashion it within the logic of its own field of the imaginary.

The politics of the mirroring is such that powerful mechanisms of denial, censorship, repression and exclusion (within imprisoning structures) are brought to bear upon deviant representations and actions. This can be seen in the responses to alternative forms of schooling. Neill's Summerhill has been referred to as a reprehensible school where the children are permissively allowed to do anything they want. In fact, it is a school which aspires to generate a child's democracy, where happiness is considered more important than book learning. It is a place where those who are schooled within the state system do not know how to handle the freedom Summerhill presents to them. There is, a Summerhillian told me, the phenomenon of breaking out which can apply just as much to teachers as it does to children: 'they go crazy' until they learn that freedom also requires self responsibility (cf. Neill 1973: 122). State schooling, it would seem, teaches un-freedom, rather than free responsibility. When state schools have in the past attempted to incorporate new freedoms they have sometimes, quite dramatically, incurred the wrath of the *status quo*.

During the latter half of the 1970s education increasingly came under media attack for its so-called progressivism. The arts of representation were brought to bear upon the creation of images of education which became central to a whole range of political attacks carried out by the Thatcher government in the 1980s. In a publication called *Lunatic Ideas* the media representation of educational events and issues were studied during the summer of 1977. Newspapers were analysed in terms of the kinds of stories that they tell where 'Just as the cast of characters is known and recognised, so the plots of the dramas are recurring and well known. They have their expected outcome. Good triumphs: the boys in blue triumph over the left-wing bully boys, the wives of ordinary men triumph over the militant strikers, little Billy, who has a hole in his heart, is saved by miracle surgery and even Elvis ends up "In peace at last" (*Mirror*, 2 September 1977)' (p. 7 Patricia Holland). The very sameness of the structure locks living individuals into place, makes them accountable within the frameworks of storying chosen by the newspaper:

> In order to become characters in the drama, the people who feature in the news are subjected to a series of transformations before they are presented to the public. Meanwhile the 'public' are thought of as a totally different set of people. In certain cases the subjects co-operate with the transformation – for example,

> politicians, the police and to a certain extent, show biz personalities. Thus politicians can hide their 'real' personality behind the screen of their press image; show biz personalities can employ public relations men to create images for them; the police can make sure that they are always the heroes and never the villains of the stories in which they star.

The newspaper constructs a 'mirror' of reality which is framed by the whole economic system which constructs people as consumers whether consumers of education, of health, of welfare or of the shop displayed products and services of the market economy. The newspaper as authority figure, with the best interests of all parents in mind, readjusts the political mirrors back to the *status quo* in order to meet the challenges of those who, like Nicky Wragg, cried out for a sense of justice.

IN MIRRORS THAT CONCEAL THE SECRET: FASCISM, RACISM AND STRUCTURAL DISCRIMINATION

Schooling promotes a disregard of education amongst millions, particularly in Britain where little more than 20 per cent take the higher qualifications. If, then, their access to information, to knowledge and to skills is restricted to employers' needs and their choices, and through market strategies conditioned further through the media, then it can be reasonably asserted that discrimination is built into the system. Set within this discriminating framework the mirrors that present images of being free to choose, free to take educational opportunities, are deceptive. To reveal the deceit is to engage openly in the forbidden politics. It is to construct a counter curriculum, a forbidden curriculum through which an alternative text representing people's lives and experiences can be expressed.

Democracy is not free, if it continually reconstructs within itself the forms of domination and the continual search for the leader who would save the world. This is simply the old politics reborn, or rather, its corpse resurrected with vampire lusts. Western democracy cannot just shrug off the memory of Nazi Germany, locating it within a specific historical culture and people. That would be to forget the fascism that survives within current societies, not just in the gangs of skinheads, but in the institutional racism, the everyday jokes and expressions, the rituals and codes of practice which define in-groups and out-groups, drawing power, wealth and privilege into the hands of a very few. This is why the images, the emblems, the signs and sounds of fascism still fascinate.

The nature of the obstacles controlling the development of a counter-curriculum that challenges the fascination can be seen in historical studies, current legislation, policing, or the attitudes and values displayed in news accounts of incidents. It is a shoddy history, made explicit by such studies as Fryer's (1984) account of black history in Britain extending back to Elizabethan times. When needed, black people have been recruited to fight wars, or to be cheap labour to industries and services; when no longer needed they have been treated as immigrants who need to be controlled and who 'should be sent back to where they come from'. Discrimination has revealed itself openly in the form of colour bars. It was reinforced implicitly by Acts like the 1962 Commonwealth Immigrants Act which blew 'the guts out of the "Mother Country" hallucination' held by many of the West Indian immigrants (Kapo 1981: 11). While employing a discourse of preventing illegal immigration, the Thatcher government in 1981 published its British Nationality Bill which immediately drew criticisms of racial discrimination. More complex to uncover are the everyday social attitudes and actions that result in lower achievements in education, lower prospects in employment and higher rates of unemployment. When these are allied to surveillance and control, explosive social situations are inevitable. As Phillips (1981) suggested, police treatment effectively criminalised black youth. Black youths were more likely to be stopped and searched than whites. Indeed, the police effectively created the black crime of mugging that was picked up in the press (Gutzmore 1984).

Whether consisting of anecdotes or media recordings and representations of experiences, a kind of curriculum is built up that shapes attitudes and action. In January 1981 an unexplained fire swept through a house where a party was taking place in New Cross in London. Thirteen black people died. There were demonstrations because people felt the police were acting too slowly. In a BBC 2 documentary a local person recalled that neither Thatcher nor the Queen offered their condolences (*Black Britain*, 8 January 1991). The people felt angry and marched with their placards: '13 dead nothing said'.

In 1983 Colin Roach was driven by a friend to Stoke Newington police station. Shortly afterwards Roach was killed by a sawn-off shotgun said to have been placed in his mouth. The police issued a statement that a young black man with a history of mental illness had committed suicide. The death occurred about 11.30 in the evening. At about midnight the father was taken to the police station and questioned for three to four hours before being told that his son was dead. He was distraught. Friends mounted a demonstration. The inquest decided it was suicide. The question remains: how could it have taken place in a police station?

On 30 September 1985, the *Star* reported a dawn police raid on the home of Mrs Cherry Groce looking for her son:

> Inspector Douglas Lovelock, 42, led Saturday's dawn raid of seven men. Mrs Groce was downstairs with her common-law husband, Leon Lawrence, 35, and her three youngest children, Lisa, eight, Lee, 11, and Sharon, 13.
>
> As police tried to keep them in one room Mrs Groce is believed to have tried to go upstairs where a noise was heard.
>
> She was warned to stay still but kept moving, say police.
>
> Inspector Lovelock fired two shots, one of which hit her in the shoulder and lodged in her spine.

The shooting was considered accidental. A riot followed the incident. Several newspapers at the time ran variations on the theme of police training methods and on having to make up one's mind quickly in situations of danger. The *Star* told the story:

> Inspector Douglas Lovelock would have been gripping his Model 10 Smith and Wesson .38 calibre revolver with both hands as he kicked down Cherry Groce's front door.
>
> But before he even plucked the weapon free from his leather press-stud holster he knew he had only three-eighths of a second to judge whether he could shoot.
>
> Only last Wednesday I faced the same nerve-racking decision. Suddenly in front of me stood a black woman dressed in jeans holding a shotgun.
>
> *I hesitated. And, academically, I was dead.*

The reporter went on to describe his experience of being in the shooting gallery of the Metropolitan Police Force. The imagery is clear. It is *Miami Vice,* Clint Eastwood, or a dozen others. It is the imagery of industrialised culture. In this imagery there is no choice.

Without choice, the actions become inevitable. It is a curriculum that not only prescribes and justifies action but that is a lesson in reading events for the generally white readership. Its power is in its implicit messages of when it is all right, even necessary, to shoot people, in these instances black people. It is all carried within an heroic white identity symbolising the protecting forces of law and order against, in these cases, black danger.

The parallel is with the way fascist imagery pervades a society providing powerful simplified images of identity and of the pure and impure. Fascism in Nazi Germany represented the ultimate in control of the masses, in self-loss in the leader and the imagery of racial purity. In a study of these images in the paintings of Anselm Kiefer, Hyssen (1989) describes the power of the fascist myth:

> Fascism had ... perverted, abused, and sucked up whole territories of a German image-world, turning national iconic and literary traditions into mere ornaments of power and thereby leaving post-1945 culture with a tabula rasa that was bound to cause a smoldering crisis of identity. After twelve years of an image orgy without precedent in the modern world, which included everything from torch marches to political mass spectacles, from the mammoth staging of the 1936 Olympics to the ceaseless productions of the Nazi film industry deep into the war years, from Albert Speer's floodlight operas in the night sky to the fireworks of anti-aircraft flak over the burning cities, the country's need for images seemed exhausted. (p. 34)

The creation of the Great Spectacle, the production of imagery which fascinates, this is the underlying achievement, the precursor of modern mass persuasion techniques and industrialised culture that are the foundation not only of propaganda but also advertising to the mass consumer upon whom the whole economic circuitry depends. We have been created in the image of the Great Spectacle of consumerism: it has sucked up the oral traditions, the great cultural works. Male and female, we are constructed into narcissistic relationships through the multiplicity of forms in which we are made to see ourselves. The counter-cultural expressions which attempt to see through the dominant mirrorings are the focus of tactics to suppress, deny, minimalise, ridicule. Only demonstrations remain to outraged citizens.

Media spectacles provide ways of coping with the past and the present without critical awareness. However, there are more mundane, more invidious forms of spectacle. The forms of discrimination are more subtly intertwined with the great political values of 'service', 'welfare', 'public interest'. Schooling provides an initial spectacle for each child of the power of the state, the power to provide and coordinate the workings of experts in control of major aspects of the lives of masses. Simply walking down the high street provides the mass spectacle of monopoly capitalism in every shop window. The display of conspicuous consumption is all-pervasive. During the last two years of the 1980s, the fall of the Eastern totalitarian states seemed to confirm the whole spectacle of the West's social, economic and political order. Against the desolation of the East, its rationing, its inefficiency, its obsolescent factories, the West seemed a domain of plenty – of food mountains, of product duplication, of built-in obsolescence. Were it not for the fact that there have been record levels of unemployment, of homelessness, of poverty in the world markets, it would seem that the problem of scarce resources had been overcome and economics had created, or is about to create, the golden age. In Britain the welfare state was created on the philosophical and moral premise that no one should worry about paying for their health, nor should they worry about unemployment. But this in the 1980s was called the nanny state and scarcity had to be, if not re-invented, then returned to its proper place at the centre of market economics. The natural level of unemployment was rediscovered as an antidote to the principle of full employment. If there is a 'natural' level of unemployment – as assumed in the monetarist economics underlying the Thatcher 'revolution' – in the market place, then no government need worry about the ethics of naturally occurring high levels of joblessness. If inequality is natural, since all have different talents and ability levels, then differences in income, wealth and privilege can be justified. Potential plenty, it could be argued, would undermine the natural order of inequalities. If that is so, then scarcity needs to be reinvented by the market place in order to regulate the distribution of power. It is not real work, real creativity, real inventiveness that regulates the construction of wealth to meet needs, but the institution of money as the sign of wealth that regulates the work that people can undertake. To untie these knots is to articulate the words that cannot be said.

Where, in everyday discourse is the critical edge? Images, icons, literary traditions are turned now to the adornment of products for sale. It has been called characteristic of the post-modern condition. There are no absolute criteria dictating choice. Rationality as expressed through science has not fulfilled its promises. Hewison (1990) uses the term post-modernism as negative, as describing a void at the point where modernism has collapsed. The post-modern refers to an age that is in some sense over. The dream of communism underpinning the Eastern Block can be seen as an expression of modernism. Now collapsed, the suppressed undercurrents, ethnic tensions, disputes, the need to assert old identities, have re-surfaced. At one level, as Jencks (1987) argues with respect to architecture, the post-modern expresses pluralism and returns to a human scale through an eclectic mixture of styles in the production of 'taste communities'. Is Fascism just another taste community? because 'no orthodoxy can be adopted without self-consciousness and irony, because all traditions seem to have some validity' (p. 7).

The spectacle of the West in its self-imagined heroic and mighty response to Iraq's invasion of Kuwait in 1990–1 is riddled with ironies as it fails to unseat Saddam Hussein and prevent the slaughter of Khurds and Shi'ites. How can the 'master narrative' (Lyotard 1984) of the West's supremacy be read without irony as news broadcasts daily showed the 'ethnic cleansing', the concentration camps in Bosnia, and daily show the West's inability or unwillingness to prevent it? And elsewhere, in Somalia, a million people were dying of starvation. News media create an apparent all-seeing access to global events which only serves to underscore the powerlessness to act, the failure of modernism to solve the world's problems. In the retreat to self-interest, market values, market solutions, there is no profit in solving such problems, only charity, begging, the arousal of pity through the display of powerful images of torn bodies, starving children.

How do we handle the images of ourselves as they stare back at us? We are all implicated, although historical figures and Nations may serve as convenient focii to help us distance the implications from our own consciences. In the end the production of a political and economic *cordon sanitaire* (Hyssen 1989) represses the images to the darkness of nightmares, places them out of ourselves, locates them in 'some other place' which has a different history, a different system, and 'there is nothing we can do about it'. Who can deny the power of this repression? Its power is revealed in the general commodification of women and the positioning of men in the role of 'manliness', 'machoness' as warriors, hunters, heroes; the representation of East and

West, North and South, White and Black, First World and Third World. These are the relationships of domination and of exploitation which are at the heart of the myths played out in both fascism, racism and pornography. At the heart of domination is the market concept of specialisation, division of labour, where the wholeness of life is cut up into pieces and individuals reduced to parts to be examined, controlled, profited from: 'This is pornographic living: the reduction of other beings to a decor to stimulate and enhance personal fantasy without any sense of the weight or reality of those beings' existence' (Cook, *The Listener*, 13 December 1990).

THE EDUCATION OF THE CORDON SANITAIRE

Real investigative journalism, fundamental social research, philosophical critique – all provide insights and sources of alternative understandings. However, only relatively small sections of the community have access to them. Schooling has done its job. It has associated serious reading with boredom, with something difficult, something that requires 'brains', with snobbery, with 'Them' not 'Us'. Traditional forms of schooling, with their emphasis upon rote learning, 'right answers', the categorisations of children into abilities, winners and failures, and structures of domination by the few of the many has associated education with the most joyless, unfree processes of learning for ever in the minds of the majority. Knowledge has been reduced to the paradigm case of such television shows as *Mastermind*; the reiteration of historical dates, the meanings of isolated terms, the names of kings and queens, heroes and villains.

Progressive education seemed to be an answer. However, there was no unified movement (Dale 1979a). According to Dale (1979b: 103): 'Generally speaking, a progressive is one who believes in the possibility and desirability of progress, that is of improvement in moral, social or rational understanding of the human condition, and so he holds a view which implies a certain optimism about human nature.' In Britain the ideas of progressive education spread in the primary schools, rather than in secondary schools. Secondary schooling was dominated by the exigencies of an elite examinations system and, until the 'comprehensive movement', was dominated by a split between schools for the most intelligent (grammar schools), the vocationally oriented (technical schools) and those who were left (the secondary modern schools). Progressive education and comprehensivisation (where children of all abilities could be taught in the same school and class) were the major challenges to traditional forms of schooling in Britain.

Progressive education, where it was practised in the state schools, adhered to a philosophy of 'child-centredness', rather than teacher- or subject-centredness. There was a tendency towards children learning at their own speed, learning through play, learning to read from real books (that is, real children's stories rather than those specially designed to introduce vocabulary in structured ways), and integrating subject areas in project work. However, the extent to which such forms of progressive education were actually practised with any rigour remains in doubt. Sharpe and Green (1975) in a study of a progressive school showed how the wider social, economic and political constraints within which schools operate act to undermine the progressive values they hold, thus reducing 'the progressive educator to little more than an unwilling apologist of the system' rendering 'his utopian solutions ineffective' (p. 226).

The egalitarian principles of the comprehensive school were also undermined by the context of operation. Ball (1981), in a study of a comprehensive school, showed the same kinds of pro- and counter-cultural pupil attitudes towards schools as seen by Hargreaves (1967) in a secondary modern school, and Lacey (1971) in a grammar school. Right from the beginning, there were hidden or even overt forms of streaming children which 'like selection under the tripartite system tends to underline class differentials in educational opportunity' (Ford 1969). The sheer size of schools also compelled teachers into mass control techniques which reduced individuality of response and initiative (Schostak 1983, 1986, 1988; Schostak and Logan 1984).

Since comprehensive schooling, in principle at least, threatened to reduce privileged access it is quite easy to see why it should come under attack from those who want to maintain inequality. It is perhaps less easy to see why progressive, child-centred forms of education should also come under such attack. This is particularly so given the underlying principles of many of the progressive thinkers. Dewey (1938: 54), for example, reinforced the myth of the family as the principle underlying his method where the model for teacher-pupil relations is that of the 'well-ordered family.' Rather than the role of dictator, or coercive force, in the classroom, the teacher's role was simply modified as 'leader of the group' where in disciplining a child 'it is done in behalf of the group, not as an exhibition of personal power'. The teacher never loses the central position. The teacher's role may at times seem more like a manager, where like Rousseau (1974: 278), the teacher endeavours to 'surround (the pupil) with all the lessons you would have him learn without awakening his suspicions' and taking care 'that all the experiments are connected together by a chain of reasoning, so that they may follow an orderly sequence in the mind' (p. 140). Computer techniques are now making it possible to conceive realistically of a control of the environment of learning which Rousseau could not have imagined (Schostak 1988). Overt authoritarian control has simply been replaced by covert authoritarian control, resulting in a liberal paternalism:

> One thing, however, is obvious, that a child cannot at birth be charged with the self-responsibility which he may ultimately claim and must ultimately bear. Family and school are institutions whose existence implies a joint responsibility in which parents and teachers have a share – preponderating at first, then decreasing as the years pass and the lines of the child's individuality form and harden. In the moral sphere the main duty of parents and teachers is to see that the little world in which the child grows up is as rich as may be in those elements that go to the fashioning of the better types of individuality, and that other elements are excluded. Since we here admit a judgement – and it will often be a faulty and mistaken judgement – which is not the child's own, we are, of course, limiting the abstract freedom of his self-creative growth. But such limitations are part of the inevitable conditions of life. An architect can build only with the materials placed at his disposal, but is yet free to make what use of them his genius suggests. Similarly the studies and discipline of a school, while of necessity representing those cultural and moral traditions which authority deems of vital value, should yet leave abundant room for the free development of individuality. (Nunn 1945: 14)

It is the last statement that arouses the fear of the anti-progressivists. What kind of individuality is being raised here? Is it something which is somehow outside the control of the authorities? There is a certain looseness in progressive philosophy and organisation which worries authorities. This perhaps explains why the tendency for increasing self-determinations in schooling is opposite to that proposed by Nunn. A five-year-old at school in many spheres of decision-making has more genuine autonomy and creative opportunity than a fifteen-year-old. Many young people who have experienced advanced forms of progressive education in primary schools may be quite unprepared for the culture shock when they move to the secondary school (whether grammar or comprehensive). However, in some of the progressive schools with which I have worked, the school has developed a self-confidence in the child which enables him or her to cope.

Progressive education, however, does not yet break the *cordon sanitaire*, merely gives it a little tweak. Nevertheless, with a concern for egalitarian forms of social process it can be a useful vehicle, like comprehensive schooling, for the introduction of such strategies as 'anti-sexism', 'anti-racism', and other forms of community action. Despite this, schools do not in general see it as their function to change the underlying circumstances of peoples' lives. A study of a comprehensive school in a very depressed area in the North of England revealed that despite its rhetoric and the undeniable commitment, compassion and hard work of its staff, its effect was to ameliorate at best and simply 'keep the lid on the dustbin' at worst (Schostak 1983, 1986).

It has been in the area of special needs education and vocational education in mainstream schools where some of the most important educational action has taken place. It is here that two strands critical to the maintenance and the destruction of the *cordon sanitaire* have been confronted by its best practitioners: the nature of everyday intelligence; and, the nature of self-responsibility. Everyday intelligence is unlike the abstract, tautological definitions that arise in intelligence-testing. Rather, it reveals itself only within practical realms of relevance in which real needs, problems and interests arise. Schooling, it can be argued, is a violation of such intelligence (Schostak 1984). It seeks to displace everyday relevance by school/exam-based curriculum relevance. There is little reason why the two should overlap other than for reasons of social class. In Britain, white middle-class interests are better served by schools than are the interests of other sections of society.

If intelligence does not reveal itself until applied in some domain of relevance, then what counts as relevant to children becomes as critical as that for adults. To have children as partners in the construction of curricula is for many anathema. Yet, in some forms of special needs education with disaffected young people, and with progressive practice with very young children, it is precisely this that is the basic educational strategy. It may take the form of contracts – if you do 'x' for me, then you can choose to do 'y' – or it may be a genuine collaboration involving the identification of the child's needs and interests *from the point of view of the child* as the basis for curriculum development.

Freire, working with adult literacy amongst peasant groups in Latin America, provides insight into the work of education as a process of freedom. It is in such work that the *cordon sanitaire* around the forbidden discourses of freedom begins to be thrown off:

> In the culture of silence the masses are 'mute', that is, they are prohibited from creatively taking part in the transformations of their society and therefore prohibited from being. Even if they can occasionally read and write because they were 'taught' in humanitarian – but not humanist – literacy campaigns, they are nevertheless alienated from the power responsible for their silence.
> (Freire 1970: 30)

The process of cultural action requires students to participate creatively in their own culture, not be passive recipients, or passive reproducers of the culture of others. Thus:

> The adult literacy process as an act of knowing implies the existence of two interrelated contexts. One is the context of authentic dialogue between learners and educators as equally knowing subjects. This is what schools should be – the theoretical context of dialogue. The second is the real, concrete context of facts, the social reality in which men exist. (pp. 31–2)

In dialogue 'the facts' of the real situations of people as active subjects in the process are represented. The representations of the social realities that arise become the representations forbidden by schooling discussed in earlier chapters. The real social conditions that affect real communities cannot be the subjects for analysis and action within the dominant school curricula. Otherwise, schools would become centres of revolutionary action. That, however, is not their function.

The role of the forbidden discourse is to set in motion a play of suspensions: the permitted and the forbidden each suspend and colour the other. Schools are at the front line of the battle. Knowledge, skills and the understanding necessary to service the complex physical and social processes of the world are essential to the power elites, the ruling classes, the people with privilege in a world of massive inequalities. However, to engage increasing numbers in the processes of knowledge and action is to risk catastrophe in the delicate balance between knowledge and ignorance: it is to risk cracking open self-enclosing mirrors, forever echoing the formulae of 'reality'; to see and hear in the geography of everyday living the echo and re-echo, the displays, the boundaries, the pathways of a terrain marked out for self loss. A city can be read in the way that a book can be read for the way in which it positions and reflects upon and against the self. There is an almost total narcissistic entrapment which it is the function of education to open up, releasing the individual from the culture of silence.

EDUCATION: PATTERNS OF DOMINATION AND SUBORDINATION

Education is at the heart of freedom. To reach that heart it suspends all faiths for a period of exploration. An ideal democracy could be constructed to support the play of education in a process through which all faiths can be explored, thereby enriching the culture of the self and of communities. Existing democracies are controlled essentially through a complex cross-patterning of relations of domination and subordination. These patterns are set into play within some model of the happy family: male–female; husband–wife; adult–child. These are then echoed in every major institution of society in terms of church as family, the firm as family. The institutions of law and order and of defence are all organised around the imagery of the protective state as father/motherland. Only the processes of education releases the carnival of ideas that can undermine the blind acceptance of the naturalness of all this. It is, thus, the processes of education which have been the object of the gravest and most terrible forms of censorship. It is education that can both represent and de-construct the 'real', the 'natural', the 'right'. Education is the other face of the forbidden discourse.

It is for this reason that throughout the centuries access to education has been regulated through schooling, and in this century of mass education and mass information, access to information has been regulated through the narrow ownership of the institutions of the media and the political control of schooling. It is necessary, therefore, to call a complete distinction between schooling and education (Schostak 1983, 1986, 1988). The role of education in the de-construction of the forces of repression will be discussed at greater length in Chapter 10. At this point in the discussion, it arises in the context of prying open the battleground of representation.

All representation is essentially a violence, according to the contributors to Armstrong and Tennenhouse's (1989) collection on the literature and history of violence: 'successive phases of imperialism – extending down through other classes within the imperial nations as well as outward to the colonies and informing foreign policy to this day – have turned the violence of representation into the ubiquitous form of power' (p. 9). The contributors to this volume trace the evolution and institutionalisation of violence within textual and discourse practices. Jed focuses on fifteenth-century humanism through which the violence of the Ancient Greek and Latin texts are still promoted as literature but not so 'the "literature" of fascist Italy' nor the violence represented daily in court records, in documents emanating from the Pentagon, or in a communique issued by the death squads in El Salvador. Yet, in each case, we are dealing with pieces of literature, though generated by different codes (pp. 37–8). What makes the one legitimate and neutral as literature and the other dismissed and lethal? Between the humanistic literature of ancient Greek tyrants and the modern death squad there is a relationship. However:

> There seems to be a tacit prohibition in humanistic studies, corresponding to the incest taboo: never identify the metaphorical relation or relation of similarity between the literary figure and the interpretative code of which it comes to form a part. Or, in terms of our examples here: never identify how the violence of the tyrant in the field, codified and transmitted by the humanistic tradition, may have influenced the workings of the code. (p. 39)

As a straightforward illustration Jed provides the account of the humanistic teacher Cola Montano, whose 'ambition was to transmit the tools of humanistic literacy to the noble youth of the city in the hopes that their conceptualisations of politics and violence would be grounded in reference to the humanistic code'. Three of his students were inspired to slay the duke in the Milan of 1476.

> Still today, the messages exchanged among humanists about 'tyranny' and 'freedom' have as their referent the code of humanism promoted by Cola Montano. And the violence represented in these codified texts is sublimated in the suppression of every kind of 'literature' which cannot be assimilated to this code. (p. 40)

What counts as literature to be studied is not a narrow debate to be played out amongst academics. By branding one set of writings as literature, attention is systematically turned from other kinds of writings so that important connections which fundamentally influence behaviour are missed. Following this argument, speeches of politicians, the articles in the *Sun, Daily Mail* or any other popular as opposed to literary or high-brow newspaper should not be excluded from literary analysis. Inclusion or exclusion are political acts of real consequence. It is in the popular press that the battles of dissent are framed, the discourses arranged, and the effort of interpreting issues in the world reduced to 'straight speaking'. Through it education is suppressed in the interests of a political struggle against knowledge that would subvert the *status quo*.

During the decade of the 1980s in Britain, children's literature became a battle ground. It is here that state, family and church were mobilised in a powerful attack on 'liberal', 'permissive', 'socialist', 'progressive' forms of thinking. Singled out as a major threat to the sanctity of the family – and hence to the state, church and the social order – has been feminism or women's studies which critiqued patriarchism itself. Associated with this in schools has been the teaching of sexuality and of alternative family forms and sexual preferences. In 1986 a conservative politician, Peter Bruinvels, criticised a number of sex education texts which he considered should be banned from schools. The fact that few, if any, of these books were used in schools was ignored. More important was the moral point of view to be communicated to the voting public: that the traditional family based on traditional understandings of Anglo-Saxon love and marriage was under attack from the lunatic left. To this core of the family ideal a range of other themes was associated in the headline stories of mass circulation newspapers: race, multi-culturalism, gay love, patriotism. Together they present a powerful, coordinated message of distrust and fear which keeps children schooled in the bodies of belief that brand as dangerous or evil any alternative forms of thought and conduct that would challenge the reproduction of unjust allocations of wealth, opportunity and freedoms. Education presents alternative readings for debate, thus opening for children a variety of discourses. The suppression of the concept of multiple discourses clearly underlay the lead up to the election campaign of 1987, when several of the national mass circulation newspapers ran stories about 'loony left-wing' councils.

One major story concerned the 'Baa baa green sheep' headlines. The Media Research Group of Goldsmith's College, London tracked the story from its first appearance in the *Daily Star* on 15 February 1986. It reported that a nursery school in Hackney had banned the singing of 'Baa-Baa Black Sheep' because it was racist and had replaced it with 'Baa-Baa White Sheep'. This story was then picked up by a local newspaper, the *Hackney Gazette*, then by the national daily the *Sun*. Eight months later the *Daily Mail* reported:

> Hackney Council ordered playgroup leaders to attend a racism awareness course, on the threat of withdrawing their grant, where they were instructed that in future children must sing 'Baa-Baa Green Sheep'. Other newspapers repeated the story without using the council's denial: the *Birmingham Evening Mail, Liverpool Echo, Yorkshire Evening Press, Birmingham Post, Sunday People, News of the World, Sunday Times* and *Sunday Telegraph.*
>
> (Francis Beckett, *Times Educational Supplement*, 5 June 1987)

Neither the ban nor the threat had ever been made. This and a number of other equally groundless stories circulated. Why were they believed, or at least believable? Beckett, in her article, argued that because of left-wing rhetoric 'It is frighteningly easy to be branded as racist, or sexist, or even heterosexist (anti-gay) when you are not.' This, however, cannot be enough of a reason in itself. There must be a deeper insecurity. Whatever reality we believe in, or take for granted as real, hard, certain, is held together in our minds by a discourse concerning it. This discourse is elaborated between self in relationship to some other. That is, the discourse is played out by a dramatis personae which unifies self with others in a dramatic interplay. In the above narrative, there are those who play members of the 'loony left', those who play members of the 'victims'. The victims are typically white, mothers and children: that is, the family. The 'loony left' breaks down into such players as: the gay rights activist, the anti-racist, the permissive free-love exponent – and so on. The discourse clearly marks the lines between one side and the other. It also displays the boundaries, the 'edge' of respectability and acceptability. There is thus a 'twist' or 'warp' in the relationships of the dramatis personae as each member on one side of the boundary confronts those on the other side as a problem to itself, a threat to its existence. Overstepping the boundary, being on the edge, going too far – these are all metaphors marking the distance between self and those acts on the other side denied to the self. Yet, each member of the dramatis personae is defined in relationship to the other, hence is elaborated by action in relation the other. In a pluralistic society, there are many edges, many boundaries making the plain and simple, obscure and complex so there are many occasions where the one is a threat to the other. The discourse of the one is forbidden by the other. The boundaries which maintain the distinctions are assiduously surveilled and enforced. If there are equally acceptable world-views and life-styles, then these boundaries are no longer absolute, no longer necessary and no longer clear. This opens out another level, or theme of the discourse forbidden by the happy family which must retain rigid boundaries or else dissolve itself.

The self of the happy family, therefore, must express itself only through a narrow range of discourse. The rest is forbidden. Essentially, the family as a guardian of tradition is the bourgeois 'happy family' of the politicians, priests and marketing agencies so scorned by Cooper (1971) as 'the family that prays together and stays together through sickness and health till death us do part or releases us into the terse joylessness of the epitaphs on our Christian tomb-stones erected, for want of any other sort of erection, by those who mourn for us in the curious mode of remembering very hard to forget us very hard' (p. 5). To Cooper, the clear task of the individual is to get rid of the happy family. It is the source of neuroses, psychoses. The modern form of the family, operating under the complementary myths of the happy family and the permissive other, leads only to contortions of the self. The full expression of the self as a source of alternative world-views and modes of self-expression is denied. It is the forbidden self and it is denied representation in the official arenas of expression. It appears elsewhere – dreams, back streets, red light areas, secret assignations in hotel rooms – as the forbidden hero of desire, need, and terror, tamed and sold through the hidden economy or packaged as image and sold with chocolate.

8

SELF-ASSERTION AND VIOLENCE

Violence may be the only way perceived by the dispossessed, the discriminated against, the suppressed to break through the cordon sanitaire and tell of their pain, their anger, their frustration. With each eruption, the myth of the Hero and the Villain must be retold to manage public interpretations and suppress again the voice of protest. In the myth the function of violence and battle is to reduce the complexity of the individual to piece-like moves, as in the tactics of 'crowding and massing' at Orgreave. The power of the 'player' (say, the police commander) is increased as the bits (the baton-wielding police, on horse back, or behind shields on one side and the 'rioters' on the other) are moved in ways which resemble the unambiguous positioning and placing of pieces on a chess board. The role of the media then is to 'story' the events so that clear-cut 'sides' emerge, with the appropriate heroes and villains emerge. The struggle in such incidents as Orgreave, or the poll tax riot at Trafalgar, cannot be simply reduced to the Thatcherite concept of the 'enemy within' without doing violence to the idea of individual (that is social) freedoms, rights and interests.

The counter-discourses which prompt reflection upon rights, interests, needs, are part of the process through which alternative understandings and actions are drawn out and challenges made, but do such processes of challenge inevitably lead to violence? During the eighteenth and nineteenth centuries, when schooling for the lower classes and then mass education was discussed, violence was precisely the result that many feared and predicted as the lower classes were educated above their station in life:

> Should the working class legislate in their own interest, 'our entire system of industry and commerce would undergo a revolution and with it every institution of property'; if the manual labour class 'usurped such a predominance as to give the practical control of

> the House of Commons', the resultant evils could 'assume the monstrous proportions of a destructive revolution.'
>
> (Simon 1974: 357, describing the views of Kay-Shuttleworth, a noted educationist, 1860)

If people know what is happening to them, what they are being denied, and what they could have access to, they may become dissatisfied, angry, rebellious.

Under situations when rights are at stake, self-assertion may be interpreted by authorities as rebellion, threats to the social order, violence. It begins with the felt sense of violation that individuals and communities of individuals feel in the face of repression, censorship, silence. The display of power to repress the demands of those who assert their rights leads to a counter reaction.

The violation of the individual, of communities, of forms of self and cultural expression is structural in a world that is policed in the interests of multinational monopoly capitalism. The political construction of culture versus anarchy maintains the structures of violation by marking assertions counter to the dominant cultural forms as subversive, rebellious, illegal, thereby stifling any real discussion of rights and the examination of alternative positions. Is violence, in certain circumstances – the deposing of a tyrant, or the protest against unjust laws – a proper outcome of education?

RIOT: IGNORING THE CAUSES; BLAMING THE POOR

In the image of the golden age of Britain, it is conceived of as a peaceful country where anybody could walk the streets without fear. This is fantasy, as any study of the history of violence on the streets reveals (Robottom 1976; Humphries 1981). Furthermore, there has been a continuity of radical revolt in Britain since at least the 1300s (Hampton 1984). A challenge to the prevailing order evokes the discourse of protest, a forbidden discourse.

> Rebellion among the young against the old is no new phenomenon, though we tend to see current manifestations of 'youth culture' or the 'youth revolution' as peculiar to our own time. The hippies, the provos and the New Left of the West today, and even the young Red Guards of communist China, have in a general sense their roots in generational conflicts that date back at least to Greek and

> Roman times; and in a far more specific sense the rebel German students now reading Marcuse, Reich, and Che Guevara are also the direct heirs of a long line of Lutheran non-conformists descended from Thomas Muntzer and the Peasant's Revolts of the sixteenth century. (Heer 1974: 7)

Heer sees protest as the search for new fathers. What was once forbidden under one regime becomes permitted under alternative fathers. Norman O. Brown's (1966) interpretation of Freud leads him in a similar direction. He sees in the history of political associations, the delinquent gang, the gathering of the brothers into fraternal organisations to overthrow the father:

> Political parties are primitive secret societies: Tammany's Wigwam; caucus; mafia; cabal. The deals are still always secret, in a smoke-filled room. Political parties are conspiracies to usurp the power of the father, 'a taking of the sword out of the hand of the Sovereign.' Political parties are antagonistic fraternities, or moieties; a contest between Blues and Greens in the Hippodrome; an agon between Leather Seller and Sausage Seller to seduce and subvert Old Man Demos; an Eskimo drumming contest; organised not by agreement on principle, but by confusing the issues to win; in a primitive ordeal or lottery in which the strife is justice, might makes right, and the major is the sanior pars. (p. 29)

The Oedipal myth is powerful in its themes of authority, sexuality and intergenerational conflict. It seems to explain so much that its imprints appear everywhere. The danger is that it acquires the status of inevitability where debate is replaced by deals, conspiracies and contests for power against intransigent authorities, competing cults, gangs and cabals.

The unofficial histories of revolt are carried within folklore or popular culture as in the tales and ballads of Robin Hood. It composes what I have called the violent imagination (Schostak 1986). When histories are written for school texts, these unofficial histories with their alternative discourses of morality, political organisation and action are typically ignored. During political discussions when unemployment was about to rise to three million in 1982, the then leader of the opposition, Michael Foot, made the connection between riots and lack of work:

> Mr Foot's question caused uproar among Tory MPs. Mr Whitelaw angrily replied: 'I find this wholly deplorable. I would have thought everyone in this House wished to see peace in our cities and no riots in the summer.
>
> 'To suggest that such riots might occur is highly irresponsible.'
>
> (*Guardian*, 31 March 1982)

Typically, the tabloid media and the government of the time described riots as if they were inspired by a few politically motivated trouble-makers leading mindless masses, as if they were acts without causes, without relations to social contexts.

During the riots of 1985 the same picture of a young black man carrying a bottle (a petrol bomb) appeared on the front pages of several newspapers (11 September 1985). The *Star* wrote 'This is the menacing face of riot-torn Handsworth yesterday.' The *Daily Mail*, under the headline 'Bloodlust', wrote that 'Copycat riots could hit other cities following the bloodshed and destruction in Handsworth, Home Secretary Douglas Hurd warned police forces yesterday.' Hurd was quoted as dismissing the 'suggestion that economic and social hardship could be blamed for the violence.' The Labour opposition blamed social conditions and the local councillor 'blamed police for allowing tension to build after two men were held at a police station' (*Star*). For the *Star* the riot was due to the poor state of the cities, the drugs, unemployment, crime. For the *Mail* it was due to 'the criminally vicious mob' composed of West Indians, with the victims being Asians:

> So was this a 'race riot'? No, it was not. It was an orgy of arson and looting by the have-nots against the haves, most of whom in Handsworth happen to be hard-working Asian shopkeepers.
>
> If we have to pin a one-word label on this predominantly black riot, it would be 'tribal'. Tribal like the predominantly white marauding bands of football thugs are tribal, tribal like the predominantly Catholic teenage stone and petrol bomb throwers from the Bogside are tribal. However daunting it is to establish individual guilt when there is a rampage, every effort must be made to bring to justice those who killed, burned and plundered.

By reducing the causes of the riot to 'tribal' to 'bloodlust', 'criminality', the people themselves have been reduced to the myth of the savage, the uncivilised tribe, the lawless criminal. Real social conditions have simply disappeared. Shipley in the *Daily Telegraph* (12 September 1985) was certain that:

> ... riots are above all local affairs with local causes. They are triggered when a succession of apparently unconnected events – an attempt to stamp on the drugs trade, a stop in the street that draws a crowd, an unexplained fire in a derelict building – combines to disturb the delicate balance of the inner city.
>
> In themselves they are everyday events in street life, but they spill over into violence where there are just too many ingredients bubbling in the pot, and when they escalate they reveal a legacy of simmering tensions and deeper causes which only the most serious disturbances bring to the surface.

The solution put forward was increased police powers and numbers. He referred to the report on the riots in Brixton in 1981 by Scarman which outlined 'three areas of need – housing, education and employment' remarking that if anything, these problems have grown worse over the years. Finally, 'political extremists are moving in to fan unrest'. In the key areas of education, housing and employment little has been done for those who most need it. Although real spending on these has risen, the *Independent* (13 December 1990) reporting the National Children's Bureau findings, states that 'The number of children living in poverty has doubled in the past 10 years.' It went on: '"Improvements in living standards of the better-off have not trickled down to low income families with children," the report said. "Homelessness, housing conditions, childhood sickness, drug abuse and probably children's diets have got worse."'

The reasons for riot are both complex and simple. They are complex because the histories of social tension out which they erupt are complex. They are simple because of the felt sense of violation, injustice and oppression experienced with poverty, discrimination and exploitation. The real complexity of such violence resides in the multi-layered contexts through which the awareness of causes, conditions and intentions are clouded, sealed off from group to group and can only be guessed at. Has education (as opposed to schooling) any real strategies in the face of protest, the intransigence of authorities seeking only to stiffen their authority, and the absence of structures for debate?

THE EDUCATION OF TERROR AND HORROR

The forbidden discourse depends upon and operates under a series of different kinds and levels of awareness, contexts which determine the conditions under which self and other are represented to each other. These are kept in place by real or imagined violence, horror and terror which together constitute the violent imagination:

> Every felt sense of injustice contributes to an overall resentment which permeates the developing drama between self and other, between those like Me and those like Them. This is the stuff of the violent imagination – the dramas, the myths, the folktales, the personal anecdotes which tell of the many violations against the self perpetrated by others. Through the contents of the violent imagination an individual recognises incidents as either violatory or non-violatory, justice or injustice. Such images are passed on through the generations by the voices of those who enter into community with each other. It is in the developing intelligence of the community – intelligence in the widest sense of practical knowledge, or wisdom, or information concerning the world (...). The violent imagination becomes a way in which people make sense of the world, identifying structures of justice and of injustice, freedom and slavery, creation and destruction, war and peace.
>
> (Schostak 1986: 33–4)

Within the violent imagination, between the permitted and the forbidden are marked out the tear lines in the facade of social order where the sense of contortion, the experiences of violation render the presentation of self brittle, placing it under pressure. In the presentation of the stable image of the permissable-self or of some social institution, the underlying pre-conceptual 'babble', the multiplicities of conflicting roles to be performed, the tensions between social identities are erased for all practical purposes. The self rides like a conceptual bubble over the confusing flux of experience whether in the performance of the public self in face-to-face situations, or in situations which involve a kind of face-to-facelessness (where self confronts such abstractions as 'the system', 'Them', and so on). Although the marks are erased, or the earlier formations of the self are forgotten, they remain like lines of fragility to be exposed under pressure. Horror depends upon such a principle. Under conditions of horror, what we know, what is held within the grasp of theoretical certainty and rationality, the conceptual bubble of the self, is blown away. The terror is real. Horror films depend upon the techniques of shifting perception away from the taken-for-granted basis for reality and knowledge, and into the realm where even the most ordinary items become disassociated from their sense of familiarity, firmness and rationality. Everything is subject to a sudden realisation of fragility once the controls are loosened. Hence, in the experience of horror or terror, the controls are reaffirmed as having their necessary place in the maintenance of social order and the preservation of the self. In order to enforce control, the techniques of terror themselves have a place: the fear of terror is then used to justify the application of terror to enforce controls. Whether the terror is international (as in the case of Mutually Assured Destruction (MAD)), Hobbesian or Machiavellian, for the control of a nation, or more casually for the control of children in families or classrooms – threats, the play upon fears, the generation of images, devils and evil forces of all kinds are fundamental to everyday social control. The political use of panic words and devil words are routine. If such and such a course is followed then the apocalypse will follow. Underneath ordinary life runs a seam of panic and terror. At any time the madness can erupt through the fissures. Education de-fuses the unity of the conceptual bubble, exposes the tear lines and opens up the possibility of new conceptual formulations. Schooling defuses the potential for fragmentation through strengthening the lines of authority, reclosing the doors on possibility and marking alternatives as forbidden, impossible, crazy.

The media is a powerful vehicle in the maintenance of a strong vein of terror, as it adds day-by-day new variations on old themes to the stock of stories, images, anecdotes of unaccountable violence which, without the strength of the authorities, would bring society to chaos.

In 1987 Michael Ryan took up his Kalashnikov AK47 and killed fifteen people in the town of Hungerford. The *Sun* (20 August 1987) carried the front page headline: 'MAD RAMBO IN MASSACRE', and the front page story started:

> CRAZED Rambo gunman Michael Ryan shot himself dead last night after slaughtering FIFTEEN people in Britain's worst massacre.
>
> Armed police surrounded a school where Ryan – dressed in U.S. military uniform and a Rambo-style headband – had holed up with a fearsome arsenal of guns.

The mere use of the name Rambo fixes the event within a story, legitimating a whole play of associations. This was not an inspirational use of imagery by the *Sun*; the headline on the same day in the *Daily Express* was: 'MASSACRE RAMBO KILLS HIMSELF'. The *Star* gave its front page headline as: 'RAMBO MASSACRE'. Extracts from a story on the character of Ryan included:

> FRIENDS and neighbours spoke yesterday of 'nice guy' Michael Ryan and his obsession with guns.
>
> Mrs Guytha Hunt, who has lived next door to the Ryans for 25 years, said of the gunman:
>
> 'He was a nice enough lad but I always thought he was a bit strange.
>
> 'He was a real loner and went in for all sorts of guns and collected them since he was a teenager.
>
> .....
>
> 'His mother doted on him and always bought things for him. He always had a new car and lots of different girlfriends.'
>
> .....
>
> Jobless musician Chris Bowsher, 28, a friend of the killer who witnessed the rampage, said:
>
> 'I saw him this morning dressed in camouflage. He seemed strange.
>
> 'He was always a bit of an oddball but no psychopath and was once a bouncer at concerts.
>
> .....
>
> 'His father died two years ago and it may have affected him ....'

The Rambo allusion was carried media wide. Here it was an image of horror. Yet elsewhere it is an image of heroism. The ambivalence in the imagery is its strength. It marks a fissure, a line of fragility in the social structure. The signs of military protection – uniform, guns, munitions, survival tactics and training – are also the signs of terror. It is this ambivalence which marks the entrance to the fields of the forbidden. In the Hungerford–Rambo story the nature of the forbidden emerges in a powerful set of images surrounding:

forbidden identities	Rambo
forbidden acts	killing
forbidden transformations	from quiet son to killer
forbidden fruits/possessions	guns and other weapons
forbidden ideas/knowledge	the arts of killing

signs of the forbidden	bit of a loner, strange dress, father died two years earlier, doting mother

This list is not exhaustive. Each category adduced in the mind of the reader has an ambivalent status in society, taking on different valuations in different contexts. Within the dramatis personae of the Hungerford–Rambo narrative are: father, doting mother, girlfriends, and 'nice lad' Ryan with Rambo as the alter ego. Each of these will be interpreted differently according to who reads it and how it is used (cf. Hodge and Tripp 1986). The Hungerford–Rambo story is highly complex in the way that it reads fiction into reality and reality into fiction. It carries the desirable qualities of the macho-Rambo image, its excitement and love of guns into an arena of horror. The ambivalence reveals that it is in the social nature of the forbidden to be both desired and condemned and variously interpreted and valued according to context and the biographical and social position of the interpreter. The imagery of Rambo has shown that it can be articulated for a multiplicity of purposes. To distinguish between the forbidden and the permissible in the imagery requires access to the codes indicating the forbidden as well as the forbidden codes in which the forbidden operates. Each such story, whether of 'crazy' or 'rational' violence, provides a lesson in the appropriate codes of interpretation. Through the code that designates the Hungerford incident 'crazy' a blind is drawn over the underlying horror and attention is focused on and the terror defused into the bounded story, there to be packaged and set aside as day-to-day living resumes.

MALE VIOLENCE

The process of Oedipalisation through the family locates violence structurally with the male as patriarch, as son, as brother. The hero and the villain is typically male. Morgan (1989) begins her exploration of the sexuality of terrorism with a narrative of a woman walking and hearing footsteps behind her. They are not just any footsteps: 'It is the footstep of a man she fears. This moment she shares with every human being who is female. This is the democratisation of fear' (pp. 23–4). Male violence against women and children has been only recently properly recognised (Breines and Gordon 1983). However, men's violence has long been a major ingredient of news coverage:

as wars, riots, rebellions, muggings, rapes. Sexuality and violence are all interwoven with everyday scandal. The British Channel 4 TV programme *Hard News* presented by Raymond Snoddy of the *Financial Times* devoted a broadcast to the issue of rape reportage in the major newspapers (16 November 1990). It showed close up headlines of *reported* rapes, acted reconstructions, interviews with those editors who agreed to be interviewed, the Home Office minister, John Patten, and interviews with the victims. This was set against the background statistic that all sex offences account for less than 1 per cent of recorded crime. A major finding of their survey was that rape was over-reported. The editor of *The Times*, Simon Jenkins, remarked that a rape story has all the ingredients of salaciousness of a good story stereotype. John Patten commented that he thought something happened in the 1970s and 1980s circulation wars where it was thought that sex sold newspapers. He added that he supposed the reporting of rape cases was one way of getting that sort of story into the papers. It was the *Sun* and the *Telegraph* that reported rape cases most. *The Times* reported them least.

Hard News analysed the rape coverage of ten national newspapers. It therefore must have covered virtually the whole of the newspaper-reading public. What was left unsaid, therefore, was that the sexual salaciousness associated with rape is a major national fantasy. The reportage of rape is a way of writing pornography. Sex and violence sells newspapers. In common with Red Riding Hood, according to the reportage, most rape victims carry some blame: they ask for it. The broadcast clearly indicated this through the words of the victims themselves. They are doubly victims: raped by the rapist and by the headlines that follow. One victim was reported as being in a 'sex slave ordeal', although the victim herself said that she had never used such terminology. Frequently, rape stories are set alongside other sexual images: the 'Page Three Girl' or other such images and stories.

The source of most rape stories are the law courts. Journalists, as one interviewed from the *Independent* said, look for the unusual. This turns out to be the usual, that which is most redundant, that is, most predictable in the good stereotypical story: she wore short skirts, was drunk, was out alone at night, or that she somehow enjoyed it, or that it was bizarre or 'kinky' in some way.

Women as a target for male harassment received worldwide attention in the Judge Clarence Thomas case. The judge was nominated by President Bush for the Supreme Court. He was accused by a law professor, Anita Hill, of sexual harassment when she had previously worked for him at two government agencies. Although the Judge won, the case brought the issue to public consciousness. Accounts of sexual harassment appeared in newspapers and magazines all over the world. At its mundane level, sexual harassment as a fact of life reinforces male authority. The raising of issues of harassment, of women's rights and issues, is experienced by many men as a threat against their authority, their identities as males. To set these issues under a feminist banner, it has been argued, particularly by the New Right, has done women no good. Faludi (1991) has written of this backlash as an 'undeclared war against women'. She describes at length, in every sphere of life, the attacks against women by the New Right under the Reagan–Bush administrations in America and the Thatcher–Major governments in Britain. At one level it is the very mundaneness of dominance, discrimination and harassment in every workplace that feeds images of power and of fear. At another level, the threat to male dominance in the counter-images of women talking and fighting back produces counter-images of dominance reasserted, the male taking charge again after having been misled by soft liberal ideas. The 1986 Yankelovich Monitor survey of American social attitudes tracked over two decades was reviewed by analysts at Yankelovich who had to create a new category of angry young men: 'the contenders'. It is a group that 'feared and reviled feminism' (Faludi 1991: 88). They represented a group of young men who earned less than their fathers and were disproportionately unemployed.

> The backlash's public agenda has been framed and promoted by men of far more affluence and influence than the Contenders, men at the helm of the media, business and politics. Poorer or less-educated men have not so much been the creators of the anti-feminist thesis as its receptors. Most vulnerable to its message, they have picked up and played back the backlash at distortingly high volume. In the US the Contenders have dominated the ranks of the militant wing of the eighties anti-abortion movement, the list of plaintiffs filing reverse-discrimination and 'men's rights' lawsuits, the steadily mounting police rolls of rapists and sexual assailants. (pp: 88–9)

Faludi follows this with a catalogue of male outrages against women.

In Montreal 1989 at the Ecole Polytechnique, Marc Lepine, a young male engineering student, having a score to settle with feminism, killed fourteen women. Such a crazed display of violence can be interpreted as the act of a single crazy person. The Killean massacre in Texas, October 1991, in which 23 people were shot by a man with a hatred of women, could be similarly interpreted. Craziness located somehow in a single individual inhibits a deeper critique of society. It is like Freud ignoring the texts of Judge Schreber's father in analysing the crazy output of the son. The master texts of 'family values' – the rallying cry of Bush's presidential campaign – become reconstructed in contorted form by those who feel under threat and unable to identify and name the deeper causes of their ills.

CALCULATED TERRORISM

The Hungerford incident, rapes, child brutality and so on are horrifying because they seem irrational. They burst upon the ordinary scene, striking ordinary people in ordinary streets. The real terror is that they reveal the connections with universal fantasies – the horrific sense that somehow, all this might be in all males. Terrorism seems to differ by being calculated and cannot be critically understood apart from the whole complex of state and revolutionary or counter-revolutionary networks. Terrorism depends upon the manipulation of awareness, emotion, and the reduction of choice to choicelessness. When a 'human bomb' – driven by a victim forced to deliver it by car – exploded at an army checkpoint in Ulster, it was reported in the media as, of course, an outrage. *Today* (25 October 1990) described the IRA as murderers who 'plumbed new depths of cowardice'. It reported the outrage of politicians, the sorrow and the grief of the victims. The terror succeeds again in its purpose of polarising and preventing dialogue. The weight of history envelops each new outrage, adding to the sense of inevitability that another and another outrage will occur in a cycle of revenge and repression.

The definition of terrorism is in many ways straightforward: 'In essence, terrorism is the use or threat of violence against small numbers to put large numbers in fear; or, as well put by an ancient Chinese philosopher: "Kill one, frighten 10,000"' (Clutterbuck 1986: 20). It is deciding who to apply the definition to that becomes more complicated. Clutterbuck divides terrorists into: political terrorists (sub-dividable 'by their motivation into nationalist, religious or ideological' or some combination), state terrorists (Soviet Union under Stalin,

Nazi Germany, Gaddafi's Libya, Khomeni's Iran etc.), domestic terrorism (French resistance fighters during the Second World War, ETA in Spain, the IRA in Ireland and so on), international terrorists (Palestinians, Libyans, Iranians and so on). He places the industrial changes due to microelectronics at the centre of social changes which he considers will place strains upon the decade of the 1990s, just as in the case of the new technologies of previous generations. The access that people have to information will be unequal and 'inequalities will stretch, in both the old and the new industrial countries, between the "haves" who learn to use the information explosion and the "have-nots" who, having scorned or otherwise failed to take the opportunities to qualify for the more rewarding kinds of brain work, will seek solace in cheap entertainment and do dismal jobs or none at all; there will be a new "them" and a new "us"' (p. 9). He sees these pressures as increasing the potential to dissent.

In presenting the images of terrorism and of the terrorist, the role of the media is critical. Clutterbuck views its role as 'a malignant rather than a restraining effect on public order and this is likely to increase in the future as channels proliferate and news spreads faster, and in more dramatic form, into people's homes.' He sees television as reinforcing prejudices and inflaming conflicts, setting up the possibilities for copycat riots (citing the UK 1981 riots as evidence). Information technology too, will give rise to new forms of terrorism through the disruption of computer networks.

The discussion is presented as risk management within the context of security and civil rights. The dilemma is pragmatic: 'if ... restrictions are greater than the situation appears to the public to justify, or if they cause excessive inconvenience or harassment to innocent people, the essential public support may be lost' (p. 50) In asserting that the essential right is the right to live, 'one of the arts of governing a liberal society is to ensure that the public understands and approves of the measures which are necessary to preserve this principle' (p. 50).

But there are different levels to consider. It is undeniably true that all want the right to live. However, this must be set in the context of governments or their agencies which endanger these rights through clandestine operations in support of regimes which the people of the liberal democracy could not in all conscience support. Terrorism cannot be removed from its full context. It is explainable only within its complex history and cannot be separated from state terrorism carried out on an international scale in the pursuit of the political and economic interests of Western 'democracies'. Herman (1982) describes the extent to which totalitarian regimes have been supported by the

West. Discussing the CIA concept of 'international terrorism' he finds that it 'does not include those responsible for the 90,000 "disappeared" in Latin America, nor the leadership of the Garcia regime in Guatemala, the direct managers of the murder of thousands in the last few years' (p. 12). He goes on to write that 'With the accession to power of Reagan, Haig, and Kirkpatrick we have entered the *post*-Orwellian era' (p.13). Thus:

> In the world of Jeane Kirkpatrick, the *Sandinistas* are 'promoting terrorism' in El Salvador, 'terrorism' referring to the actions of the rebels, who are possibly being given some marginal assistance by Nicaragua. Local church sources and independent observers have uniformly contended that the daily murders and mutilations by government and government-sponsored paramilitary forces account for well over 80 per cent of civilian killings. These forces were, and still are, armed, trained and given crucial support by the United States, either directly or through one of its client states. Kirkpatrick excludes the massive official murders of civilians from the category of terrorism partly by arbitrarily removing government from the category of terrorist; but she also resorts to the tired ... cliche that much of the official violence is by irregular forces who are 'out of control'. (pp. 12–13)

Occasionally a scandal arises to disturb the scene such as the Iran–Contra and the Noriega affairs. Without any sense of historical contradiction the war of nerves against Saddam Hussein since the summer and winter of 1990–1 had been pursued as if the West had no role in maintaining this dictator in power. The *Sunday Times* (2 December 1990) revealed that despite an embargo since 1984 on selling arms to Iraq, Alan Clark, then a trade minister, 'allowed firms to break the spirit of the government's arms embargo' by encouraging firms to export machine-tooling equipment that could equally well be used for peaceful or military purposes. Cockburn and Cohen (1991) described the extent of Western military aid to Iraq. During the eight-year war between Iraq and Iran the US provided 'satellite intelligence, helicopters, agricultural credits and naval protection in the Gulf' (p. 2) and secretly shipped weapons. On the date of the Iraqi invasion of Kuwait, 2 August 1990, 'a fifth of Saddam Hussein's arsenal was French' (p. 3). In the view of Cockburn and Cohen, it was a war made possible by Western policies, an unnecessary war. The catalogue of support for terrifying regimes is extensive. Indeed, the sale of British weaponry to Third World countries has been a steadily increasing industry due in part to 'vigorous government promotion' since the establishment of the Defence Sales Organisation within the Ministry of Defence in 1966 (Collinson 1989: 29). Protest seems impossible. The terrorist strike suddenly appears, as if from nowhere, a vicious reminder of wars and social conflict elsewhere. The terror lies in the breaking of the illusion of separation, of non-connection between the one world and the other.

THE DOMESTIC RIGHT TO PROTEST

The Vietnam War offers a peculiarly acute theme for the elaboration of the right to protest. Consider the following letter (Michener 1973):

> Authority, law and order are the backbone of our society, for its protection. Would you want authorities to stand by if your home were threatened? Well, Kent State is my home by virtue of taxes spent funding it. What's more, it's their home by virtue of tuition paid. Playful children destroying a disenchanting toy.
>
> How dare they! I stand behind the action of the National Guard! I want my property defended. And if dissenters refuse to obey the final warning before the punishment, hurling taunts, rocks (stones they say), sticks, brandishing clubs with razor blades embedded, then the first slap is a mighty sting.
>
> Live ammunition! Well, really, what did they expect, spitballs? How much warning is needed indeed.
>
> Hooray! I shout for God and Country, recourse to justice under the law, fifes, drums, martial music, parades, ice cream cones – America, support it or leave it. Ravena housewife

This letter was written in defence of the killing of a number of students at the Kent State University by the National Guard at a time when one section of America's youth were protesting against the Vietnam War while another section were fighting it. The letter is remarkable for its profusion of unremarkable images of home, children, education, the forces of law and order, the forces of disruption, property, God, patriotism, country and the military. These are conceptually tied in a network of associations. In a brief space they present a way of mapping out the world. In a sense the letter is paradigmatic, that is, it presents a taken-for-granted exemplar of how things are to be seen, and more than that, it provides principles of conduct through an illustration of exemplary conduct: 'I shout for

God and Country, recourse to justice under the law, fifes, drums, martial music, parades, ice cream cones – America, support it or leave it.' Where in this letter does the forbidden reside?

The forbidden is not necessarily 'the silent', nor is it necessarily 'the hidden'. Protest is neither silent nor hidden when it is happening. The demands of the protesters are expressed openly, not covertly, through the stratagems of dream consciousness seeking to express the repressed. The forbidden can erupt upon the social scene. The processes of repression into the realm of the forgotten come later if they come at all. Typically, the forbidden evokes the forces of oppression, of defence, of control. The National Guard took this role against the students who were likened to 'playful children' caught in the act of destruction: fathers against children who were rising up against the fathers.

However, to set the issue solely within the Oedipus myth is somehow to belittle the moral issues involved. The right to protest may be inconvenient to governments in a hurry to win wars; however, the assertion of alternative moral frameworks is fundamental to democratic debate. When these are suppressed, then protest and civil disobedience seem the only outlets. Orgreave and Wapping became the focus for what could only be called a class war, where the trade unions were explicitly referred to by Thatcher as the enemy within. In placing protest within the discourse of policing, reinforcing it with laws and clandestine actions which reduce the ability of people to discuss conditions of work, the siting of nuclear power stations, the deployment of nuclear weapons, and so on, a lack of faith in democracy is betrayed. Protest is polarised into 'us' and 'them' confrontations where knowledge and the power to act is inequitably distributed rather than canalised into debate and the education (drawing out) of alternatives. Or is the ideal of democracy and of education only an illusion which will always founder upon the basic impulse to violence and war at the heart of our species?

WAR

War seems pervasive. At any given time there are 60 or more wars going on around the world. On 17 January 1991 America launched an attack on Iraq in order to regain Kuwait which had been annexed by Iraq in August 1990. It was a war remarkable for its media coverage. Right from the start, when news reporters from Cable

News Network in Baghdad covered the first air raids, this was a war which was mediated moment by moment around the world. The world knew, in fact, before it had been officially notified. People in their front rooms often seemed to know more than front-line troops. Expert analysts discussed the strategies, the political implications and the might of the forces arraigned against Saddam Hussein. Interviews with returning aircrews were repeated over and over again in the regular 'updates' and news round-ups. There was excitement, fear and the elation of having returned home safely.

There was also surprise, almost disbelief, that Hussein seemed to be doing nothing. The anti-aircraft fire over Baghdad could not reach the high-flying bombers. There had been no casualties in the initial runs. Even by the end of the first week there were only a few aircraft reported missing. The initial feelings were of optimism that the war would be over very quickly, perhaps in a matter of days. Yet, as Deedes in the *Telegraph* (19 January 1991) commented, despite the 'fog of information' being provided by correspondents around the world, 'Twenty-four hours after this first assault, described as the biggest air raid in history, we knew no more of the immediate local consequences than we did after Dresden, Hamburg or Hiroshima in the Second World War. In all our recent wars, government has shown itself slow to strike the right balance between too much information and too little.'

The drama continued when Iraq fired about eight Scud missiles, one of which was blown up by an anti-missile missile over Saudi Arabia, another falling on Israel, the others in the sea. Hussein had carried out his threat to try to drag Israel into the war. He was not playing by the rules. Even if it could be argued that aggression and violence were genetically inherent, wars are always explained in terms of rules, values, beliefs, ideals. A war is socially constructed out of speculations and what can and cannot be said about it. It is perhaps the paradigm case of the product of forbidden discourses in the age of modern mass communications.

In an article reporting from Dhahran (*Independent*, 19 January 1991) Robert Fiske reminded his readers that 'Winston Churchill ... spoke of the need for a nation at war to surround itself with "a bodyguard of lies"' or, the preferred term of diplomacy, misinformation. Fiske provided examples:

> When they talk in front of the cameras, American air force and Marine pilots speak comfortingly of the accuracy of their waves of

air strikes over Iraq and Kuwait. Off camera, when the notebooks have been put away and the recorders switched off, they acknowledge that perhaps only a third of president Saddam's Scud batteries – estimated as 200 by intelligence officers – have actually been destroyed and that may be an unwitting exaggeration.

Knightley (1989) has charted the role of the war correspondent since 1854 when William Howard Russell reported the Crimea war in terms of 'Hero, Propagandist and Myth Maker' pointing out 'that since armies fight as people think, it is essential to control that thought' (p. 434). During the Falklands War 'no correspondents other than the British were allowed to accompany the task force; there was no room for neutrals' (p. 434). Indeed, even these had to be accredited. As for the Gulf War, since so many nations were involved other approaches to control coverage were taken. Lessons had been learnt from the coverage of the Vietnam War as the *New York Times* (4 January 1991) noted: 'Televised images of combat in Vietnam helped to build opposition to the war in the United States.' Consequently, the article reported:

> Under the Pentagon's plan, combat operations in the gulf would be covered by specifically designated 'pools' of print and broadcast journalists, subject to tight restrictions. Pool members would have to remain with military escorts at all times, and all interviews with servicemen and women would be on the record.

On 8 January the *New York Times* reported that a further requirement had been made by the Pentagon, 'that military censors review all reports before they are disseminated'.

The emotional impact on the American people of the news that war had started was captured by Barron in a front page article (*New York Times*, 17 January 1991):

> In one long moment yesterday, word that the United States had attacked Baghdad swept the country.
>
> In split-level suburban homes on the East Coast where dinner was in the oven, in big-city restaurants in the mid-west where bars were jammed with the happy-hour crowd and in sky-scraper offices on the West Coast where people were still at work, there was an odd mixture of apprehension, sadness and relief.

> In malls, shoppers emptied out of stores and cried. In supermarkets, cashiers rushed to call relatives and share the news that after five months of waiting and wondering America was at war.

The whole of the United States is imagined here as one community, sharing the same feelings. In the images selected to represent both geographically distinct and occupationally distinct individuals the unstated text of nationalism unifies them with the phrase 'America was at war'. There was then a single national purpose.

In further 'educating' this purpose horror stories have to be generated because 'They affect votes in both the Security Council and the Conference on Security and Cooperation in Europe by altering the mind-set of an electorate who would never dream of reading a UN resolution. They establish the conditions which make it possible to be involved in a war' (Waldron, 1992, reporting John MacArthur, publisher of *Harpers* magazine and author of a book on the Gulf War, *Second Front*). Indeed, a public relations company, Hill and Knowlton promoted a 'Dead Kuwaiti Babies' story which later proved dubious. The story relied heavily on an eye witness who testified to the Congressional Human Rights Caucus:

> The 'eye-witness' was subsequently revealed to be the daughter of the Kuwaiti ambassador to Washington who had been 'told' about the killings by witnesses who have never since been produced.
>
> 'If this had been known at the time,' John Edward Potter, senior Republican on the caucus said, 'she would have not been allowed to testify'. But the story of the story was not published until January this year, nine months after the end of Desert Storm.

What were they fighting for?

As John Simpson (1991) pointed out, 'For Britain, the United States and the West generally, the war against Iraq is essentially a police action. There is no threat to our national life or our political system'. Were there higher values at stake? Noam Chomsky, addressing the annual conference of the Catholic Institute of international Relations, castigated the claims by President Bush that America was fighting to maintain the new world order. Rather it was to protect the old vested interests of business elites who saw oil 'as "our resource", as if the fact that it is located in foreign countries is merely a "geographical accident"' (*Independent*, 19 January 1991).

He made comparisons with other situations where the West did not leap to the defence of an oppressed people.

Protests around the world were shown during news reports with snatches from speeches focusing on America's self-interest. Alternative views were aired in late night talks and in the 'quality' press a few articles still argued for peace negotiations.

Before the outbreak of fighting, John Diamond in the *Daily Mirror* (15 January 1991) asked his readers to imagine being a politician asked by the parents of a young man killed in action, what exactly their son had died for. If it was to rid the world of a frightening regime then 'why has Britain not gone to war to deal with the equally iniquitous regimes in a dozen other countries?' It could not be to protect the sovereignty of countries: America had invaded Grenada and Panama; China had annexed Tibet; the USSR entered Afghanistan. Most ironic of all, Russia during the course of the Gulf War was in the process of suppressing Lithuania. Real debate had left the political scene. The front page of the *Daily Mirror* that day was split in half. The top half showed 'The Heroes' – two colour portraits, one of a young soldier, the other of a veteran RAF pilot; the lower half, 'The Villain'.

To the tabloid press in general, it was a simple case of heroes and villains. On the day that war broke out, the *Sun* had given over the whole of the front page to a Union Jack having at its centre the face of a young soldier, symbolically closing all further debate. That evening the fighting started. By the weekend, the tabloids were full of stories and stunning colour pictures of the machine might of the Allied forces with its 'pin point bombing'. Each paper provided pictures and drawings of the technology involved or as the *Daily Mail* (19 January 1991) called it, 'The sci-fi war that defies imagination'. The film *Top Gun* provided the imagery for the American pilots. The pin-up girls in the *Sun* and the *Star* sported the imagery of uniforms. On Saturday the *Sun* included two pages of colour pictures of girls willing to write to 'our boys'. Wives and mothers tearfully spoke of their menfolk at war. These papers with the largest share of the readership provided no opening for debate, no sense that before hostilities opened the UK was divided about the wisdom of going to war. Television coverage was overwhelmingly the repetition of what little real news there was together with endless discussion of options, strategies and guesses of who will do what next. However, the simple hero–villain imagery became muddied with the possibility of Israel entering the battle. Neither Syria nor Egypt could countenance fighting on the same side as the Israelis. The complex levels and flows of sympathies and allegiances in the Arab world could not be easily tidied away.

During one of the night-time broadcasts on 17–18 January John Pilger, a veteran war journalist, reminded his questioner that a journalist's duty was to represent a range of views, to seek out alternative sources of information, and to present the reality of what was happening. By the weekend, however, it was reported that four out of five people in the USA supported the war, 'elated by the early success' (ITN 9.45 *News* Saturday, 19 January). Britain too, had moved in its attitudes with opinion poles in the weekend press revealing 80 per cent in favour of the decision to fight. War cannot afford debate. The success proclaimed in the press was clearly having its effect upon opinion.

VIOLENCE: NATURAL OR UNNATURAL?

Education can only be a temporary amelioration rather than a solution, if violence is essential to human nature. Freud considered people to be fundamentally aggressive: 'man is a wolf to man' (1963 edition, p. 48). Through the 'successful' Oedipalisation of the child by the family, one could at least hope to contain the aggressions. However, for Freud the inner violence of the individual always threatens to tear society apart. As in Hobbes' (1651) 'war of all against all', where only the power of some central authority holds society together, Freud does not see people lightly giving up 'the satisfaction of this inclination to aggression' (p. 51). Within this Freudian perspective, the violence of the passions against the father, indeed, against all, is the forbidden discourse at the heart of traditional discourse concerning the civilised values of respect for authority. Looking at modern world history, the world wars, Korea, Vietnam, Cambodia, the fascist regimes of South America, the racism and dictatorships in Africa, the fundamentalist wars of the Middle East and so on, it is hard to contradict Freud, that at the heart of civilised, polite conversation is the Oedipalised forbidden discourse of violence. It is the battle of Eros and Thanatos; the Life instincts and the Death instincts. To Freud, it was at best an open question as to who would win.

Yet, it is possible to find tribal communities which have lived at peace for centuries, perhaps millenia, with rare outbreaks of violence for centuries, perhaps millennia (Montagu 1978). The continued existence of these communities suggest that violence is more learnt than innate (Fromm 1974). If that is the case, then the boundaries and the contents of the forbidden are shifted. Non-violence and peaceful organisation become the forbidden discourse in a society which is underpinned by the beliefs, institutions and ideology of violence. The discourse of violence, then, is not the natural outcome of inherent violent urges, but must be continually constructed and re-constructed through the vocabulary and imagery of aggression, revenge and war.

Peace studies in schools as an alternative to the traditional histories of wars came under attack by the government in the UK during the 1980s as indoctrination, rating with the Campaign for Nuclear Disarmament as a source of subversion. During the Gulf War CND together with some Labour party MPs and other socialists marched in protest, pointing to the doomsday scenario waiting to be unleashed in the form of nuclear, chemical and biological weaponry. The unthinkable, in the war debate, is the thought of total destruction and the atrocities of wars won or lost on the one hand; and on the other, the silenced cry for peace. Both peace studies and anti-nuclear movements bring these to attention. The marches for peace during the Gulf War recalled the great marches against the bomb and against the Vietnam War. John Pilger on 17 January during a Channel 4 discussion, made the comment that issues at a variety of moral, political and emotional levels were in play, one being that psychologically, America was re-fighting the Vietnam war, but this time to win. Similarly, from the rhetoric of the British press, it could have been argued that Britain was reliving the 'glory' of the Second World War. Certainly, it was widely reported during the first week of the Gulf War that Saddam Hussein was confident of victory because of his 'reading of history' – that a modern democracy could not sustain a long war, as America's experience in the Vietnam War seemed to demonstrate.

The Vietnam War, like all wars, left a powerful cultural imprint, worked and re-worked through a thousand war films. The sedimentation of popular cultural imagery that had accumulated was expressed in the run up to and during the course of the Gulf War: appeasement, Hitler, Rambo, Desert Rats, the Few, Top Gun, Star Wars, Saddam Busters (Ghost Busters – a popular film of the 1980s). Each image calls into mind a story, an event, with its emotions, its implied moral positions and its dramatis personae. One of the clearest expressions of the process of how 'storying' touches the life of the individual is by Ted Hughes, writing generally about how stories are experienced, understood and used:

> If the story is learnt well, so that all its parts can be seen at a glance, as if we looked through a window into it, then that story has become like the complicated hinterland of a single word. It has become a word. Any fragment of the story serves as the "word" by which the whole story's electrical circuit is switched into consciousness, and all its light and power brought to bear.
>
> As a rather extreme example, take the story of Christ. No matter what point of that story we touch, the whole story hits us. If we mention the Nativity, or the miracle of the loaves and fishes, or Lazarus, or the Crucifixion, the voltage and inner brightness of the whole story is instantly there. A single word of reference is enough – just as you need to touch the power-line with only the tip of your finger.
>
> (Ted Hughes, *Times Educational Supplement*, 1 September 1977)

The word not only becomes a sign of the whole but provides a sense of looking through it as looking through a window into a landscape. Following Hughes' metaphor, the whole exists like the electric circuit; that is, all the structural or logical relations necessary to make the circuit of electricity work are already in force. Similarly, the grammatical relations of language are already given before any one individual speaks. Finally, a similar structure exists when a particular narrative is well known, like Sleeping Beauty, or Beauty and the Beast, or the conquest of the American West. So, when the Ravena housewife expressed her support for the National Guard who killed defenceless students at the Kent State University, she utilised this same process of selecting words which stood for, or switched on, the electrical circuit of the national myths of god and country and the protection of the home from villains. She did not intend to draw upon the Oedipus myth, yet the structural relations of this myth were fundamental to her expression of support for the deadly action of the National Guard in killing the rebellious children. Examining the letter more closely, there are two kinds of discourse here and contained within each, a multiplicity of others. Crudely, take the two broad viewpoints contained in the letter: Ravena housewife and student protesters. The two viewpoints arise in mutual conflict – and the conflict is deadly. To see them together in this mutual bond of conflict is to see them ironically. They, perhaps, would see themselves as mutually exclusive, each working for the defeat of the other. From the one viewpoint the other is a forbidden discourse. The protesters offend the housewife's principles of good citizenship, which are in turn founded upon what she considers to be proper conduct for children. The housewife in turn offends against the student's principles of the right to protest. To see their indissolvable ironic relation – that too is forbidden, and the strength of the forbiddenness is seen in the outcome. The same feelings, principles and discourse was again voiced during the Gulf War. The storying does its work.

The assertion to good citizenship, and the assertion to protest cannot be made without the possibility of either. The realm of the forbidden is always deeply ironic for its contents must, at some point, be always personally desired and socially determined. That is to say, in Hughes' terms, the forbidden discourse with its ironic structure is at the social level like the electrical circuitry and at the level of personal action like the desire or impulse to touch the power cable which switches on the system – and shocks. Re-writing history to include the sources of protest, the challenges to the dominant interests is the urgent task of education, not only in peace time, but most importantly during war. At the centre of the re-writing is the individual. It is a re-writing which recovers from the 'experts' responsibility, critical thinking and decision-making in which the discourse of peace may replace the discourse which constructs war as 'natural' or 'inevitable'.

WOUNDING INDIVIDUALITY

The rewriting of history has no foundation without the recovery of the self's biography and in biography the enquiry as to whether individuality, in the form of creatively expressive, reflective and critical thinking, has meaning. All wars are fought by individuals. They do their job. Their biographies differ but the mythologies, the popular culture that invades their lives is interconnected, intertextual. At every level, however, individuality is wounded, its uniqueness violated. This violation is the basis for all socially constructed violence (Schostak 1986).

At one level, there is no problem with the definition of 'individual'. Ordinarily, it is taken to mean the singular individual. However, upon closer inquiry, there is the problematic uniqueness experienced concerning one's self: the 'my-ness' of experience. This 'my-ness' is closed off from public experience, and hence objective scrutiny. 'I' cannot experience 'your' experiences as 'you' cannot experience 'mine'. As Ortega y Gasset (1957) describes it, we live lives that are non-transferable (p. 46). In this way, we are different from the dead singularity of a grain of sand or for that matter the dead universality of a mathematical abstraction. It is a uniqueness that is at once the essence of human life and the horror of its finality. Violence, in the last analysis, is always personal, uniquely felt, its horror is 'mine'. Violence is a personal violation. It arises when individuality is wounded by others, by the demands of institutions, by the impersonality of the structures of society. Consider in this context the discourse of a fifteen-year-old girl in a unit for children considered 'maladjusted'. She talked of her temper as a problem. 'I want to stop it if I could but I can't see how I can':

> *Carol:* People out there that can turn round, you know, [and say] 'control your temper' and things like that 'cos (...) and I've only been like this about three years ago, since we left my dad I've been like this.
> *J.F.S.:* Since leaving your dad?
> *Carol:* Yeah, think me dad made me like it. 'Cos I lived with me dad. He beat me up an' everything. Just turned me vicious to everybody then because of what he *done* to me. I can't stop myself being ...(inaudible due to outside noises).
>
> (Schostak 1986: 124)

Although this is only a brief extract from a larger case study, it can be used as a key into the whole case study. Carol, in her few words here, presents not an arbitrary association of words but a connected set of associations which point like signposts towards further, as yet, unspecified associations. She speaks of her dad and this, in association with the facts that he left the family, that he beat her, connects in our cultural experience with a range of further associations with 'violent fathers', 'broken homes', 'child abuse'. According to Carlson (1984) there are about 3.3 million children who witness violence between their parents annually. Connect this with child abuse, with bullying at school or in the streets, with the normal patterns of violent discipline (slaps, canings, shouts and threats) at home and school, racial and sexual discrimination and a cultural of violation begins to build up with a structural continuity or parallel from one extreme to the other. Each incident calls up the imagery associated with other incidents in the development of a violent imagination.

There is thus, at every level, an 'inter-textuality' by which the text of one script refers to the texts of other scripts and makes sense in the light of other scripts or, more generally, other signifying systems: the youth and adult focused media, the comics, the teenage magazines, the music press, the pop videos, the TV soaps and the TV-video-film market in general. However, there is no simple straightforward way in which an onlooker, a professional (teacher, social worker, police officer and so on) or Carol can read her life into, or from, such a repository of stories.

Carol's personal history has to be re-discovered. Her rage, like that of so many millions of damaged people around the world is real. All around her, and us, are the powerful mirrors of violence directing her rage and our rage towards the simple heroes and villains of the media, a structure which seems to set the world straight. Underneath, her personal imagery, like that of many, however, evokes not a mirror leaving her whole to face the world, but one that fragments her experiences, crushes them – her world is more like the kind of reflections formed through broken mirrors. She sees herself as, in some part, a representation of her father, expressing this through her inability to control her temper: we can set up the mirroring strategy easily enough. It becomes an explanation. And Carol is trapped, already scarred, aggressive. To recover her personal history for protest, for renewal, for growth is an educational journey as yet unwritten. Yet, it begins here with her, with individuals who feel violated. This is the single greatest educational challenge in the promotion of self-assertion and the defeat of the discourse of violence.

9

THE THATCHER YEARS:
No Turning Back

The 1980s will be remembered in Britain, if not the world, as the Thatcher decade. Whether the years will be remembered as making a permanent change in the political and social life of the country remains to be seen. During the decade itself there was considerable talk about the idea that politics would never be the same again. At the same time, the decade was promoted as a return to traditional values, in particular, Victorian values. The avowed purposes were to eradicate socialism, undo the supposed damage of the permissive 1960s, abandon Keynsian economics and return to the classic market conditions supposedly assumed in monetarist theories. To do this required a re-schooling in the old values, a re-shaping of the economic and social structures to make a better, fitter course of life where Britain would reassume its rightful role in the world, a role lost because of socialist and wet liberal ways.

There is little doubt that for everyone, the decade of the 1980s is personified in the face, the voice and the handbag of Margaret Thatcher. She was often portrayed as a stern headmistress, or an equally stern nanny, lecturing the population, her cabinet, or her foreign ministers. To the extent that politics attempts to change attitudes, beliefs, conduct, knowledge, its purposes if not its methods and its results are educational. To achieve its purposes it constructs a curriculum consisting of political texts and discourses in order to influence the ways people reflect upon their experience, mark the difference between the reality, illusion, truth and falsity, establish social and cultural values, promote desired conduct and justify action. I have elsewhere defined a curriculum, at its most general, as a course of reflection upon experience, of expression and of action (Schostak 1983, 1988). Curriculum derives from Latin roots meaning to run, and chariot racing. It conjures the image of racing round a course. One is either forced on such a course, or one takes up the reins of one's own destiny, choosing one's own course. Continuing the metaphor, the course has a material structure that guides and supports directions. There is an audience to watch the winners and losers. There are prizes to be won. There are reputations, bets, investments at stake. To train for the course requires a spirit of competition, a dedication to a purpose. The mind has to be trained to reflect upon the improvement of performance, to learn appropriate ways of doing things.

Through reflection upon experience, the imaginative grasp of possibility and the formation of action plans, each individual constructs a life course from the economic, social, and cultural opportunities that are either made available to them, or grasped by them. Changes in political, social and economic organisation directly affect the realisation of opportunity. Some groups of individuals are positioned into privileged locations to use resources in order to make their opportunities real. Others find that the resources for similar opportunities are beyond their grasp. A political curriculum can be defined as one that promotes the knowledge, beliefs and forms of conduct appropriate to the organisation of resources intended to realise courses of action that are, in turn, supposed to result in the 'good life'.

Any curriculum can be criticised from an educational perspective. Education, as I use the term, is a perspective capable of critiquing social and cultural practices. It has to do with the ways people reflect upon, critique, learn from experience and express themselves to represent their experience. As such it must always be capable of suspending the taken for granted, peering beyond the boundaries and confronting the forbidden in the exploration of and creation of new possibilities. Political beliefs, however, limit the possibilities to establish particular ways of life for particular purposes. The political role of the major public institutions – schools, media, churches, business enterprises, health, the forces of law and order – is to handle the images, the possibilities for action, the desire, the anger and the pain of everyday living. Education, therefore, reflects upon political action, critiquing the limitations imposed, while keeping open the possibility of new horizons for human cultural expression and action. Where a particular political orthodoxy may claim 'there is no alternative', education maintains 'there is always an alternative'.

THE POLITICS OF 'NO TURNING BACK'

On the day after Thatcher was forced to resign, the *Sun's* cartoon on page 6, by Franklin, showed 'Maggie' lined up on a pedestal with other great military and war leaders of the past – Nelson, Wellington,

Churchill, Monty. She is in the centre, twice the size of the rest, grinning, handbag hanging from her arm. The caption reads 'among the greatest'. It consists of the imagery of domination, of a person surrounded by pygmies. The editorial of the *Sun* described her virtues as:

> **Honesty. Principle. Vision. Stubborn courage. Sheer guts. She displayed all the qualities this country rightly prizes most of all.**

The situations before and after coming to power are then summarily contrasted. Before there was 'stinking rubbish' in the streets, seen as 'a visible symbol of industrial power' that defeated the preceding Labour and Tory governments. Then there was 'the Thatcher Revolution' which:

> ROLLED BACK the frontiers of the State, returning to people control over their own destiny.
> ROUTED the once-invincible Arthur Scargill, destroying the ability of the big industrial unions to hold the country to ransom.
> FREED the great State industries one by one.
> SLASHED the controls that bedevilled private enterprise.
> CUT taxation again and again.

In caricature-like form this outlined the political agenda of the 1980s. It is a curriculum with the avowed aim of 'returning to people control over their own destiny'. This was accomplished, it was claimed, by removing obstructions to people's freedom that socialism and wet liberalism had constructed. Yet it had been a government that had increased centralisation, maintained the highest levels of post-war unemployment, and increased wealth inequality. Despite this, the left was unable to gain an image of sufficient credibility to win during the 1980s, nor sufficient credibility to win in 1992 against Major during the longest recession since the 1930s. In effect, a sufficiently powerful counter-curriculum did not emerge.

Any curriculum distinguishes what it claims as knowledge from ignorance, acceptable social values from those that are unacceptable, and the means of achieving them. However, a particular political curriculum has to be accepted as representative of social reality and people's interests before it begins to dominate other possible curricula. The broad post-war political consensus formed such a curriculum, defining acceptable economic and social values, aims and strategies.

Despite winning the 1979 election, there was at that point no guarantee that the Thatcher curriculum would prove acceptable to sufficient numbers to bring about changes in the course of life. In fact, before the Falklands War Thatcher's government was proving to be the most unpopular since the Second World War. By 1983 she was a triumphant war leader, the opposition was split between the Labour Party and the new Alliance and the government was returned to power with an increased majority. In particular, according to Butler and Kavanagh (1988: 6):

> in each year since 1981 there was a steady rise in the living standards of those in work. Surveys regularly showed large majorities expressing the wish for more money to be spent on welfare services, even if this entailed an increase in taxation. Yet when asked what mattered to themselves and their families, more public spending or tax cuts, a majority preferred the tax cuts.
> (Marplan, March 1987)

Such a split appeared again in the 1992 election where in the end the fear of tax increases if Labour were elected was exploited by the Tories under Major. The electorate can be split into distinct categories. As implied in the above, there were 'those in work' as against 'those not in work', or 'those whose income increased substantially' as opposed to those whose income either did not increase or even fell. There were those who required public welfare services and those who did not; and so on. Each such category, however defined, represented a distinct audience having different needs, values, interests and opportunities. To win power, it was not necessary to satisfy each category. A political text can be constructed that targets appropriate audiences and manages discourses in order to mark one possible interpretation of events as 'true' and others as 'false' or forbidden. Thatcher, as the 'Iron Lady', spoke of her resoluteness in the face of adversity. For her, no matter how rough things became, 'this lady is not for turning', there was 'no turning back' to the bad old days of the post-war consensus. If the population became discontented then the problem was not the policies but in trying to 'get the message across', of ensuring that the right interpretation was placed upon events.

The role of Bernard Ingham, Thatcher's press secretary, has long been recognised in 'leaking', 'smearing', 'marginalising' colleagues, providing disinformation and managing the interpretations that the press place upon statements and events. The *Sunday Correspondent* (11

February 1990) described him as a 'spin doctor', one of those 'men, who through bullying or flattery, seek to put the best gloss on the day's news'. This, together with a Conservative-dominated press and attacks upon the BBC, promoted the view that a new era had been reached: the classless society, or at least one in which the old classes were in decline. Thus, there was the need for new forms of organisation, a view which many even in the left accepted.

Trade union activity even among many trade unionists after the defeat of the miners in 1985 began to be seen as 'doomed', or outmoded, like the dinosaurs. This, however, is not to say that rhetoric alone can sustain power. As German (1990) argued, the general rhetoric of an economic miracle and a transformed political scene was composed of little more than illusions which were 'rudely shattered in early 1990' at the introduction of the poll tax. By late 1990, before the resignation of Thatcher, the economic recession had disrupted illusions of any sustainable economic miracle, tensions were increasing and discontent was being voiced from industrialists as much as from the government's opponents. Nevertheless, for a period the illusion was sustained by apparently real economic results. These results had been achieved, in part, by fixing the figures. As pointed out by Peter Jenkins, 'in order to bring British living standards up to those of West Germany it would be necessary to grow by 1 per cent faster than the European economies for some 30 years' (1987). The economic buoyancy that did occur was created largely through a credit boom engineered by Lawson, together with a manipulation of statistics such as the frequent changes to the way in which unemployment figures were collected, and a dogged repetition that more was being spent and more freedom was being delivered in every sphere of life, the rhetoric involved always rejoicing in the positive and overlooking the negative.

There were many who did do well out of Thatcherism, who could feel its benefits. Mostly these were the 50 per cent who own 93 per cent of all wealth (CSO 1990). Thus:

> Recent studies all underline a growing gap between rich and poor. While living standards rose 23 percent in real terms between 1979 and 1987, this rise was not equally distributed. The income of the lowest 10 percent saw virtually no rise. For many within that bracket this means a fall in living standards. The income of the poorer half of the population has increased overall by 10 percent. But their share of total income has gone down from around a third to

below 30 percent for the first time since the war. At the same time the incomes of the top 1 per cent have risen by 80 per cent.

The rhetoric of economic miracle arose as a necessary reward, diverting attention from and defusing in the minds of the winners the realities of the hardship and pain experienced by the manufacturing sectors, the poor and the unemployed. The new information technologies which boomed during the first half of the 1980s in the domestic market provided another dimension to the rhetoric. During the first half of the 1980s western economies were facing a crisis in the world market system, and information technologies were seen to be a solution (Schiller 1986). In Britain the government saw the silicon industries and the financial services of the city as the main areas for economic growth. The old heavy industries were seen as a drain upon public resources. The resulting sharp recession of the early 1980s due to the rundown of the major industries, saw unemployment rising to its highest level since the great depression of the 1920s and 30s.

It was in the management of the rhetoric of unemployment that the control of knowledge and ignorance could be seen at its clearest. In July 1982 unemployment was 3,190,621. At 13.4 per cent of the working population this was the highest since records began. During the summer of riots in 1981 there was a continuous rhetorical attack by the right against any notion that unemployment or poverty was to blame; Peregrine Worsthorne in the *Sunday Telegraph* (12 July 1981) used the then current right-wing demonology to press the claim that 'Unemployment is NOT to blame':

> All sections of society today are dangerously prone to lawless violence, and it is the merest cant to blame Mrs Thatcher for a development which is social, even spiritual, rather than economic. When the miners besieged the Saltley coke depot in 1972, under the leadership of Arthur Scargill, driving the police from the streets by brute force, was this because of their material suffering? Then, as now, the miners were the aristocrats of labour, rioting for privilege, not against injustice.

The tactic was to shift attention. Thus Teddy Taylor, Tory MP, exclaimed through the pages of the *Sunday Express* on the same day: 'Violence has soared. Vandalism has become endemic' therefore 'we must impose tough and nasty penalties on vandals, arsonists and looters caught in the act and found guilty by the courts.'

A second strategy for defusing the perception of unemployment as an evil was systematically to undermine the basis upon which those statistics were collected. There were multiple changes in the ways in which unemployment statistics were collected; each successive change excluded groups of people from the categories of the officially unemployed. The *Sunday Observer* (24 July 1983) examined the changes and revealed that by adding back those who had been removed the figures would increase by an extra 900,000 at that time. No real comparison between the unemployment figures for 1990 can be made with those of 1980. By redefining unemployment the problem could be reduced. By abandoning any commitment to full employment and making unemployment appear natural, monetarist economics effectively took unemployment off the political agenda and replaced it with inflation.

Since the mass of the unemployed, disproportionately in the northern parts of the UK, were likely to be labour voters they could be ignored when considering political strategy. A similar argument could be applied to the issue of poverty. However, poverty pricks the conscience and the discomfort caused has to be defused. Since there were accusations that the richest were profiting from the Thatcher years at the expense of the poorest, the definition of poverty became an issue. During a discussion on poverty in the summer of 1986, the government argued that the supplementary benefit was not the poverty line despite having been broadly accepted as a measure of the numbers in poverty. They showed a rise from 'six million in 1979 to 8.8 million in 1983' (Frank Field in the *Guardian*, 4 August 1986). Arguments have centred on the concept of relative poverty. Government ministers refused to accept the concept, preferring to speak of some absolute notion of poverty: because people were not starving to death as in some areas of the Third World, then the term poverty could not be applied in an absolute sense. Alongside this attack upon the notion of poverty was the idea of the 'trickle down' of wealth from the rich to the poorer people: set free the rich, provide them with tax incentives and they will create work. The poor could always be accused of being lazy, of being scroungers, of being spendthrifts. They needed to be educated into living within their budget. If they were unhealthy it was because they smoked too much, or their diet was poor. Thus they needed to be re-educated into healthy living. If they were unemployed, it was because they had the wrong skills and needed re-training. If they were unmarried, it was because of a lack of morals, or because of the irresponsibility of the absconding father, who must be made to pay. A web of reasons drawing upon the prevailing mythologies surrounding poverty are strategically applied to assuage the sense of guilt. And, of course, in the final tactic, justifying changes in the level and categories of benefit, where there is real need, benefit will be targeted so that the needy and not the scroungers get the money.

Another key term throughout the Thatcher era, was 'choice'. People were to be freed from the welfare state and from nationalisation in order to exercise choice. By putting the nationalised industries into private hands the taxpayer would be relieved of the burden of supporting them and would therefore have more money through which to exercise choice. In education people would be able to make choices between schools, though their governors, and parents would be able to choose to opt out of local authority funding. There would be more choice in the health service, as hospitals would also be allowed to 'opt out', control their own budgets and compete with other hospitals. Council house tenants would be able to choose to buy rather than rent their homes. Choice appeared to be everywhere.

Choice has the effect of shifting responsibility and therefore blame. Poverty, lack of success, even poor health, could be blamed upon making wrong choices. Choice has a powerful role in defusing tension, awareness of discrimination, and guilt surrounding privilege. People have the choice. Competition provides choice. However, most products and services delivered by the market are so similar that they are only distinguishable by brand name, thus concealing the real identity of the product. The market for a wide range of products and services is dominated by monopolies or by just a few very large firms in competition with each other. Frequently, real choice is only illusory. Marketing and propaganda set the limits to choice. The role of the market is to coordinate actions, whether as workers or as consumers; its role is to reduce the individual to the mass, and within the mass to prescribable roles. Cities and towns are largely dedicated to the pursuits of the market place. Transport systems predominantly serve the function of ensuring that people get to work and get to shopping centres. A whole lifetime is largely spent in carrying out the duties of work and of consuming. Those with great wealth may choose not to; the rest have no real choice. Few really choose unemployment, or the life of the street. Yet the illusion of real choice is powerful. So long as one accepts the framework of the market place, the freedom to choose when, where and how to spend money provides as much freedom and power as most people want.

If freedom and power are defined by money, then people are, in the main, coordinated by the mechanisms that control the flow of money. If enough people experience freedom and power defined in terms of money, then those who have little or no money (and thus little or no freedom and power) can be ignored or be made the subject of charity, thus promoting another freedom of the wealthy, the freedom to give. Through such processes real participation is denied while the illusion of participation is maintained. Participation or not even becomes a choice in itself: the essence of freedom, the choice not to participate, the justification of inertia.

MANAGING THE 'REAL'

The images employed in the depiction of events are portrayed to construct the sense of a seamless web of reality tying reader, reporter and event in a chain of valid interpretations and judgements. Photographs, eye-witness accounts, the detailing of 'facts' all render the reportage 'real'. Everyone knows, however, that the sense of the real can be constructed through 'special effects', false reporting and so on. Film-makers spend millions on constructing this sense of realism. Both hide the constructed nature of knowledge. Information is always managed and selectively impacts upon audiences.

When Gareth Peirce, solicitor to the Orgreave miners, wrote her article describing the case in the *Guardian*, a paper considered liberal, with a relatively small readership when compared to the right-wing press of the *Sun*, the *Star*, the *Daily Express*, the *Daily Mail* and others, this was apparently an example of the alternative voice being permitted a hearing. However, it was a voice swamped by the dominant media images, and unlikely to be read by the readership of the right-wing press. The *Guardian* itself is positioned as something to be laughed at, scorned by the tabloid press of which the *Sun* has been the most powerful image creator.

However, despite the predominance of a right-wing press, the government felt aggrieved, in particular, at its treatment by the BBC. Throughout the decade attacks had been made by the government, demanding objectivity and balance, and prosecuting journalists for making revelations. During a discussion on the leadership battle after Thatcher resigned the hard-right Tory MP Norman Tebbit stated that one of the really great achievements of the 1980s was that there was no trade union representative pontificating about things that were not their business (BBC2 *News Night*, 22 November 1990). This was a powerfully revealing statement.

In response to claims made by the right-wing Media Monitoring Unit of political bias by news journalists against the conservatives, the BBC was reported to have held a confidential investigation into its interviewing techniques (*Sunday Correspondent*, 18 February 1990). The article reported that an IBA survey claiming that '27 per cent said the BBC was biased towards the Conservative party and 9 per cent said it was biased towards Labour'. On the same day the *Observer* reported the story as: 'The BBC is worried that Government Ministers have learned to outsmart their top newsmen, according to secret minutes of a high-level corporation meeting.' This article went on to illustrate tactics employed by the ministers. One was choosing the time at which to be interviewed: for Radio 4's *Today* programme, it was claimed 'some will agree only to be interviewed at 7.50am, knowing they have a full five minutes before the weather forecast. They refuse to go on at 7.52am, realising that they would get only three minutes' air-time.' Another tactic is '"synthetic indignation" if they think the interviewer is not being courteous, or if they are filibustering on a sticky wicket'. Moreover, 'Ministers can pick and choose from their invitations to be interviewed.'

There is, of course, another major tactic which relies upon faulty memory, lack of viewer interest in following difficult or protracted arguments, and the fact that the past can always be reinvented and reinterpreted for a multiplicity of purposes. It is very difficult in the short time-slots allotted to interviewers and interviewees on news programmes to carry out any detailed analysis, to call up evidence from a variety of sources providing immediate checks on the use of 'facts' and statistics, or to re-run previous statements to check emphasis and the exact words employed (although slow-motion replays are a feature of most sports programmes). Interviewees can reinterpret questions, provide alternative stresses and slants on previous statements, and deny having said or meant anything. The past, under such circumstances, is always deniable. The strategy of feigned indignation is frequently employed against any who have the temerity to point out the implications flowing from an unguarded assertion.

There are a number of ways in which the appearance of viewer or reader control can be constructed. Newspapers print letters to the editor, and carry out surveys where 'you can have your say'. Similarly, on television there are shows like *Right of Reply*, or *Comment* where viewers are able to write in or even speak on the air giving their views. There may be 'phone-ins', or shows with audience participation. There are shows like *Question Time* and *Cross Question* where selected members of the audience are allowed to ask questions of a panel of politicians or other 'experts'. In this way, 'having your own opinion', 'having a say' is made possible. It seems to show democracy at work, allowing and sustaining the variety of opinions. However, these are highly managed occasions. Shows like *Question Time* firmly control the direction of debate, allowing little time for the development of arguments, particularly from members of the audience who are asked for their 'opinion'. They are situations where it is difficult to call upon evidence. There is no facility for checking facts or drawing upon data bases to test assertions. By keeping all argument within the realm of 'giving your opinion', rational debate is limited and action constrained. If evidence is limited, then personalities take over: abrasiveness, wit, charm, fill the gap.

THE MANAGEMENT OF DESIRE, TERROR AND HORROR

As discussed in Chapter 2, it is the family that regulates the conflicting sexual feelings, identifications and expressions. Through the image of the family possible readings are controlled into two groups: those containing comfortable arrangement for the conflicts and contradictions; and those creating discomfort. Returning to the *Sun's* glorification of Thatcher on the day after her resignation, pages 6 and 7 employed the comfortable range of sexual readings to enmesh the reader's desire. Directly opposite the large cartoon of the warrior Thatcher with her handbag, the greatest hero of heroes, is a large, virtually half-page, photo of a naked, seated twenty-three-year-old woman holding, just below her breasts, a rosette symbolising political allegiance as 'the sort of candidate who could unite any party'. Directly above this is the main headline, 'GUTLESS TRAITORS', followed by the subheading 'Maggie's daughter lashes Tories'. The main images coalesce to provide: mother, daughter, mistress alongside the cartoon which positions her as the dominant figure among male warrior heroes. At different levels of attack (sexual, maternal, familial, martial, patriotic) messages are being coordinated towards 'Maggie' and all that she symbolises for the *Sun* and against her betrayers in the Tory party and her enemies: the left, the unions and foreign aggressors. The apparent contradictions between Thatcher leading the party of the family with its moral implications concerning pin-ups, the salacious covering of rapes, the sexual misdemeanours of the famous, and violence, are fused into the safe imagery of these two pages.

Subliminal seduction is the the term given by Key (1973: 58, 59) to the use of imagery to package products, persons and institutions:

> In the mass media of communication, the preoccupation with love and death symbolism is apparent in every newspaper, magazine, and television programme. Genital symbolism is universally used in the media, though rarely recognised by the audience as such. Commonly used phallic symbolism includes neckties, arrows, flagpoles, automobiles, rockets, pencils, cigars and cigarettes, candles, broomsticks, snakes, trees, cannons, pens – the list is endless ... Death, or the fear of death, underlies virtually all the symbols of state, authority, governments, political parties, military, commercial, and social institutions.

Politics is fundamentally about the sexualisation and the re-sexualisation of the body, its expressions and its world, whether in play or work, to unify purposes and actions. Underlying the political project of sexualisation is the horror of difference, of the other, of the beyond symbolised as death, of the dissolution of the prevailing order. This is behind the imagery of the fear of communism, the fear of 'gays', the fear of the 'dangerous classes' symbolised for the Tories in the riots, crime statistics and trade union actions of the 1980s. For Thatcher, overcoming these fears and perceived dangers required 'getting rid of socialism' (*Independent*, 24 November 1986) with the help of her 'spin doctors' and the infra-structure of media allies, big business and the secret state as discussed in Chapter 6.

Socialism was seen as weakening people, taking away their initiative, rendering them dependent. Ministers talked of getting rid of the dependency culture that had built up under the welfare state. No longer were people to think they had a job due to the power of the unions. People were to be set free to look after themselves, to be small shareholders in the increasing numbers of de-nationalised industries. The problems in the nationalised industries, in the health service, in education, were all to be solved by the market. To the faithful the defeat of Thatcher at the hands of her own party was a tragedy. The *Daily Express* presented its tribute with a cartoon of Thatcher as Britannia with shield and trident and lying beside her, a tearful lion. It likened the day of her resignation with the day that

President Kennedy was killed: all would remember where they were at the time. It celebrated her achievements:

> Mrs Thatcher presided over radical change. She threw off the suffocating shackles of socialism and union power. She created a climate in which ever increasing numbers of Britons owned their own homes and 400,000 launched their own businesses. She taught us that our destiny was in our own hands, not that of a bureaucratic nanny-state. She taught us that the Government has no money: The funds at its disposal are taken in tax from your wallet and purse.
>
> And on the international stage, together with President Reagan, she confronted the soulless, totalitarian dictatorships of Eastern Europe. She brought the old tyrants of communism to their knees. She helped their people see they could be free. And now they are free. (*Daily Express*, 23 November 1990)

There was no mention of the record levels of unemployment that had been achieved during the Thatcher years, the devastation of manufacturing industry, the increase in the gap between the richest and the poorest, the increase in homelessness, the demoralisation that had occurred in the caring professions: nursing, teaching, social work. Nowhere was there provided any conceivable reason for her to be removed. Yet she was removed, dramatically. With a resignation speech by the then deputy prime minister, Geoffrey Howe, all the resentments that had built up over the years were unleashed and the process of challenging Thatcher from inside her own party began. The day after that speech all the press recognised it for what it was. The *Daily Mail* summed it up as 'SIR GEOFFREY THE ASSASSIN' (14 November 1990). This was to be the death and betrayal of 'the greatest peacetime prime minister this century'. The *Mail*'s political cartoon showed a giant pair of high-heeled shoes outside of 10 Downing Street with the three leadership contenders anxiously looking at them – 'Who's big enough?' (23 November 1990).

The events of the decade and of the leadership battles at its end were firmly placed into familiar narratives. There is the narrative of the great leader, strong, virile, who triumphs over the fearful monsters that threaten the peace and security of the realm. She had battled the all-enveloping monster of the welfare state; against it she had reasserted the time-honoured male virtues of competition, survival of the fittest, and had made Britain a respected nation in the world: Maggie in male warrior mode rather than nanny. The overwhelming horror was that in socialism's ideal of egality there would be the loss of difference, the threat of being absorbed into the all-providing, all-suffocating womb. In the imagery of the Tory press this is connected with the real tortures and terrors of Eastern block socialism rather than the totalitarian puppet states supported by Western military and business interests. Socialism, in the imagery associated with it, represented the fall of manhood, the castration by the indifferent womb which cast all down as equals, without difference, without privilege, without the virility of individualism. With the fall of Eastern block regimes, all credits were heaped upon Thatcher by the right-wing press. Indeed, at the Tory Party Conference during the summer of 1990, representative after representative from the new emerging states in the East were presented on stage to pay tribute.

Through the management of news – particularly through the role of the press officer Bernard Ingham – the narcissistic echo was created which re-presented the images of success, of military might, of triumph in the face of adversity. But in her fall, just as in the myth of Narcissus, it all proved finally beyond grasp.

There is, then, at another level in political consciousness, the narrative of betrayal within the innermost family. The sons overthrew the leader, the symbolic father. It is an Oedipal story filled with further narratives by the fact that the symbolic father is a woman: a she-man who combined with powerful effect the business-like imagery of the authority of the male – often described as the only real man in the cabinet – with the national imagery of Britannia being 'like Boadicea with the Romans, scything her chariot through (the trade union) ranks with four massive pieces of legislation' (*Daily Mail*, 23 November 1990). The double imagery had been recognised in the attempts by the image-makers to make her seem more feminine, to soften her appearance and her tone of voice; but also to ensure that she was associated with Churchillian and warrior-like imagery.

The she-man as a phenomenon in film has been discussed by Straayer (1990), commenting that 'Ironically, women had to declare/display their own active libidos through male clothing', or in the case of Thatcher, through male imagery. This male imagery was well captured by the harsh, cigar-smoking, business-suited puppet in TV's satirical *Spitting Image*. Following the logic of mythic imagery, the woman steals the phallus.

It is this image that was the love-object of her followers. The cabinet was shuffled and re-shuffled to reflect the correct image.

Each minister was chosen to reflect the chosen line, to speak with the same voice, to act the same deed. If in the imagery she was the man, then each could be said to be identified with her in terms of the missing part in themselves. In the logic of the myth, the spectacle presented for all was a symbolic castration, recoverable only through an internal possession, through the obsessive adulation of the iconography of Thatcher.

For those who could not follow her blindly, the political castration of the many ministers and 'Tory wets' throughout the era was real. They were cast-off, sent into the wilderness, powerless to influence. Those who remained but disagreed were equally powerless to influence, as revealed in the resentment caused by the lack of cabinet discussion which eventually led to Howe's speech of resignation as deputy prime minister. At her resignation, there was panic amongst the faithful. Would the forces that had been vanquished now rise?

The media faithful to her campaigned for her chosen successor – John Major – against Heseltine who was seen as one who would undo all the work. On the wider political scene, Thatcher and the government were at their lowest in the opinion polls. With her gone, the picture was transformed with leads as much as 16 per cent being recorded for the Tories depending upon which candidate for leadership they chose. Coincidence or not, no woman was elevated to enter the new cabinet under John Major.

These are the narratives of political life and the stuff of political thrillers, horror movies and fantasies recycling the fight between the good empire and the evil empire. The myths continually reconstruct the need for rescuers to fight the monsters. The media, throughout the Thatcher era, has sold to its public a political spectacle with all the ingredients of the myths underlying political and personal life. But at her resignation, the myths are simply renewed and recycled for the new conditions. The dominant myths of the social order are played out at a variety of levels to the viewing public each level reaffirming the essential emotional, social and political logics of society.

The underlying terror and horror which marks out the boundaries between order and disorder is deployed in fantasy through the violent thriller and horror genres in popular culture. This does the work at the level of fantasy that the mass news media organises at the level of 'reality' as it represents the horrors of natural disasters, terrorist attacks, random killings and rapes. This underlying horror has to be defused in ways which sustain the sense of the normal, the sense that despite apparent senselessness, reason, courage and faith prevail. Yet, the defusion can never be made complete, rather it is diffused, always there to gather again into real horrors. Thus, the imperative always to be on guard. The panics are recycled and sold again with new heroes replacing the old.

MAKING UP ONE'S OWN MIND

If asked, most people would claim to be uninfluenced by the media: they simply read the facts and make up their own minds. The myth of making up one's own mind is reinforced by all opinion moulders. It was clear in the media campaigns to influence the general elections; it was equally true in the fusing of emotion, fear, thrill and patriotism in the management of opinion during the course of the Gulf War.

First, Miller in *New Statesman and Society* (26 October 1990) reported on the British Election Campaign Study on the influence on voting behaviour of the major national newspapers. The difficulty has always been that people tend to choose newspapers that reflect their political views. It was found a year before the election in 1987 that labour readers chose the *Guardian* or the *Daily Mirror*; conservatives went for the *Daily Express*, *Mail* and *Telegraph*; but *Sun* and *Star* readers were the least interested in politics and least likely to watch the 'highbrow' news programmes. This market differentiation is important in the strategy of de/fusion. It allows the targeting of paradigmatic narratives and the relative closure of possible readings by castigating or vilifying aberrant positions. The conclusion was that:

> The influence of the tabloid press was particularly strong on the uncommitted. Among party supporters, the Conservative lead never increased by more than 10 per cent, irrespective of what paper they read; but, among relatively uncommitted voters, it increased by 28 per cent among *Express/Mail* readers and 50 per cent among *Sun/Star* readers. In sharp contrast, there was no drift to the Conservatives among uncommitted *Mirror* readers.

In 1992 it was again a matter of debate whether the tabloid press influenced the vote. The *Sun* was in no doubt; it was they 'wot won it'. As MacArthur commented:

> If newspapers aren't powerful, why did the Tory tabloid editors devote so many columns to hammering Kinnock throughout the campaign?
>
> Why, if newspapers aren't powerful, were 31% of the reports in the three Tory tabloids on April 9 negative about the Labour party compared with a score of 8% against the Tories, according to a study by European Information Technology? Why did The Sun devote eight pages to the Nightmare on Kinnock Street if its editor didn't think it would sway votes?
>
> (*Sunday Times*, 24 April 1992)

Finally, MacArthur quoted a Mori analysis that 'enough Sun voters changed their minds on election day, when 45% voted Tory, compared with 36% who intended to vote Tory earlier that week, to tilt 12 of the 17 most marginal seats to the Tories'.

Winning an election has a lot to do with marketing strategy, identifying target populations of relatively uncommitted voters and giving them what they want, with the object of associating these desires with politically structured explanations. A comparable media onslaught occurred in the reporting of the Gulf War.

THE COURSE OF LIFE: A REASON TO DIE

If people are to die, reasons have to be given. Meaningless death is unacceptable, the ultimate horror. Of political importance, therefore, is to provide good, clear reasons to die: to make death meaningful. If there is room for doubt or for confusion the certainties fall apart. This was very much the concern expressed during the ITV broadcast *War in the Gulf* (19 January 1991) presented by Brian Walden. The issue was framed within the context of opinion polls of British, American and French support (all at, or close to, 80 per cent for the war), suggesting that there was a feeling that this was a just war. This was followed by clips of Vietnam where film of civilian and child casualties helped to foment anti-war sentiment. The message that democracies could not sustain long wars could not be drawn, the documentary argued, because it was not the casualties but the lack of commitment that led to the final withdrawal. When there was commitment, the will was there. In support of this, clips from the First World War, the Second World War and the Falklands War were shown.

The initial strategy of the broadcast, therefore, was to set the Gulf War within a selective historical framework, calling on the images of resoluteness, pride and patriotism revealed in the clips from previous wars. The Vietnam War was made to be a different kind. The fears that people doubted the reasons for the war or were confused were briefly explored from the point of view of an American talk-show host. The discussions that followed with a sample selected by a market research group picked up these issues, showing the diversity of views. Next, clips were shown of Bush and other politicians presenting a confusing variety of reasons for going to war. Finally, a discussion took place between two politicians, David Howe (Conservative) and Gerald Kaufman (Labour). Howe set the context primarily within the context of not letting aggressors get away with aggression, else the price later would be much higher – a lesson from the 1930s. Secondly, he turned to the fundamental importance of oil for world economic growth, ultimately bringing prosperity to the underdeveloped nations. Saddam Hussein should therefore be stopped from seizing and using this resource for evil ends. Kaufman agreed that Hussein's objective was oil but disagreed that it was Britain's aim. He focused attention on the authority of the United Nations. Here there would be a worthy moral aim. It was not a war fought only for oil but for the development of a new world order under the authority of the United Nations. This, then, provided a rational aim capable of defusing rational doubts.

Such a programme presented issues and doubts under a gloss of rational debate, carefully structured, appealing to a certain kind of audience, impressed by its 'scientific' approach. The larger audiences represented by the daily tabloid press had no such gloss of rationality. Employing all the techniques already discussed, dissenters were firmly marginalised, set into the stock dramatis personae of heroes and villains, fools and clowns. The majority of the Gulf coverage in all the tabloids revelled in triumph and emotional stories of tearful mums, wives and girlfriends. The *Sun*, 19 January 1991, amidst the celebratory images gave space to 'Kick out Fanatic Muslims', who were 'praying for Saddam to win'; to an article on Iraqi warplanes being 'saved from the Allies' air attack by bunkers built by two-faced BELGIANS'; and a tiny note on page 6 proclaiming, 'TV too even-handed' in its coverage. Within the structure of heroism and treachery, doubt simply disperses, as challenge and even a balance of views are rendered unpatriotic.

THE VALUE OF THE COURSE

A curriculum ends in the distribution of values. What is the value to society of a human being? What is the function of society in relationship to each individual? A society that aims towards full employment places a different value on the individual to one that aims for low inflation. As Norman Lamont, Chancellor of the Exchequer in the Major government put it, unemployment is a 'price worth paying'. In 1992, despite all the changes to the ways in which the figures are constructed, employment steadily increased. In July the figures reached 2.75 million, but 'The true total is nearer four million when account is taken of about one million people excluded by 32 changes in the way the count has been calculated since 1979' (Mike Edwards, the *Observer*, 12 July 1992). In addition a further 450,000 on various government training schemes had also been excluded. Piachaud (*Guardian*, 4 March 1992) compared average unemployment for four decades:

1950s:	338,000
1960s:	459,000
1970s:	976,000
1980s:	2,714,000

Even the massaged figures of the 1980s cannot disguise the results of a change in social values regarding full employment. In a BBC2 broadcast in the *Pandora's Box* series in June 1992, Professor Alan Budd, who advised the government, was shown wondering whether policy-makers had deliberately created unemployment, saying he 'has a nightmare' that 'raising unemployment was a way of reducing the strength of the working classes'. Thus 'what was engineered, in Marxist terms, was a crisis in capitalism, which recreated a reserve army of labour, and has allowed capitalists to make high profits ever since'.

With business failures rising daily and unemployment set to remain high to the end of the century, crime creates an alternative course of action to achieve value in life. The *Guardian* (17 August 1992) estimated crime as the fourth largest industry, with a turnover of £14 billion, employing 130,000 police officers, 50,000 civilian staff, 34,200 prison officers, 10,000 staff in magistrates courts, 2,000 in crown courts, 175,000 security industry personnel, 1,200 barristers, 69,000 solicitors doing criminal practice, and of course, the professional criminals themselves. When individuals can imagine no other response to the conditions of life than crime then the dominant political curriculum fails to provide the means of imagining and realising a community capable of mutual regard and support. Education must challenge the limited imaginings of current politics.

10

THE EDUCATION OF ACTION

The first step to change begins in imagining alternatives. Mass education was feared at its introduction because of its power to put ideas into people's minds. The works of imagination are feared because they open the mind to the possible, the images of desire and the bizarre creations of nightmares. Education and imagination together create the imagined communities that provide identity, belonging, self-value and purpose. However, a distinction must be maintained with schooling. Where schooling moulds and fashions belief, education, through a playful suspension of disbelief, opens up the imagination for reflection, and experimentation. In the imagination there are other faces of the self, other forms of conduct appropriate to the new face, other dramatis personae and the new possibilities for action and relationship that go with the new worlds of experience.

In general, the process of education, as conceived here involves a suspension of hierarchy between people, groups and in the forms of cultural expression. Every age has its favoured forms of expression. It requires a break with those forms to represent new experiences, new imaginings. This process, however, is de-stabilising. The ethical framework, principles and procedures of educational processes and action are critical where personal and social structures are placed in question. The attitude of play in education is a way of handling the uncertainties underlying any process of reformulation and reconstruction. Education plays with the relations between self and others, beginning first with the imagined world of the family and ending in transformations of the imagined communities that constrain subjectivity and the possibility of action.

RESTRUCTURING THE FAMILY AND SUBJECTIVITY

Education is not a mere add-on but directly plays with the forms of the self, its public and covert, its permissible and forbidden representations. These forms draw from the stock of paradigmatic narratives in the framing of courses of life as key elements of the forms for living. In the family the self is sexualised, the realm of the imaginary fused with the prevailing moral orders. It is here that the reformation begins. There is a great deal at stake in making transformations to the imagined structure of the family. At its heart is the transformation of society to meet new needs, new aspirations, new possibilities.

Reconstructing the family is not a new idea. Rabine (1989) has described a radical attempt by the 'Saint-Simonians' in France in the nineteenth century. The movement under Saint-Simon promoted a doctrine of economic socialism. After his death in 1825, the new leader, Enfantin, transformed the doctrine 'in which the emancipation of women played a minor role, into a romantic-socialist doctrine that would seek to build a new order cemented by bonds of love rather than greed and exploitation' (p. 37). Early capitalism, Rabine argues, could not satisfy the desires it had aroused and Enfantin appealed to these unconscious desires by offering 'a new liberating form of religion and a new liberated form of the family, both governed by a new sexual morality' which 'placed women at its centre' (p. 38). Enfantin became the father and at first wanted to place a real woman as the mother. As this did not work, he 'recreated her as an absence, a mystic "Femme Messie," whose coming the sons of the Saint-Simonian family were to desire with great fervour' (p. 38). The absent woman could thus become the object of the true quest:

> Enfantin transposed the desires that structure romantic fiction into a theory of social action, and so succeeded in making utopian socialism into a popular movement. The trajectory of the split, alienated hero of romantic novels, questing a mirror-woman who can unify and complete him, becomes with the Saint-Simonians the search for a transcendent, erotic 'Mother' who will liberate them. (p. 39)

It was, as Rabine argues, in effect a re-writing of the Oedipal relations of the family. She sees similarities with psychoanalytic discourse in its post-structuralist form 'in that it valorizes the devalued, marginalized term of the symbolic structure: for the Saint-Simonians, sentiment, love, harmony, woman: for the Lacanians, the disruptive margin at the outside of phallocentrism, the Other, the feminine' (p. 39).

Rewriting social relationships gives a different value to individuals, groups, communities. What was once marginalised may be lifted to prominence. In effect, a new text is created through which self and other are represented to each other and through which a new community is imagined. It is an approach which attempts to supplant the older vision of community. An alternative approach involves re-experiencing current social realities as strange, by 'causing trouble'. This is a method practised by Garfinkel (1967) in his social experiments. One approach is to adopt an attitude like that of a scientist, but applying it in the context of ordinary polite conversation. The attitude jars with what is expected and causes trouble. By causing trouble, the unstated restraining structures or rules of social conduct, he argued, would be manifested. In this way the 'unwritten' text, consisting of taken-for-granted rules, knowledge, understandings, values, comes to be made explicit. Making the unwritten explicit renders it open to critical reflection and releases the potential for change. As an example of his approach to the study of social structures Garfinkel would ask his students to act on arriving home as if they were total strangers, always needing to ask permission, or ask instructions about how to handle familiar situations. Or, upon being greeted by an acquaintance in the street, instead of providing the usual ritual replies to the question 'Hello how are you?' to respond by requesting further information as to what the question meant 'Do you mean how am I in my health, or my financial situation, or my sex life or …' In causing trouble through ritual performances, the taken-for-granted rules of behaviour and of conversation were immediately revealed. Frequently the responses were dramatic, even violent. This, however, is simply a specialised use of a general phenomenon. Feminism, anti-racism, the assertion of human rights or of individuality can all have the effect of disturbing what is expected or taken for granted as normal in the dominant culture, thus revealing the underlying taboos, the hidden constraints, the gaps in explanations. In such a way, what has been hidden, forbidden, or left unremarked can be made explicit for re-evaluation, criticism, debate, and can be made open to change. What was once dirty, unmentionable, swept out of sight can be re-valued in new texts.

Through imaginative expression new possibilities can be worked out in the form of thought experiments, raising issues that would not otherwise be raised. Feminist Utopian novels have presented futuristic portrayals of possible worlds in which are explored 'ideas about different types of social structure other than based on the nuclear family; about alternative priorities to those of capitalism; about different approaches to technology and its uses and, crucially, about the erosion of gender stereotypes' (Vincent 1986: 19). At another level, feminists have begun to construct their own fairytales or versions of fairytales (Zipes 1985). The creating of futures and the materials of imaginative life in raising new agendas brings a re-exploration of subjectivity itself.

Imagination is already conditioned by the historical and biographical constitution of subjectivity. In order to find empowerment, therefore, work has to take place directly upon and within the sense of the self. Haug (1987) and the group with whom she worked recovered their biographies as women through a process of 'memory work', as a form of social scientific method involving a 'search ... for possible indications of how we have participated actively in the formation of our own past experience'. It is a process which has implications for the relation between subject and object in research methods. Memory work sets up subject and object as 'one and the same person':

> Even notions of 'subject' and 'object' had to be problematized in our work, amongst other reasons because they posit both as fixed and knowable entities, neither of which is subject to change. Since what interests us is the human potential for liberation, we conceived of human beings in collective and co-operative terms. However, enchanted we may have been by princes and other fairytale heroes whose great deeds – often no more than a kiss at the right moment – release the spellbound from their chains we were none the less determined to strip these dreams of their tempting character, and instead to rehearse the painful lesson that liberation is dependent upon liberation of the self. Our intervention is itself an act of liberation. (p. 35)

Haug's group re-called the sexualisation of their bodies. This involved focusing upon bodily sites through which aspects of gender had been constructed in their lives: the legs, the hair, the form of the body itself; and the development of particular themes such as the slave-girl project. These led to the construction of narrative materials as the basis for group reflection, discussion and critique. The method is compatible with the construction and educational use of paradigmatic narratives elaborated in connection with the course of life, a process to be further developed in the latter half of this chapter.

Such examples of de-constructing, re-imagining, re-valuing, and re-forming are deliberate, specialised and accessible by only relatively small committed readerships (or action groups). The issue of the preconditions for wider accessibility is crucial if such educational initiatives and actions are to be productive, given that schools do not necessarily provide a good or appropriate institutional context.

POPULAR CULTURE AND THE RE-WORKING OF SUBJECTIVITY

Is the agenda of popular culture changing? Feminist and anti-racist discourse has clearly worked its way into popular culture through news and entertainment genres. The reactions of 'moral-right' and narrow-minded conservatism have made that clear. The right-wing claim of the emergence of a 'classless society' – a centrepiece of John Major's election to Prime Minister after the resignation of Margaret Thatcher – is an attempt to defuse legitimate claims for equal participation and the fair distribution of opportunities and reward. The cry is 'any one can make it, look at me.' Anyone who does not make it must either be lazy, untalented or have had bad luck. What results in the media is a kind of oscillation. The minority 'high-brow slots' contain debate and often real investigation at the margins of the viewing audience. The broadcasts of mass popular appeal vacillate in their responses, often providing ambiguous pictures.

The challenges to subjectivity made through the conflicts and contests of alternative discourses can be seen in TV and film portrayals of the family and the institutions of the world. Many commentators have claimed that male subjectivity is undergoing a confusion of identity, portraying men as not knowing what women expect of them while portraying women as able to play their new roles, easily able to adopt male imagery in the business world while expressing themselves also in more traditional female roles. Margaret Thatcher, for many, symbolised the woman able to adopt male roles, parade male imagery whilst also deploying female roles and attitudes (jewellery attractively arranged, flirtatious fluttering of eyelids during television interviews, display of housewifely handbag during the early election campaigns to underscore metonymically a simplistic housekeeping view of national economics).

The popular notion of a sex war between feminists and 'men', provides good copy for newspapers. In the magazine of the *Sunday Times* (9 December 1990) Neil Lyndon opened for the men, stating that 'something ruinous and evil has happened between men and women' and explaining that women now routinely make contemptuous remarks about men, that there are many forms of discrimination against men: different retirement ages, discrimination in pensions. Kate Saunder (*Sunday Times*, 16 December 1990) replied for the women. The tone adopted was 'Gosh, those poor little dears' and a number of women in the publishing and political fields were drawn in to add their comments. The obvious discrimination against women in work and politics was sketched and a couple of sexist comments unleashed. For example, in response to Lyndon's claim that the penis was under-researched in comparison with female sexual organs:

> Carmen Callil, the director of the publisher Chatto and Windus, is initially more sympathetic. 'I thought it was rather tragic about the penis being under researched, whereas the womb basks in all that attention.' But she goes on to ruin the effect with great whoops of mirth: 'I laughed and laughed. There must be something wrong with him – perhaps the size?'
>
> Yes poor old Lyndon was quite right about the feminine talent for making sexist remarks. Many of the women I canvassed felt there had to be a personal reason for his diatribe. Clare Short thinks he may be 'unhappy and insecure in his maleness'. And nine out of ten asked if Lyndon's wife had left him.

This sense of battle has its basis in the real structures of power. Men still dominate the public stage of work and politics.

Television sitcoms and soaps have responded to the changing views but not in a uniform manner. *Wonder Years* follows the adventures of a thirteen-year-old boy growing up in the mid 1960s. It is home centred, safe, but 'it's hard struggling for manhood when your Mom weighs fifty pounds more than you.' It is a nostalgic look back to the kind of home where Mom and Dad have their respective undisputed roles and young boys dream of girls and try to assert their manhood. Its virtual opposite is *Roseanne*. She is loud, strong and rules the home. Relations between herself, her husband and her children are enacted with a barbed humour, both subversive yet reinforcing the strength and closeness of the family. Probyn (1990) sees the changing fashions of the last two decades as a move from 'new traditionalism' to 'post feminism':

> In many ways these homes correspond to different visions of generations of feminism, a sort of 'vulgarization' of feminist

> discourses. Thus, underlying *Who's the Boss?* is the seventies liberal feminism insisting on women's rights to equality of employment; underneath *Wonder Years* lies Betty Friedan's articulation of the suburban home housing the 'problem which has no name'; *Roseanne* updates the seventies line and gives the wife and mother all power: economic, social as well as affective control over her family; and then with *thirtysomething* we have a post-feminist vision of the home to which women have 'freely' chosen to return.

It is difficult to consider any of these a thorough rewriting of the old scripts. They are rather more like updating old pop songs for new audiences. The new household contains the same old economic structures. Women have written themselves in as equal players with men in the same old games of power and exploitation.

Mr Mum, a film made in 1983, provides a mediocre example of the role-reversal genre. The husband loses his job, his wife gets a job. He is shown first as incompetent in such housewifely situations as the supermarket, and doing the housework. Then he becomes demoralised, grows a beard, wears the same old shirt for two weeks, watches too much soap opera. He quarrels with his wife over this after she returns from work. In his demoralised state he has a soap-opera style daydream of an attractive neighbour seducing him, his wife finding them kissing, and shooting him. Immediately he returns to a disciplined sense of self, quasi-militaristic in making sure the kids get up early for school, and in the management of house. He thus becomes the good housekeeper with a sense of pride in doing a worthwhile job. Finally, after each are tempted by an adulterous relationship which neither accept, they return to a normal household as the husband is offered his job back. There was never a real question of the husband preventing his wife from working. The values of independence were accepted but finally undercut in the return to the *status quo*. There was a sense of competition, which the man needed to win, but not an out-and-out sex war, merely a conservative account of the temptations and suspicions that may be released.

Capital City, a series about financial dealers, placed women and men on apparently equal terms. In one broadcast the issue of one of the main characters entering into a lesbian relationship was raised, in other broadcasts an on-going relationship between a married woman in an open marriage and one of the unmarried dealers was developed. Ethical investment was also raised as an issue on a number of occasions, in relation to the support of firms involved in questionable deals and activities likely to pollute or exploit. Such issues were raised in a way which rarely involved more than a light critique of the market solution, yet nevertheless raised real issues. So, has there been a real destabilisation of the old verities, has the old agenda taken a real knock?

As if in answer, the *Daily Mail* (2 January 1991) gave front page prominence to the television 'chief watchdog' (chairman of the Broadcasting Standards Council) Lord Rees-Mogg's comments on the 'children of the Sixties who make programmes in which they impose their permissive values on viewers'. Examples which had upset viewers, according to the BSC's director, were: 'a scene in the BBC's *East Enders* in which two homosexuals exchanged a kiss, a lesbian scene from *Capital City*, the BBC2 drama *Oranges are Not the Only Fruit*, describing a passionate affair between two adolescents, and *Portrait of a Marriage*, about the love affair of Vita Sackville-West and Violet Trefusis'. The battleground is very much the family where, according to the article, 'In ordinary family life the balance was imposed by what the mother would allow in the home.' Power in the family may be changing due to challenges to awareness but it is clear that the real rights of children scarcely exist except in the form of rights to be protected. Rights over economic matters, sexual freedom, freedom of movement and so on do not exist in the same way as for adults (Holt 1974 ; Freeman 1983). Earlier chapters have focused upon the ways in which agendas can be defused and suppressed. Nevertheless, there is an oscillation which pervades popular consciousness as people demand more of their rights in society, yet cling to the old constructions of self-identity. This is nowhere more apparent than in the modern form of marriage.

During the latter half of the twentieth century, some have argued, marriages have seemed increasingly open and democratic in response to real changes in subjectivity. However, while a study in Britain by Burgoyne (1990: 662) of how money is handled in marriage revealed a move towards sharing, there was still a bias towards male control. Pooling money did not necessarily remove the psychological sense of ownership. In addition:

> Perceived ownership of earned income also legitimizes a pattern of control which can disadvantage a partner whose contribution is less visible because it is unpaid. This had important implications for women in the event of marital breakdown. Most of the men in the study assumed responsibility for long-term security in the

> form of insurances, investments, etc. This means that dependent women are less likely to develop important financial skills, and, if the relationship ends, they are less likely to benefit from such things as investment in occupational pensions ... Moreover, the (unwarranted) assumption that marriage provides women with financial security can leave them in a very vulnerable position if the marriage breaks down, hence the prevalence of poverty in the case of lone mothers ...

The economic structures that pervade society, placing men in the position of economic power, will inevitably influence marriage relationships unless there is a strong counter-definition of marriage roles and relationships. This entails a deconstruction of the family, which is something many cannot countenance. However, the family is already being opened up and represented in a light which destabilises its old foundations. It is having to respond to real changes in the social agenda. AIDS, the legal recognition of rape in marriage, equal opportunities legislation, homosexual marriage – all contribute to a re-evaluation of sexual relations, sexual practices and gender identities both in the family and in relations at work. There is evidence, then, albeit, fragmentary, incomplete, contradictory, non-systematic and highly conditioned through media-imposed popular culture, that the preconditions for mounting educational challenges are already in emergence. Education works upon the existing conditions, the tensions, the contradictions, the pleasures, the pains, through a play of perspectives in which the alternative agendas for social and cultural action can be constructed, and alternative texts for imagining and representing new communities of relationship developed.

EDUCATIONAL SUBJECTIVITY

The individual's imaginative grasp of the world is composed of the representations of it made by family, friends, school, media and so on. Most of what we know of the world comes from what we are told and from what we read or see mediated by cinema and television. We experience very little of it directly. Our perspective on it is shaped largely, therefore, by powerful imaginative representations of the world, whether these are scientific, works of literature or the folklore, beliefs and anecdotes of everyday life. However, there is no single perspective. In a pluralistic society there are always competing views. The process through which we adopt a perspective, or perspectives, is largely unconscious. Through the everyday processes of socialisation in family, school, peer group, workplace and so on, a perspective on the world is formed and fashioned. It comes to be largely taken for granted, accepted as real or natural without further reflection. The educational moment (Schostak 1989) takes a particular attitude towards such perspectives:

> Perspectives always ask for belief, they set out their criteria for validity, certainty, plausibility and so on. Education exists at that moment when all such perspectives are merely possible; when each one is just a possibility to play with, to vary, to 'see what happens if ...'. The educational moment exists like a hinge from which hang all other possible perspectives. From this hinge all other perspectives are articulated just as a door opens the way into other rooms or domains. In general terms, then, an educational moment is successful and powerful if it opens up alternative possibilities. Each of these possible worlds provides alternative forms through which to cohere a self. And each world is a frame for energies by which the powers of the self to sustain itself emerge. At this hinge-like moment, the self plays with possible worlds and possible self-expressions. Through the play, the consequences of choice are drawn out.

Education elucidates the connections that tie the self to the world, a world grasped in imagination, in ways which increase the power of understanding, control, action and self-expression. The object is to deconstruct, re-frame and analyse who 'I' am and how 'I' relate to the world of others and objects. It is, in the first instance, a work of subjectivity where both the subject and the object of the work are the same thing: the self. The project of the self and the self's relations to others generates its own agenda which ties at many levels to the wider structures and processes of social life. This results in the expansion of the agenda in which the repressed and the silenced is voiced, and the marginalised and dirtied revalued.

A number of 'alternative schools' and practitioners of education can be singled out as pioneering examples. Neill's Summerhill (1973) can be seen as a form of educational action through which children's rights to happiness, to self-determination are placed on the agenda. Bettelheim's Orthogenic school at Chicago worked with the most emotionally and psychologically damaged children, children who were considered a danger to themselves and to others, inverting the traditional views on how to handle such children, placing their needs, their security at the centre of school organisation, removing altogether the surveillance and control mentality of prison-like 'secure homes'. Freire's work in literacy encouraged peasants to re-own their culture, to enable them to step out of the culture of silence and challenge the director society. The socialist, anarchist/libertarian traditions described by Smith (1983) set the traditions of educational action within a long and international history. Each of these initiatives articulated within subjectivity the play of alternative perspectives that had been sealed off from the experience of the child or adult through social conditioning.

A start must be made to take education out of the domain of 'one-off' experiments and accounts by outstanding teachers. Education has so far failed to achieve the status of an independent discipline alongside philosophy, sociology, psychology, as a critical perspective and creative source of expression and action. It has been too firmly tied to schooling as an agency of social control and the delivery of politically constrained curricula. There should not be an area of life and endeavour that escapes the educational perspective: whether personal, national or international. It is not enough for individuals to learn about the wars or the achievements of 'great' people. Education is integral to all the debates concerning war and peace. Political strategy in the absence of educational debate is dangerous. Education is the condition of subjectivity and of intersubjectivity in which freedoms are born and survive.

PRECURSORS TO EDUCATIONAL ACTION

The appropriate beginning to educational action is with the given, the experienced conditions of the self, the construction of its subjectivity and its relations in intersubjectivity, that is, the relations between subjectivities through which shared or sharable and expressible experiences arise and are made public. Through conversation, discussion or critical debate these public experiences may be accorded various degrees of validity, plausibility, reality and so on. Much that is accorded the status of knowledge, of 'reality', of true faith is transmitted as such through the processes of socialisation and enculturation as a child grows up into everyday structures of belief and knowledge which are taken for granted as real and true for all practical purposes unless circumstances arise which compel a rethink.

Aspects of the process of education, the exploration of new possibilities for the self, may arise quite naturally and hardly be recognised as such. For example, Sarland (1991) provides accounts of the relationship between texts and the ways in which they are used in the everyday talk of children at school. He shows first the relationship of the Rambo stories (both novels and movies) to the experiences of young working-class males. They found themselves in the text, found echoes of experiences, of feelings. Rambo, for them, articulated their sense of personal violation. Of more interest are the alternative gender readings made of the texts that boys and girls read. In Sarland's studies the boys valued the macho imagery in Rambo, the hardness, the size of the guns, the action. For the girls, this imagery was 'pathetic', it caused them to laugh, to deflate the exaggerated sexual connotations. For them, the feelings and the character development they read into the stories were of more importance. In such stories, the children were able to position themselves in relation to their own sex, their own social class and their own particular experiences and feelings. With regard to the girls reading the Rambo book (*First Blood* by David Morell, 1972), they were able to read against the grain of the book, construct aberrant readings. Fiction and fantasy are forms which promote the play with aberrant readings and the forbidden elements of desire:

> In expressing desire, fantasy can operate in two ways (according to the different meanings of 'express'): it can *tell of*, manifest or show desire (expression in the sense of portrayal, representation, manifestation, linguistic utterance, mention, description), or it can *expel* desire, when this desire is a disturbing element which threatens cultural order and continuity (expression in the sense of pressing out, squeezing, expulsion, getting rid of something by force). (Jackson 1980: 3–4)

In reading *First Blood* they were locating the sexual imagery within their own lives, forming judgements framed within their own cultural experiences and expressing (expelling) male desire in terms of the deflation of macho pomposity. As such they were reading a text for their own purposes: educating, or drawing out, alternative meanings and in the process reconstructing themselves in relation to the macho perspective and disconnecting the macho imagery from its relationship to guns and power. It is not something new and strange for children to do. They have considerable experience in reading the 'texts' which form the curriculum of everyday life. They must know how to locate themselves, read the intentions of others from the signs they betray or publicly express in their clothes, their conversations, their postures, their gestures. They must be able to make any experience, any text, accountable in relation to their own lives. In the act of reading, something of one's own agenda is found or inserted. This either acts to reinforce already well-established polarisations, or can be employed to promote debate, negotiation, reconstruction.

There is, in general, a need to insert a margin of free space into the constrictions of the prevailing ways of seeing, interpreting and acting in the world. This space may be created through the discourse of struggle and resistance adopted by the oppressed or marginalised. Or it may lead to rebellion or the criminal act by which the social barriers can be broken. It may be a temporary excursion into the misrule through the traditional carnival of May, or the carnival of perception due to altered states of reality. In each case, the agenda is split: one side is written off, the other claims to be the only representative for moral and legal debate. Yet, if the forbidden re-emerges, the circumstances of its re-emergence is strictly controlled; every culture has ways of legitimating or at least overlooking certain forms of its return.

In all cultures substances have been used to alter conscious states of mind and to experience other realities or different levels of personal freedom while social inhibitions are lowered. In a study on youth subcultures and alcohol, one young man believed:

> it brings out your personality. If you go to a party and you get merry and you start joining in with people you've never known before you say 'hello, how're you doing, you alright? Can I buy you a drink and all this stuff.' When you sort of come back, I feel that some of that experience has sort of gone onto your personality, anyway, even when you don't need drinks, you're sort of more open, more extroverted; it brings you self-confidence; you can say 'I can do it with drinks and I can do it without drinks.' It's like a gate, if you like; have a drink, open the gate, and you sort of have a chat, you say 'hello' things you'd never do to a complete stranger. Then when you see the gate close, but you sort of remember it, and you want to go over there again.
>
> (Schostak and Davies 1990a)

Alcohol, like any other drug, is a prop which aids the attainment of a desired state of mind, of experience. The reasons for its use in the literature on drug abuse are many. Most point to a lack in the personality of the individual which the drug in some way helps to fill. It is viewed as a pathology. The dangers associated with drugs are obvious and alcohol, though socially accepted, is one of the most dangerous to health and to public safety. However, the experience of opening up the mind, of the creation of freedoms through reducing social inhibitions, altering perceptions, should not be overlooked either as a valid experience or as an explanation. Typically, if children's experiences with drugs, sexuality, aggression and so on are on the agenda in school they are marked as bad, dirty, mad because of the censorial or moral framework of a kind of paternalistic rationalism which seeks to persuade rather than to listen and learn.

In a study involving young people in a special school, many of whom had experienced drugs, one young man talked eloquently of his glue-sniffing activities, giving a detailed analysis of his experiences. He had learnt how to manage his hallucinations:

> 'you are not really out of your head, you know what you are doing.' And more particularly: 'As long as you got something in your head saying, no, none of this is true, then you are alright. That's the main thing, see that's alright. Because then you can make hallucinations out of it, that's what I sometimes do. If not, they sometimes come to you.' (Schostak 1986: 153)

This was really the first time he had been allowed, in an educational setting, to talk about his experiences. He had been sent to the school because he, like many of the others there, was considered aggressive, stupid and emotionally disturbed.

Posing his own experiences as the agenda for discussion allowed him to take the first steps towards deconstructing his own experiences. He described his imaginative world of experience, gave voice to the alternative perspective that hallucinations provided him in a way that allowed serious debate. This act of debate neither condoned nor censored glue-sniffing. What it did was allow the emergence of the underlying issues, feelings and experiences that had led to the act of glue-sniffing. Many of the children in the school had experienced violations in their own lives which had left them deeply scarred. By turning their own experiences into projects for debate and self-expression, steps were made in which many began to unpick the sense of violation concealed by the scars that left them hardened to the world and disempowered. But these people were only at the special school for a year, two at the most. Though their educational achievements typically improved, often dramatically, for many it was simply too late. The educational process must be integral to their experience of school right from the beginning.

In these examples, we see a combination of 'memory work', of perceptual work and works of expression in both the senses of 'telling of' and 'expelling'. They arise quite naturally in the course of life but not necessarily in ways which fully articulate educational potential and, on occasion, in ways that become self-defeating, even self-destructive. This then raises the issue of intervention.

EDUCATIONAL INTERVENTION

Education is not limited to its traditional or official sphere of action: schools. The practice of psychoanalysis has frequently been discussed in terms of a pedagogy (Rank 1936, 1978 edn). Marketing often talks in terms of 'educating the public awareness' for a particular product. The media, families and churches are considered major institutions of education. Each intervenes in the lives of others. In traditional forms of schooling, intervention is not a problem. Modern mass schooling has been conceived of as an intervention in the lives of others. It is compulsory. Teachers are placed in a custodial role, keeping children in school, controlling what they do. Some do it with care and love, others because it is a job. Education, as has already been discussed, is best distinguished from schooling. Intervention is not as straightforward an issue in education as it is in schooling. If, in education, the self is both subject and object, then intervention robs the self of its subjectivity (in terms of agency), rendering it only an object in submission to the intervention of the other who intervenes. Rather than take each possible arena in which education can take place, I will focus on schools as an illustration of the issue of intervention.

Teachers share the same problem as any parent, psychoanalyst, journalist, politician or social worker: that in wanting to promote educational experiences and full access to information, double-binds develop: education cannot be compelled; responsibility for the safety of others when they experiment and explore cannot be fully withdrawn; necessary skills and information may not be learnt by choice. The occasion for intervention always arises.

In a study (Schostak and Coathup 1991) of the work of a progressive first school, it was precisely these issues that were being confronted. The solution resided in the creation of a culture through which responsibility for conduct and curriculum choices may be expressed and shared by both teachers and children in processes of negotiation. The issue was particularly acute since the children of the study were only four to five years old. As a first mundane example:

> With the younger children clear boundaries between what is or is not permitted are perceived as necessary. The reasons for the boundaries must be rationally communicable:
>
> *Michael*: Can I go to the toilet?
> *Teacher*: Why are you asking?
> *Michael*: So you know where I'm gonna go.
> *Teacher*: So what do you need to tell me?
> *Michael*: That I'm going to the toilet.
> *Teacher*: (To another pupil) What's the matter?
> *Joe*: [Do you have to ask to] go to the toilet?
> *Teacher*: You haven't to ask me. I'm not going to say no you can't go. But he does need to ... tell me where he's going, so I know.
> *Joe*: He's going to the toilet.
> *Teacher*: Fine
>
> The children can go to the toilet as and when they wish but on the condition that they let the teacher know where they are going. It is a compromise between trust and the necessary surveillance of children to ensure safety. In this way children can be inducted towards responsible behaviour. Learning to act responsibly, experiencing being trusted, and being valued can only take place if there are real occasions for choice-making.

Schools start from conditions of constraint and compulsion. There is in schools, as elsewhere, the assumption that all decisions made by the experts are in the best interests of the 'inexpert' or 'the public'. The issue then is to widen the possibilities for choice-making in ways that are progressive, allowing the child to take on more and more responsibility for decision-making not only in matters of conduct but also in academic matters. Equally, for politicians, for journalists and other experts in the public domain the issue is the extent to which they are willing to deconstruct their own authority and powers of decision-making in order to empower 'the mass'.

The negotiation of the curriculum is an approach which has been taken in a wide range of school situations. It is a part of progressive primary school practice where children negotiate a timetable for a day, a week, a term. The negotiation may take the form of 'if you do this, then you can do that'; or it may be more open-ended, drawing upon the current interests of the child, with the teacher acting as a curriculum development consultant: 'if you want to do this, then you'll need to think of "x" and you'll need to know about "y".' Such forms of negotiation typically arise in the form of project work which at once taps a particular interest and integrates a range of curriculum areas. This form of curriculum development means that teachers have to deconstruct their own power in the situation, otherwise the negotiation will be loaded against the students – teachers have to 'come clean' (Boomer 1984).

Empowerment becomes the key term. However, empowerment is not simply about being able to choose between a menu of offerings permitted by the schooling system. It is also about deconstructing what is on offer:

> As a part of liberatory culture, critical teaching challenges the limits on thought and feeling. A critical classroom pushes against the conditioned boundaries of consciousness. The enveloping realm of the routine is extracted from its habitual foundations. When the class examines familiar situations in an unfamiliar way, transcendent changes become possible. Such an animation of consciousness can be formulated as *extraordinarily re-experiencing the ordinary*. This key rubric locates an empowering theory of knowledge in the re-perception of reality. (Shor 1980: 93)

The curriculum becomes the 'everyday' re-perceived and thus re-experienced. Critical teaching is a particular kind of intervention which systematically challenges the given experiences of students. It thus defuses the given unities of perception, of experience, exposing the hidden relations, structural comparisons and underlying processes. The process of empowerment implies that something has to be done to the students to 'raise awareness' or wake them from a kind of uncritical sleep. This may be so. However, a different approach arises more naturally.

Empowerment comes from being able to make, shape and bring about changes in the real world that meet the agenda of interests and needs of the individual. Everyone has to meet their everyday needs. At their most basic there are the needs to have food, shelter, clothing. Poverty in Britain, like other major Western countries, means that many millions of children are frequently deprived in their basic needs. In a study I carried out in a large North of England comprehensive school, unemployment was high in general, poverty widespread. When the children left school in 1982 only about 11 per cent were able to find real jobs (Schostak 1983). In 1990 nothing has changed. There was considerable violence and criminality in the area. It constituted an alternative economy and power structure. Schooling was perceived by a large proportion of the children to have little relevance to their everyday life. Empowerment, in such conditions, means knowing how to make changes in their real circumstances. If school cannot help, many are likely to be attracted to alternative 'teachers'. As well as basic needs there are issues relating to their developing sexuality, the need for friendship, their need for self-esteem. Beyond these, there is a developing idealism, a vision of justice, of how communities and people should be treated. There is curiosity about how things work, why the world is as it is, a need for self-expression through the arts and sciences. In interaction with the social conditions in which they find themselves, these needs, interests and curiosities construct the agenda of everyday living. For each item on the personal agenda a discourse situates the individual in relation to the agenda and the likelihood of achieving it. What can or cannot be done, what can or cannot be said, seen and heard concerning the items on the agenda is already defined by the prevailing forms of the forbidden discourse.

In large areas of schooling, children have little control over what is to be learnt, the manner in which it is learnt, the pace and time of learning. The discourse is the discourse of expertise, not their expertise, but the expertise of others who know what is 'in their best interests'. It is a lesson which generalises throughout life. Politicians act 'in the general good' or 'the public interest'. Businesses act in 'the interests of shareholders' or of consumers. What is silenced, in this discourse of interest, is the empowering expertise of the self to act in one's own best interests. In *Letter to a Teacher* (1969), a member of the school of Barbiana wrote:

> Barbiana, when I arrived, did not seem like a school. No teacher, no desk, no blackboard, no benches. Just big tables, around which we studied and also ate.
>
> There was just one copy of each book. The boys would pile up around it. It was hard to notice that one of them was a bit older and was teaching.
>
> The oldest of these teachers was sixteen. The youngest was twelve, and filled me with admiration. I made up my mind from the start that I, too, was going to teach.

These were children rejected by the Italian school system of the time who wrote a book of their experiences, winning a prize for science in the process. Education and empowerment are inseparable. Without empowerment there is only schooling.

Contemporary schooling is largely incapable of offering an empowering curriculum because that would mean actively engaging with the real conditions of people's lives and with the processes of promoting change. Where it occurs, it is typically in relation to special needs education, with those children who are disaffected (cf. Booth and Coulby 1987, Barrett 1989), or in relation to vocational education (Fiddy 1982) or pastoral care (Schostak 1983). A number of radical teachers have provided insights and have reminded us of children's real needs and social conditions (e.g. Kozol 1967; Stuart 1969; Kohl 1971; Postman and Weingartner 1971; Richmond 1982a, b). There is in Britain a tradition of curriculum development which does place serious world, community and personal issues on the agenda (Stenhouse 1975; MacDonald 1970). From this tradition a teacher research movement, employing the techniques of action research, has developed through which teachers research their own classroom practice in order to meet the educational needs of their students (Elliott 1990). It is a process which in its most educational forms engages students of all ages as co-researchers.

When children are asked to formulate their own agenda in conditions of mutual trust and support, a surprising, sensitive and controversial range of themes and issues can emerge. On one occasion when I asked my student teachers to engage in some action research of their choice, one person decided to interview her nine- to ten-year-old pupils to see what they considered important in their lives. When she reported back to the seminar group she admitted embarrassment and a feeling of inadequacy. They had told her about their experiences with drugs and sex. A lively discussion then took place amongst the seminar group as to whether these were appropriate subjects for school discussion. In the media there are frequent moral panics on underage sex, drinking, access to drugs, arcade gambling, violence. Health education programmes may be funded to tackle the problem. AIDS made such programmes urgent. Yet, all of these evoke powerful double-binds. They are all difficult to talk about in school. Most such programmes seem to fail to meet their targets. Typically they take a preaching tone, or the tone of the expert, delivering information. What is typically missing is real engagement with the circumstances within which decisions to drink, take drugs and so on are made in the life experience of the individual. In a pilot study of the alcohol experiences of young people, an educational process was postulated drawing from the alternative traditions of curriculum development, starting from the accounts people made of their own lives:

> It has been shown that the accounts that people tell of their lives have a structure involving the relations between a *dramatis personae*, the kinds of encounters they make, what is at stake in the encounters for the self, the criteria for decision-making, the decision and the action that is taken. These accounts can be described in terms of a course of reflection and action. The educational act or intervention is to reflect again upon the structure of the account to suspend the inevitability of the course, to raise possible alternatives. By generating the possibility of critical dialogue, accounts and experiences may be shared in ways which begin to undermine the frozen boundaries and category systems which led to the original actions. Such dialogue itself must be open to critical reflection. The rules of dialogue and the actions that follow must be agreed between the participants in order to maintain a spirit of inquiry and support. The process, in summary, involves a number of phases:
>
> **phase 1:** generate a grounded description/re-presentation of everyday experiences
> **phase 2:** formulate the range of issues on individual life agendas
> **phase 3:** establish the rules of dialogical engagement
> **phase 4:** agree forms of curricular inquiry and/or expression
> **phase 5:** agree the principles and procedures of educational action
>
> *return* to phase one for further reflection on phase 5

> The intention is to generate critical feedback cycles promoting reflection upon life experience. The only relevant curriculum material is the individual's own life experience. The task of the pilot study was to show how such material could be generated, how it could be analysed and thus indicate why the mainstream attempts at alcohol education were largely failing to engage young people in real reflection, decision-making and action. In order to reverse the situation, the role of the teacher must be reformulated as a participant, not a moral guardian, in the reflections of individuals upon their own life experiences. (Schostak and Davies 1990)

The forms of inquiry required by this account are discussed more fully elsewhere (Schostak 1986, 1988, 1991). Frankham and Stronach (1990) made similar points in a study of AIDS education. It was found that a play on AIDS was a far more effective focus of discussion than informational presentations. It set the issues in relation to believable characters, situations and personal issues which enabled the audience to make identifications. The aim of health education programmes is to effect changes in the behaviour or attitudes of target populations. The direction is broadly one way: from promoter/teacher to target population. Educational empowerment, however, is not one way. It moves back into the wider social structures and processes.

AN APPROACH TO EMPOWERMENT

For the students of Freire, in the peasant cultures of Latin America, empowerment was through the recovery of their voice as cultural actors through literacy programmes. The conditions in Western democracies are different. However, in Britain there is widespread illiteracy. Channel 4, in a broadcast in 1990, documented the experiences of adults learning to read employing Freire's approach. This led them to express their own experience, inquire into their relationships in the community. By the active recovery of a voice through which to express their own experience, their own agendas, they re-wrote their relationship to others. They were not drawn into the mirrors of others but rather became active in their own production of representations, the development and ownership of their own imagery and imaginations.

Engaging people in their own culture in terms of 'memory work' and imaginative work, was an approach used, for example, in some village schools in Northern Portugal (Schostak, Labbett and Logan 1990). This work involved children developing projects based upon their own needs and interests and the needs and interests of the community. In one case this led to the development of a museum of artefacts of the region. In others it led to the collection of local sayings, stories and a recovery of the local cultural history. In another, it led to a school project on the environmental impact of the construction of a local dam. The children (about five to eight years old) interviewed workers, villagers and construction engineers. In another it led to voicing the fears and hopes of children that had previously been overlooked. By synthesising the approaches so far outlined, a general pattern through which educational action can be developed begins to emerge:

1. Identify the agenda of concerns
Through conversation or interviews, members in the educational relationship produce a list of issues that they are concerned about. This can involve aspects of the *community* or their own *personal* interests or situation.

2. Discuss the agendas of issues
A process of memory-work and of imagination provides the basic material for debate and action.

a. which issues/questions/problems can be categorised together?
b. if there is more than one category, do each of the categories fit together to produce an integrated study of a village, region, or a way of life?
c. what kinds of projects are implied?
d. what would be the purpose of doing a study?
e. how should the study be organised?
f. who should be the audience for what is produced ?

3. Decide how the study is to be organised
Nobody in the educational relationship should be excluded from educational projects. It is here that all must be very aware of group dynamics. The dominant, the ones who seem to have a lot of good ideas, can very easily take over the project, imposing ideas, closing down alternatives before their fruitfulness has been explored. It is a matter of finding strategies of support for all, protecting minority views.

a. what are the different tasks to be accomplished in order to develop the project? These may include for example:

   i. *interviewing*: parents, neighbours, experts, administrators, employers, government officials, politicians, etc.; and recording the interviews.
   ii. *observing* and making an account of for example:
      - social customs
      - traditional or modern ways of working
      - a typical day in the life of a member of the community
   iii. *collecting* artefacts, documents, artwork, songs, proverbs, stories, etc. of the community past and present – collect also the accounts of how these are used, what they mean, etc.
   iv. *illustrating* the theme imaginatively as well as historically by describing, making stories, poems, paintings

4. Identify the potential of the project for social and personal expression
What are the forms of representation? What are the boundaries between what can or cannot be said, revealed and done?
   i. as art, literature, drama, music and so on
   ii. as documentary, history
   iii. as biography
   iv. as social analysis, etc.

5. Discuss the use of the products of the study
Possibilities include:
   a. exhibitions – locally, or to a wider audience
   b. publishing books, articles locally or more widely
   c. contacting the media
   d. computer networking – i.e. transmitting data to others

Such an approach is likely to produce personal and social material that is sensitive and controversial within a community or society. Empowered action strives to reveal, make known, express, make changes. It is inevitably drawn into a political domain and subjected to the processes through which apparent taken-for-granted unities are broken apart to reveal the hidden social processes through which they have been constructed. The members involved are likely to be positioned within the *dramatis personae* of praise and blame of the official or dominant cultures; and their expressions to be made the subject of a range of readings made possible by the alternative cultures and subcultures within the world society. At this point educational action enters the ethical domain in which alternative meanings and actions are deconstructed, discussed and negotiated.

ETHICS OF EDUCATIONAL EMPOWERMENT

It is no longer advisable to take for granted a nineteenth-century moral discourse for the justification of school organisation and teaching relationships. With the move towards information technology environments in education, the principles upon which action within these environments takes place must be rethought. There has recently been some discussion within the UK on the introduction of a Bill of Rights. Against the introduction is the argument that over a period of 1000 years there has been the sophisticated accumulation of case law. Even a Bill of Rights would have to be tested within the courts of law, subjecting it to interpretation and the accumulation of rulings. Through a kind of case lore a list of principles can be postulated to help think about educational processes. Any such list is likely to include at least the following (Schostak 1990):

1. All personal or sensitive information provided in the process of the negotiation of activities will not be made public outside of the negotiation group unless otherwise permitted by the individual or group. As a general rule, in the release of such information, all names of people and places will be anonymised (or fictionalised) unless otherwise negotiated and agreed. That is, a *principle of confidentiality* will underlie all research and educational transactions.

2. A *principle of openness* will underlie all research and educational transactions. This promotes the value of laying bare the underlying agendas, interests, needs, desires, hopes, and so on that motivate, block and either make life worth living or turn it into a nightmare for the individual. It is through openness that the agenda for educational action can be formed. Such openness will be protected by the principle of confidentiality.

3. All actors involved in the research have an equal right to be informed, and to engage in any decision-making directly affecting them. These rights relate to the *principle of empowerment* fundamental to all forms of educational action and research if it is to generate change in a community of actors.

4. All actors have the right to say 'no', the right of reply and the right to have a voice in the affairs of any research or form of action that affects them. These rights refer to the *principle of freedom* fundamental to human rights.

5. All actors have the right to self-expression, initiative and action. This is the *principle of action*. Acts of domination are subjected to the principle of freedom, the right to say 'no'. As a principle which protects the rights of self-expression, it is important to underline the need to protect minority views and the diversity of opinion and forms of cultural conduct.

6. All actors have the right to support. This right refers to the *principle of mutual support*.

Underlying all the principles is the protection of rights of self-expression described in point 5. It is a principle that Bev Labbett, a colleague at the University of East Anglia, recalled as being fundamental in the operation of Lawrence Stenhouse's Humanities Curriculum Project. During discussion, a procedural device was applied by the teacher in the role of the 'neutral chair' to ensure that minority views were allowed to be aired and dominant views challenged. This is a principle that promotes the play of possibility during discussion as a basis for formulating potential courses of action. Too easily, minority perspectives can be suppressed and the educational moment subverted. While the list above may not be exhaustive, it does form a basis for further discussion about how to avoid the abuse of rights and freedoms as research and analysis takes place.

Empowerment goes beyond self-enlightenment. Knowledge is power. And knowledge of other people is power over people. Education which promotes the processes of expression, representation and reconstructive action must be subject to the exercise of ethical principles. In the light of propaganda, surveillance, control and censorship, the rights of expression, privacy and independence of action form the basis of any underlying ethical principles. With other abuses such as torture, both physical and mental, with exploitation and social discrimination the rights to life, safety, equality and dignity are shown to be paramount. These are not exhaustive. Rights that should underlie educational action are explorable within the whole issue of what counts as human rights. All involve returning to people, to individuals, a sense of being empowered in their own right.

In a culture which proclaims itself to be democratic, liberal, a bastion of freedom, empowerment is still a controversial issue. Its institutions – schools, media, churches, families, places of work, the military, the forces of law and order – all adopt a hierarchical pattern modelled on a patriarchal centring of the power to make decisions. In what ways may individuals or groups seek empowerment? And, in what ways may others seek to empower individuals and groups? This is a basic educational issue which, also, is the object of the forbidden discourse of society through which power and access to power is distributed. The major institutions of society contribute to the creation or reproduction of a narcissistic discourse which keeps in play the prevailing ideologically produced moral orders and social structures. Education moves beyond this. Education for empowerment entails developing a discourse with the forbidden in expanding the agenda of debate and the field of action. This is an educational project which challenges narcissistic power structures at every point. It sets into play a reconstructive movement: from surface text, to aberrant readings, to a carnival of the imagination, to a restructuring of the real. The given in everyday life is opened to alternative readings, to a mis-rule of the mind in order to invert, challenge and discover the structures of everyday living. Then in educational action the self, the community and their relations to the wider institutions and processes of society are represented to inform action. Placing on the agenda the forbidden, the silenced components of life, is a risk. It is not, however, a risk that can be avoided in acts of suppression. One way or another, the forbidden returns.

CONCLUSION

The world is an imaginary construction formed out of the multiple representations circulated by family, school, church, media, workplace and so on. It extends beyond our reach; it is populated by billions we will never meet. Yet we grasp it in imagination and say we know it exists, that it is real, that indeed, we know the ways of the world. However, our knowledge of the world is second-, third-, fourth-hand at best. It is fragmentary, contradictory, and largely illusory. Information is managed, manipulated, suppressed. Individuals and their communities are shut out from the arena or real debate and action.

The world in the last decade of the twentieth century is willing and able to unleash worldwide destruction with its chemical, biological and nuclear technology, whether for military or industrial purposes. The images of war, starvation, pollution, exploitation are daily seen by millions who are unable to reach out to help. The apparent televisual power to see everywhere is not complemented by an equal power to act. Instead, leaders, political parties, state and private institutions, aid organisations and so on seek to act on our behalf. How can we learn to act on our own behalf? How can we generate genuine representation of our experiences and beliefs?

Empowerment takes place through revealing and drawing out the lines of construction in the propagandistic; and by refinding one's voice, drawing up the new imagery of the self and the self's relations with others, and re-presenting the repressed and silenced cultural forms. The movement to re-presentation is an educational process. In repressed societies the forms of re-presentation themselves employ the forms of the forbidden discourse, the employment of a double discourse of irony, satire, embedding subversive imagery.

The purpose of education is to expand and enrich human possibilities for expression and action in community. Fundamental to the process is the critical exploration of what cannot be said, seen or done.

The ideal of democracy can be attained only if the contents, the processes and the structures of the forbidden are placed into debate. Educational action provides the way in which to formulate expressive, creative courses of life and social relations. The attitude requires a continual vigilance of the media, the politics of representation, in order to re-frame, and re-own communities in the service of the needs of all groups, not privileging one group over another. This is to re-make the structures of democracy in order to reflect the needs and interests of all, rather than the reflection of minority power interests. The authority structures of leader–led, expert–inexpert, superior–inferior, rich–poor pervert democracy. For democracy to be effective, all its institutions must reflect democratic relations: families, schools, churches, businesses and, above all, political associations. Education is central to this process of democratisation in revealing the hidden patterns of hierarchical authority, of vested interests, of the covert repression of information and the ideological massaging of media representation. Education is not simply a matter for career teachers. Its perspective is that of all who are concerned to liberate, to articulate alternatives, to empower the disenfranchised.

The right to know and to act cannot be separated. Knowledge is not a specialised academic pursuit, it is central to informed action. Politics is not the province of paid specialists, it is the life of all – children, men, women. Democracy should not be a cloak for the powerful few, but the tool through which information is distributed and informed decisions made by all.

REFERENCES

Abramovitz, M. (1991) 'Social Policy in Disarray: The Beleaguered American Family', *Families in Society: The Journal of Contemporary Human Services*, vol. 72, 8, 483–495.

Althusser, L. (1971) 'Ideology and Ideological State Apparatuses' in *Lenin and Philosophy and Other Essays*, New York and London, Monthly Review Press.

Amossy, R. (1986) 'Autobiographies of Movie Stars. Presentation of Self and its Strategies', *Poetics Today*, vol. 7, 4, 673–703.

Anderson, B. (1983) *Imagined Communities. Reflections on the Origin and Spread of Nationalism*, London and New York, Verso.

Aries, P. (1962) *Centuries of Childhood*, London, Cape.

Armstrong, N. and Tennenhouse, L. (eds) (1989) *The Violence of Representation. Literature and the History of Violence*, London and New York, Routledge.

Arnold, M. (1932) *Culture and Anarchy*, Cambridge University Press.

Bakhtin, M. (1973) *Problems of Dostoevsky's Poetics*, tr. by R. W. Rostel, Ann Arbor, Michigan, Ardis.

Ball, S. (1981) *Beachside Comprehensive: A Case Study of Secondary Schooling*, Cambridge University Press.

Barrett, G. (1989) *Disaffection from School? The Early Years*, London and New York, Falmer Press.

Barthes, R. (1967) *Elements of Semiology*, London, Cape.

Barthes, R. (1977) *Image Music Text*. tr. S Heath, London, Fontana.

Berne, E. (1968) *Games People Play: the Psychology of Human Relationships*, Harmondsworth, Penguin.

Berne, E. (1975) *What Do You Say After You Say Hello?*, London, Corgi.

Birdwhistell, R. L. (1973) *Kinesics and Context: Essays on Body-Motion Communication*, Harmondsworth, Penguin.

Boomer, G. (1984) 'Students and the Means of Production: Negotiating the Curriculum', in: J. Schostak and T. Logan, *Pupil Experience*, London and Sydney, Croom Helm.

Booth, W. C. (1974) *A Rhetoric of Irony*, Chicago and London, University of Chicago Press.

Booth, T. and Coulby, D. (eds) (1987) *Producing and Reducing Disaffection. Curricula for All*, Milton Keynes and Philadelphia, Open University Press.

Breines, W. and Gordon, L. (1983) 'The New Scholarship on Family Violence', *Signs: A Journal of Women in Culture and Society*, vol. 8, 3, 490–531.

Brown, N. O. (1966) *Love's Body*, New York, Vintage Books.

Burgoyne, C. B. (1990) 'Money in Marriage: How Patterns of Allocation both Reflect and Conceal Power', *The Sociological Review* vol. 38, 4, 634–65.

Butler, D. and Kavanagh, D. (1988) *The British General Election of 1987*, Basingstoke and London, Macmillan.

Butler, F. (1989) *Skipping Around the World: The Ritual Nature of Folk Rhymes*, Hamden, Library Professional Publications.

Cahill, S. E. (1990) 'Childhood and Public Life: Reaffirming Biographical Divisions', *Social Problems*, vol. 37, 3, 390–402.

Campbell, J. (1964) *The Masks of God: Occidental Mythology*, London, Souvenir Press.

Campbell, J. (1968) *The Hero with a Thousand Faces*, Princeton University Press.

Carlson, B. E. (1984) 'Children's Observations of Interpersonal Violence', in: *Battered Women and their Families: Intervention Strategies and Treatment Programs*, New York, Springer.

Carter, A. (1979) *The Sadean Women, An Exercise in Cultural History*, London, Virago.

Clutterbuck, R. (ed) (1986) *The Future of Political Violence. Destabilisation, Disorder and Terrorism*, Basingstoke, Macmillan.

Cockburn, A. and Cohen, A. (1991) 'The Unnecessary War', in: Brittain, Victoria (ed) *The Gulf Between Us. The Gulf War and Beyond*, London, Virago Press.

Collinson, H. (1989) *Death on Delivery. The Impact of the Arms Trade on the Third World*, London, Campaign Against Arms Trade.

Cooper, D. (1971) *The Death of the Family*, Harmondsworth, Pelican.

Creed, B. (1990) 'Phallic Panic: Male hysteria and *Dead Ringers*', *Screen*, vol. 31, 2, 125–46.

CSO (1990) *Social Trends*, London, HMSO

Dale, R. (1979a) 'From Endorsement to Disintegration: Progressive Education from the Golden Age to the Green Paper', *British Journal of Educational Studies*, vol. xxvii, 3, 191–209.

Dale, R. (1979b) 'Progressive Education and Politics', *British Journal of Educational Studies*, vol. xxvii, 3.

Danto, A. C. (1985) *Narration and Knowledge*, New York, Columbia University Press.

Davies, B. and Harré, R. (1990) 'Positioning: The Discursive Production of Selves', *Journal for the Theory of Social Behaviour*, 20, 1, 43–63.

Davies, R. and Schostak, J. F. (1989) *Final Report: The Culture of Alcohol in Relation to Secondary Age Pupils* CARE University of East Anglia, Norwich, UK, and AERC, London.

de Lauretis, T. (1989) 'The Violence of Rhetoric. Considerations on Representation and Gender', in: Armstrong, N. and Tennenhouse, L. (eds) (1989) *The Violence of Representation. Literature and the History of Violence*, London and New York, Routledge.

De Mause, L. (ed) (1975) *The History of Childhood*, New York, Psychohistory Press (a division of Atcom).

Dewey, J. (1938) *Experience and Education*, New York, Collier.

Doane, M. A. (1989) 'The Economy of Desire: The Commodity Form in/of the Cinema'. *Quarterly Review of Film and Video*, 23–33.

Dorfman, A. (1983) *The Empire's Old Clothes: what the Lone Ranger, Babar and Other Innocent Heroes Do to Our Minds*, London, Pluto.

Douglas, M. (1966) *Purity and Danger. An Analysis of the Concepts of Pollution and Taboo*, London and Boston, ARK edition 1984.

Eckert, C. (1978) 'The Carole Lombard in Macey's Window', *Quarterly Review of Film Studies*, 3, 1, 1–21.

Eco, U. (1979) *The Role of the Reader. Explorations in the Semiotics of Texts*, Bloomington and London, Indiana University Press.

Edelman, M. (1988) *Constructing the Political Spectacle*, Chicago and London, University of Chicago Press.

Eliade, M. (1965) *The Two and the One*, London, Harvill Press.

Elliott, J. (1990) 'Teachers as Researchers: Implications for Supervision and for Teacher Education', *Teaching and Teacher Education*, vol. 6, 1, 1–26.

Ellul, J. (1965) Propaganda. The Formation of Men's Attitudes, New York, Alfred A. Knopf; 1973, New York, Vintage Books, Random House.

Faludi, S. (1991) *Backlash. The Undeclared War Against Women*, London, Chatto and Windus.

Fiddy, R. (ed) (1982) *In Place of Work. Policy and Provision for the Young Unemployed*, Barcombe, Lewes, Falmer Press.

Fiske, J. (1982) *Introduction to Communications Studies*, London, Methuen.

Fiske, J. (1987) *Television Culture*, London and New York, Methuen.

Ford, J. (1969) *Social Class and The Comprehensive School*, London, Routledge Kegan Paul.

Forman, H. J. (1933) *Our Movie Made Children*, New York, Macmillan.

Foucault, M. (1981) 'The Order of Discourse', in: Young, R. *Untying the Text: A Post-Structuralist Reader*, Boston and London, Routledge and Kegan Paul.

Frankham, J. and Stronach, I. (1990) 'Making a Drama out of a Crisis. An Evaluation of the Norfolk Action Against Aids Drama "Love Bites"', CARE University of East Anglia, Norwich, UK.

Freeman, M. D. A. (1983) *The Rights and Wrongs of Children*, London, Francis Pinter.

Freire, P. (1970) *Cultural Action for Freedom*, Harmondsworth, Penguin (published 1972).

Freire, P. (1973) *Education: The Practice of Freedom*, London, Writers and Readers Publishing Cooperative.

Freud, S. (1963 edition, reprinted 1979), *Civilization and its Discontents*, tr. L. Riviere, revised and newly edited by J. Strachey, London, Hogarth Press and the Institute of Psychoanalysis.

Fromm, E. (1974) *The Anatomy of Human Destructiveness*, London, Cape.

Fryer, P. (1984) *Staying Power. The History of Black People in Britain*, London and Sydney, Pluto Press.

Gardner, C. B. (1990) 'Safe Conduct: Women, Crime, and Self in Public Places', *Social Problems*, vol. 37, 3, 311–28.

Garfinkel, H. (1967) *Studies in Ethnomethodology*, Englewood Cliff, NJ, Prentice-Hall.

German, L. (1990) 'The Last Days of Thatcher', *International Socialism*, 48, Autumn.

Glaser, B. G. and Strauss, A. L. (1967) *The Discovery of Grounded Theory. Strategies for Qualitative Research*, Aldine, Atherton.

Goffman, E. (1961) *Asylums*, New York, Anchor.

Goffman, E. (1970) *Strategic Interaction*, Oxford, Basil Blackwell.

Gutzmore, C. (1984) 'Capital, "Black Youth" and Crime', *Race and Class, A Journal for Black and Third World Liberation*, vol. XXV, 2, 13–30.

Hall, S. and Jefferson, T. (eds) (1975) *Resistance through Rituals: Youth subcultures in post-war Britain*, CCCS, London and Melbourne, University of Birmingham and Hutchinson University Library.

Hampton, C. (ed) (1984) *A Radical Reader. The Struggle for Change in England, 1381-1914*, Harmondsworth, Penguin.

Hargreaves, D. H. (1967) *Social Relations in a Secondary School*, London, Routledge and Kegan Paul.

Hartley, J. (1982) *Understanding News*, London and New York, Methuen.

Haug, F. (ed) (1987) *Female Sexualization. A Collective Work of Memory*, tr. E. Carter. London, Verso.

Hayward, P. (1988) 'How ABC Capitalised on Cultural Logic: The Moonlighting Story', *Mediamatic*, vol. 2, 4.

Heer, F. (1974) *Challenge of Youth. Revolutions of Our Time*, London, Weidenfeld and Nicolson.

Herman, E. S. (1982) *The Real Terror Network. Terrorism in Fact and Propaganda*, Boston, South End Press.

Hewison, R. (1990) *Future Tense. A New Art for the Nineties*, London. Methuen.

Hobbes, T. (1651) *Leviathan*, 1914 edition, London, Dent.

Hoch, P. (1979) *White Hero, Black Beast: Racism, Sexism and the Mask of Masculinity*, London, Pluto Press.

Hodge, R. and Tripp, D. (1986) *Children and Television: A Semiotic Approach*, Cambridge, Polity Press.

Holt, J. (1974) *Escape from Childhood: The Needs and Rights of Children*, Harmondsworth, Pelican.

Humphries, S. (1981) *Hooligans or Rebels? An Oral History of Working Class Childhood and Youth 1889-1939*, Oxford, Basil Blackwell.

Hyssen, A. (1989) 'Anselm Kiefer: The Terror of History, the Temptation of Myth', *October*, No. 48, Spring, 25–45.

Itzin, C. (1990) 'Pornography and Civil Liberties', *Index on Censorship*, vol. 19, 9, 12–13.

Ives, J. (1985) 'How to Halt the Battering', *New Society*, 22 November.

Jackson, R. (1980) *Fantasy. The Literature of Subversion*, London and New York, Methuen.

Jed, S. (1989) 'The Scene of Tyranny: Violence and the Humanistic Tradition', in: Armstrong, N. and Tennenhouse, L. (eds) (1989) *The Violence of Representation. Literature and the History of Violence*, London and New York, Routledge.

Jencks, C. (1987) *What is Post-Modern?* Academy Editions, London; St Martin's Press, New York.

Jung, C. G. and Kerenyi, C. (1970) *Introduction to a Science of Mythology. The Myth of the Divine Child and the Mysteries of Eleusis*, tr. R. F. C. Hull, London, Routledge and Kegan Paul.

Kapo, R. (1981) *A Savage Culture. Racism – A Black British View*, London and Melbourne, Quarto Books.

Katz, E. and Liebs, T. (1984) 'Once Upon a Time in Dallas', *Intermedia*, 12:3, 28–32.

Keller, E. F. (1983) 'Gender and Science', *Psychoanalysis and Contemporary Thought*, September, 409–33.

Key, W. B. (1973) *Subliminal Seducation. Ad Media's Manipulation of a Not So Innocent America*, New York, Signet and Mentor Books.

Knightley, P. (1989) *The First Casulaty. From Crimeria to Vietnam: The War Correspondent as Hero, Propagandist, Myth Maker*, London, Sydney, Pan Books.

Kohl, H. (1971) *36 Children*, Harmondsworth, Penguin.

Kozol, J. (1967) *Death at an Early Age*, New York, Houghton Mifflin.

Lacey, C. (1971) *Hightown Grammar*, Manchester University Press.

Laing, R. D. (1976 edition) *The Politics of the Family, and other essays*, Harmondsworth, Penguin.

Lambropoulos, (1989) 'Violence and the Liberal Imagination: The Representation of Hellenism in Matthew Arnold', in: Armstrong, N. and Tennenhouse, L. (eds) (1989) *The Violence of Representation. Literature and the History of Violence*, London and New York, Routledge.

Lauretis, de T. (1989) 'The Violence of Rhetoric. Considerations on Representation and Gender', in: Armstrong, N. and Tennenhouse, L. (eds) (1989) *The Violence of Representation. Literature and the History of Violence*, London and New York, Routledge.

Lemaire, A. (1970) *Jacques Lacan*, tr. D. Macey, London and Boston, Routledge and Kegan Paul.

Lévi-Strauss, C. (1969) *The Elementary Structures of Kinship*, trans. James Harle Bell, John Richard von Sturmer and Rodney Needham, Boston, Beacon Press.

Lunatic Ideas (1978) *Lunatic Ideas or a Lesson in What School is All About*, London, School Without Walls and the Corner House Bookshop.

Lurie, A. (1990) *Don't Tell the Grown-Ups. Subversive Children's Literature*, London, Bloomsbury.

Lyotard, J. F. (1984) *The Postmodern Condition: A Report on Knowledge*, trans. Geoff Bennington and Brian Massumi, foreword by Frederic Jameson, *Theory and History of Literature, vol. 10*, Manchester, Manchester University Press.

MacDonald, B. (1970) 'Briefing Decision-makers: The Evaluation of the Humanities Curriculum Project', in: Hamingson (ed) (1973) *Towards Judgement*, Occasional Publication No. 1, CARE, University of East Anglia, Norwich, UK.

Macey, D. (1988) *Lacan in Contexts*, London and New York, Verso.

Macpherson, C. B. (1973) *Democratic Theory. Essays in Retrieval*, Oxford, Clarendon Press.

McGowen, (1989) 'Punishing Violence, Sentencing Crime', in: Armstrong, N. and Tennenhouse, L. (eds) (1989) *The Violence of Representation. Literature and the History of Violence*, London and New York, Routledge.

Michener, J. A. (1973) *Kent State. What Happened and Why*, London, Corgi; 1971 Secker and Warburg.

Milgram, S. (1974) *Obedience to Authority: An Experimental View*, London, Tavistock.

C. Wright Mills (1956) *The Power Elite*, New York, Oxford University Press.

Mitchell, J. (1974) *Psychoanalysis and Feminism. A Radical Reassessment of Freudian Psychoanalysis*, Harmondsworth, Pelican.

Montagu, A. (ed) (1978) *Learning Non-Aggression. The Experience of Non-Literate Societies*, Oxford and New York, Oxford University Press.

Morgan, R. (1989) *The Demon Lover. On the Sexuality of Terrorism*, London, Methuen.

Murdock, G. and Golding, P. (1978) 'Capitalism, Communication and Class Relations', in: Curran *et al.* (eds) (1977) *Mass Communication and Society*, London, Arnold.

Murphey, D. (1991) *The Stalker Affair and the Press*, London, Unwin Hyman.

Neill, A. S. (1973) *Neill, Neill 'Orange Peel': a Personal View of Ninety Years*, rev. ed, London, Weidenfeld and Nicolson.

Nunn, Sir P. (1920, 1945) *Education: its Data and First Principles*, London, Arnold.

O'Brien, M. (1981) *The Politics of Reproduction*, London and Boston, Routledge and Kegan Paul.

Ortega Y Gasset, J. (1957) *Man and People*, New York, Norton & Co.

Patton, C. (1989) 'Hegemony and Orgasm – or the Instability of Heterosexual Pornography', *Screen*, vol. 30, 1&2, 100–12.

Pearson, G. (1983) *The Deviant Imagination. Psychiatry, Social Work and Social Change*, London and Basingstoke, Macmillan.

Perry, R. and Greber, L. (1990) 'Women and Computers', *Signs: Journal of Women in Culture and Society*, vol.16, 1

Phillips, M. (1981) 'Rage that Shattered Thatcher', *New Statesman*, 17 July.

Platt, A. M. (1977) (2nd edn) *The Child Savers. The Invention of Delinquency*, University of Chicago Press.

Postman, N. and Weingartner, C. (1971) *Teaching as a Subversive Activity*, Harmondsworth, Penguin.

Probyn, E. (1990) 'New Traditionalism and Post-feminism: TV does the Home', *Screen*, vol. 31, 2, 147–59.

Propp, V. (1968) *Morphology of the Folktale*, tr. L. Scott, 2nd edn revised by L. A. Wagner, Austin and London, University of Texas Press.

Rabine, L. W. (1989) 'Rewriting the Oedipal Triangle: Feminism Psychoanalysis and the Saint-Simonians', *l'esprit createur*, vol. xxix, 1, 37–49.

Rank, O. (1936, 1978 edn) *Will Therapy*, Norton Library; first published in translation, Alfred Knopf.

Reich, W. (1948, 1975 edn) *Listen Little Man!*, tr. T. P. Wolfe, Harmondsworth, Penguin.

Richelson, J. T. and Ball, D. (1985, revised 1990) *The Ties That Bind*, Boston and London, Allen and Unwin.

Richmond, J. (1982a) 'Making it Happen', *The English Magazine*, 10, 30–3.

Richmond, J. (1982b) *Becoming our Own Experts*, Talk Workshop Group, ILEA English Centre, London.

Robertson, M. F. (1986) 'Deconstructive "Contortion" and Women's Historical Practice', *Poetics Today*, vol. 7, 4, 705–28.

Robottom, J. (1976) 'A History of Violence', in: N. Tutt (ed) *Violence*, London, HMSO Social Work Development Group.

Rodgerson, G. and Semple, L. (1990) 'Who Watches the Watchwomen? Feminists Against Censorship', *Feminist Review*, 36, 19–24.

Rousseau, J. J. (1974) *Emile*, tr. B. Foxley, London, Dent.

Rowe, J. C. (1989) '"Bringing it All Back Home" American Recyclings of the Vietnam War', in: Armstrong, N. and Tennenhouse, L. (eds) (1989) *The Violence of Representation. Literature and the History of Violence*, London and New York, Routledge.

Sarland, C. (1991) *Young People Reading. A Study of the Cultural, Ideological and Experiential Factors in the Interaction between Young People and Fictional Texts*, Milton Keynes, Open University Press.

Sayer, A. (1984) *Method in Social Science: a Realist Approach*, London and Melbourne, Hutchinson.

Schatzman, M. (1973) *Soul Murder. Persecution in the Family*, London, Allen Lane.

Schiller, H. I. (1986) *Information and the Crisis Economy*, New York and Oxford, Oxford University Press.

School of Barbiana (1969) *Letter to a Teacher*, Harmondsworth, Penguin.

Schostak, J. F. (1983) *Maladjusted Schooling: Deviance, Social Control and Individuality in Secondary Schooling*, London, Philadelphia, Falmer.

Schostak, J. F. (1984) 'The Violation of Intelligence' in: Schostak, J. F. and Logan, T. (eds) (1984) *Pupil Experience*, London, Sydney, Croom Helm.

Schostak, J. F. (1986) *Schooling the Violent Imagination*, London, New York, Routledge and Kegan Paul.
Schostak, J. F. (ed) (1988) *Breaking into the Curriculum: the Impact of Information Technology on Schooling*, London, New York. Methuen.
Schostak, J. F. (1989) 'The Play of Education', *Cambridge Journal of Education*, vol. 19, no. 2, 207–23.
Schostak, J. F. (1991) *Youth in Trouble. Educational Responses*, London, Norwich, Kogan Page in association with CARE, University of East Anglia, Norwich, England.
Schostak, J. F. and Coathup G. (1991) 'Rising 5: A Right to Education, not a Duty to be Schooled', Mimeo, University of East Anglia, Norwich, England.
Schostak, J. F. and Logan, T. (eds) (1984) *Pupil Experience*, London, Sydney, Croom Helm.
Schostak, J. F. Labbett, B. and Logan, T. (1990) *Final Report of the Independent Evaluation of the 'Paneda Geres Project'*, CARE University of East Anglia, Norwich, UK, and the European Commission.
Schutz, A. (1976) *The Phenomenology of the Social World*, tr. G. Walsh and F. Lehnert, London, Heinemann.
Schutz, A. and Luckmann, T. (1973) *The Structures of the Life-World*, tr. R. M. Zaner and H. T. Engelhardt Jr., London, Heinemann.
Sève, L. (1978) *Man in Marxist Theory and the Psychology of Personality*, tr. J. McGreal, Sussex, Harvester; New Jersey, Humanities Press.
Sharpe, R. and Green, A. (1975) *Education and Social Control. A Study in Progressive Primary Education*, with assistance of J. Lewis, London, Boston, Routledge and Kegan Paul.
Shor, I. (1980) *Critical Teaching and Everyday Life*, Boston, South End Press.
Silverman, K. (1983) *The Subject of Semiotics*, New York, Oxford University Press.
Silverman, K. (1988) *The Acoustic Mirror*, Bloomington and Indianapolis, Indiana University Press.
Simon, B. (1974) *The Two Nations and the Educational Structure 1780–1870*, London, Lawrence and Wishart.
Simpson, J. (1991) 'Free Men Clamouring for Chains', *Index on Censorship*, 4 and 5, 3–4.
Skinner, B. F. (1976) *Walden II*, New York, Macmillan; London, Collier Macmillan.
Smith, M. P. (1983) *The Libertarians and Education. A Guide to the Alternative Press*, London, Methuen.

Stallybrass (1989) '"Drunk with the Cup of Liberty": Robin Hood, the Carnivalesque, and the Rhetoric of Violence in Early Modern England', in: Armstrong, N. and Tennenhouse, L. (eds) (1989) *The Violence of Representation. Literature and the History of Violence*, London and New York, Routledge.

Stenhouse, L. (1975) *An Introduction to Curriculum Research and Development*, London, Heinemann.

Straayer, C. (1990) 'The She-man: Postmodern Bi-sexed Performance in Film and Video', *Screen*, vol. 31, 3, 262–82.

Stuart, S. (1969) *Say. An Experiment in Learning*, London, Nelson.

Swinburne, A. J. (1911) *Memories of a School Inspector. Thirty-five years in Lancashire and Suffolk*, published by the author, London.

Taylor, C. (1988) 'The Master Text and the Jeddi Doctrine', *Screen*, vol. 29, 4, 96–104.

Thrasher, F. M. (1927) *The Gang. A Study of 1,313 Gangs in Chicago*, University of Chicago Press.

Tulloch, J. (1990) *Television Drama. Agency, Audience and Myth*, London and New York, Routledge.

Vincent, C. (1986) 'The Future is Feminist', *New Socialist*, July / August.

Waldron, K. (1992) 'Spin Doctors of War', *New Statesman & Society*, 31 July, 12–13.

Walsh, J. (1988) 'First Blood to Rambo: A Textual Analysis', *Tell Me Lies About Vietnam. Cultural Battles for the Meaning of the War*, Milton Keynes and Philadelphia, Open University Press.

Walvin, J. (1982) *A Child's World. A Social History of English Childhood 1800–1914*, Harmondsworth, Penguin.

Webster, R. (1990) *A Brief History of Blasphemy. Liberalism, Censorship and 'The Satanic Verses'*, Southwold, The Orwell Press.

Widzer, M. E. (1977) 'The Comic-Book Superhero. A Study of the Family Romance Fantasy', *The Psychoanalytic Study of the Child*, vol. 32, 565–603.

Willis, P. (1977) *Learning to Labour*, Farnborough, Saxon House.

Zipes, J. (1979) *Breaking the Magic Spell: Radical Theories of Folk and Fairy Tales*, London, Heinemann , and Austin, University of Texas Press.

Zipes, J. (1983) *The Trials and Tribulations of Little Red Riding Hood. Versions of the Tale in Sociocultural Context*, London, Heinemann.

Zipes, J. (1985) 'Don't Bet on the Prince: Feminist Fairy Tales and the Feminist Critique in America', in: ed. J. H. Smith and W. Kerrigan, *Opening Texts. Psychoanalysis and the Culture of the Child*, Psychiatry and the Humanities, vol. 8,. Baltimore, Johns Hopkins University Press.

INDEX